THE BOOK OF THE DEEDS OF THE
GOOD KNIGHT JACQUES DE LALAING

THE BOOK OF THE DEEDS
OF THE GOOD KNIGHT
JACQUES DE LALAING

Translated by
Nigel Bryant

THE BOYDELL PRESS

First published 2024
The Boydell Press, Woodbridge

ISBN 978 1 78327 651 6

The Boydell Press is an imprint of Boydell & Brewer Ltd
PO Box 9, Woodbridge, Suffolk IP12 3DF, UK
and of Boydell & Brewer Inc.
668 Mt Hope Avenue, Rochester, NY 14620–2731, USA
website: www.boydellandbrewer.com

A CIP catalogue record for this book is available
from the British Library

The publisher has no responsibility for the continued existence or accuracy
of URLs for external or third-party internet websites referred to in this book,
and does not guarantee that any content on such websites is, or will remain,
accurate or appropriate

CONTENTS

Map 1   France and the Burgundian Dominions.

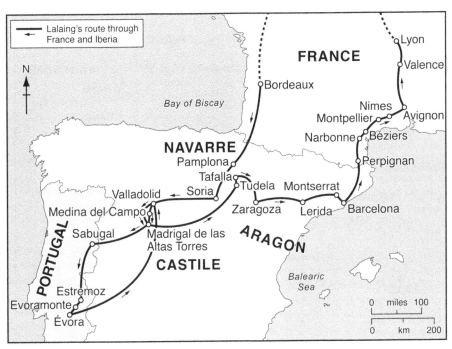

Map 2   Lalaing's Iberian Journey.

Map 3   Flanders and the Ghent War.

INTRODUCTION

Authorship

'My most honoured lord, I am sending you ... certain recollections of the high and admirable deeds of arms performed in the lists by your late son Sir Jacques de Lalaing ... and ask you to forgive me for not presenting them in fuller and better form ... But they are small memories in relation to the greatness of his deeds, and [the herald] Charolais, who witnessed the majority of his noble exploits, has written of them at length, and can write still more along with other noble persons who can speak of them. With the gathering of such writings I hope that you, my most honoured and redoubted lord, will have books made, so that those who have issued – and will in future issue – from the noble house of his birth take his high and noble deeds as an example ... [I hope, too, that] the one who comes to write of Sir Jacques's illustrious, chivalrous deeds can recover something from this letter which I, Golden-Fleece, have written ... for they are well worthy of record.'

This is an extract from a letter by Jehan Lefèvre de Saint-Remy[1] – otherwise known as 'Golden-Fleece', King of Arms of the Burgundian order of chivalry, the Order of the *Toison d'Or* – written to Jacques's father following the young knight's dramatic death, of which more anon. It is a letter of surprising length, full of heartfelt admiration – and, one senses, affection – for Jacques, and contains detailed, eyewitness accounts of many of his most memorable exploits. Given Lefèvre's status and reputation for integrity, it leaves little reason to doubt that Jacques de Lalaing was a genuinely exceptional knight, fit to be memorialised as an object of outstanding pride for Burgundy, and indeed a model of ideal knighthood. Moreover, the letter gives such clear indications of how *The Book of the Deeds of Jacques de Lalaing*

---

[1] François Morand, 'Épître de Jean Le Fèvre, seigneur de Saint Remy, contenant le récit des faits d'armes, en champ clos, de Jacques de Lalain, et publiée, pour faire suite à sa *Chronique*, d'après un manuscrit de la Bibliothèque nationale', *Annuaire-bulletin de la Société de l'histoire de France*, 21:2 (1884), pp. 177–239.

came to be written that it is more than a little strange that there should have been for a long while doubts and confusion about its authorship.

In short, the first (17ᵗʰ-century) edition attributed *The Book of the Deeds* to the Burgundian chronicler Georges Chastellain, on the flimsiest of bases that the writer's name which appears at the very end – in the last line of the verse epitaph for Jacques – is '*Jorge*'. The 19ᵗʰ-century editor Kervyn de Lettenhove followed suit, including *The Book of the Deeds* in his *Oeuvres de Chastellain* (Volume VIII). But though Chastellain may have written the epitaph, that is all. *The Book of the Deeds* was quite clearly not written by Chastellain, or indeed by any other one person. It is precisely the 'gathering of writings' proposed by Lefèvre in his letter: a compilation assembled from a variety of different sources including, almost certainly, the herald Charolais who, as Lefèvre had said, 'witnessed the majority of his noble exploits, has written of them at length, and can write still more'. Who compiled it we shall never know for sure: for a long while scholars variously assumed (on no strong evidence) that it was Chastellain, Antoine de la Sale or Olivier de la Marche; more recently it has been generally accepted, far more plausibly, that it was 'one of the Burgundian heralds whose reports were used in the compilation of the text'.[2] Especially good and interesting is Rosalind Brown-Grant's suggestion that the compiler was Gilles Gobet, Lefèvre's successor as Golden-Fleece;[3] previously Lefèvre's assistant serving as pursuivant with the name Talent, he appears in *The Book of the Deeds* in at least one episode during the Ghent War.[4] In any event, whatever his identity, the compiler refers to himself as the '*acteur*' ('author') of the work, but to call him 'the Lalaing biographer', as Brown-Grant and others often do, is really a little misleading: 'compiler' would be the word to use consistently, not least because to call him 'the biographer' is to overlook the fact that the work can only loosely be called a 'biography' at all. It is far more accurate to see it as a dossier, an assemblage of documents which together record the subject's life and career.

These documents are of very different kinds: early passages borrowed from a romance are followed by material drawn from heraldic records and, finally, from a chronicle – and also, and certainly not least, extracts from Golden-Fleece's long and detailed letter from which he had 'hoped something could be recovered by the one who comes to write of Sir Jacques's illustrious deeds'. And the styles change so markedly from source to source – and are

---

    [2] Rosalind Brown-Grant, 'Jacques de Lalaing and Chivalric Biography', in *A Knight for the Ages – Jacques de Lalaing and the Art of Chivalry*, ed. E. Morrison (Los Angeles, 2018), p. 71.

    [3] Rosalind Brown-Grant and Mario Damen, *A Chivalric Life* (Woodbridge, 2022), pp. 53–4.

    [4] Below, pp. 194, 215.

reproduced by the compiler with so little interference – that it is strange that scholars persisted for so long in looking for an author.

It is even stranger to see the work described as 'a rollicking account … like a fast-paced adventure novel',[5] and to find even Richard Vaughan, doyen of historians of ducal Burgundy, describing it as 'a work which reads more like romance than biography'.[6] Little could be less the case. The first section – Jacques's youth and the instructions given to him by his father – is indeed copied in almost verbatim chunks from Antoine de la Sale's romance *Le Petit Jehan de Saintré* (1455–6), a work which, to confuse matters (but to explain its inclusion), had been based in large part on Jacques's own exploits. But the sections concerning Jacques's travels through France, Spain and Portugal and then to Scotland read like heralds' (wholly unromanticised, almost bureaucratic) records and are clearly copied from precisely such material. The detailed (and sober, unfanciful, undramatised) account of Jacques's famous *pas d'armes* of the Fountain of Tears was without doubt written by Jehan Lefèvre, as it is copied nearly verbatim from his letter to Jacques's father. There then follows the substantial final section, the Ghent War of 1451–3, in which Lalaing participates in notable fashion before being killed at the siege of Poeke. This, far from being rollicking or reading like a romance, is patently a series of extracts from a chronicle.

Regarding the author of this last part of the text, even in a very recent work, *A Knight for the Ages*, Rosalind Brown-Grant ventures no further than to say that this narrative 'is taken almost verbatim from a fragment of a chronicle of the Ghent War which, until recently, was thought to be by Georges Chastellain, although this attribution is no longer generally accepted'.[7] Graeme Small, in his excellent book on Chastellain, simply says in two sentences that Kervyn de Lettenhove's 'attribution of the Ghent War account was made in error. The editor himself suspected as much, for towards the end of his mammoth task he recognised that the account may in fact have been the work of Jean Lefèvre.'[8]

It is odd that so little has been made of this: Lettenhove in the preface to his volume VIII of Chastellain's *Oeuvres* not only made clear that he thought the Ghent War narrative (which, to complicate the issue, he omitted from his edition of *The Book of the Deeds*, having already published it in Volume II of his *Oeuvres de Chastellain*) was probably the work of Lefèvre; he went

---

5   *A Knight for the Ages*, ed. Morrison, cover blurb.

6   Richard Vaughan, *Philip the Good* (revised edition Woodbridge, 2002), p. 149.

7   Brown-Grant, *op. cit.*, p. 70; ; also in *A Chivalric Life*, p. 47.

8   Graeme Small, *George Chastelain and the Shaping of Valois Burgundy* (Woodbridge, 1997), p. 154. Small points out that Chastellain's authorship of the Ghent War narrative is unlikely because he was appointed official historian only in 1455, and between 1451 and 1454 – i.e. for the period of the war – Chastellain is notably absent from all records (*Ibid.*, pp. 65, 63).

further, and made the important suggestion that this account of the Ghent War was in fact a missing part of Lefèvre's famous Chronicle. The very fine *Chronique* of 'the observant and punctilious ducal herald Jehan Lefèvre'[9] is otherwise known to have survived only as far as 1436. Lettenhove wrote:

> The *Chronicle* of Lefebvre Saint-Remy extended to 1460, but nothing of it has survived for the period beyond 1436. The section relating to the Ghent Wars, published in our Volume II, might it not belong to this lost fragment?[10]

In support of this suggestion, Lettenhove quoted Lefèvre (Golden-Fleece)'s letter to Jacques's father, but then, simply because of Lefèvre's phrase 'the one who comes to write of Jacques's illustrious deeds', strangely leapt to the following assumption:

> *The Book of the Deeds* must therefore have been the work neither of Lefebvre Saint-Remy, nor of the herald Charolais, but of some writer enjoying a lofty reputation.[11]

That assumption is not impossible, of course, but it seems far more reasonable to speculate that Jacques's father, prompted into action by Lefèvre's letter, would not have commissioned a non-specialist to write the book of his son's deeds, but would have asked those who had already written substantial amounts about Jacques's career – the herald Charolais and/or Lefèvre himself (who, after all, says in his letter that he hopes what he has written will be included in such 'books') – to provide that material and assemble it. It is true that by the time the compilation came to be made (at the earliest the late 1460s, more probably the early 1470s) Lefèvre himself was almost certainly dead, and the compiler refers to him in the past tense (and in glowing terms, which would be singularly immodest if it was Lefèvre's own work); but there is surely a strong probability that the first port of call for material on the Ghent War would have been the work of a man who had, as it were, proposed the *Book of Deeds* project: Lefèvre. It is notable, too, that Lefèvre was personally involved in the Ghent War, was present at the moment of Lalaing's death and his conversations with Lalaing on that day are quoted in detail in the account. In terms of style, it might be added that the writing of the Ghent War narrative sounds very like the surviving sections of Lefèvre's *Chronique*, though it is certainly the case that the prose of 15th-century chronicles can often tend to be quite similar. More significantly, the frontispieces of all three illuminated manuscripts of *The Book of the Deeds* depict a herald busily writing the book; he is wearing a tabard

9 Vaughan, *op. cit.*, p. 56.
10 Kervyn de Lettenhove, ed., *Oeuvres de Georges Chastellain, Vol. VIII* (Brussels, 1866), p. ix (my translation).
11 *Ibid.*, pp. xi–xii.

with a coat of arms suggesting that he is to be identified as the King of Arms of the Golden Fleece. This could, therefore, be a depiction of Lefèvre's successor as King of Arms, Gilles Gobet, thus supporting Rosalind Brown-Grant's interesting suggestion that Gobet was the compiler; or it could be Lefèvre himself. There is no way of being sure, but if it is the latter, one explanation would be that the compiler, even though it almost certainly was not Lefèvre, wished to acknowledge that a significant part of the work, not just the account of the *pas d'armes* of the Fountain of Tears and other combats, was material written by Lefèvre. If that is right, it would strongly suggest that the lengthy Ghent War narrative which concludes *The Book of the Deeds* is composed of hitherto lost sections of Lefèvre's fine and important *Chronique*.[12]

A Model Knight, a Model Prince

Not only does Lefèvre's letter to Jacques's father give strong indications about how the book came to be assembled; it also tells us why. It is 'so that those who have issued – and will in future issue – from the noble house of his birth take his high and noble deeds as an example'. Lefèvre's phrase is immediately taken up by the *Book of the Deeds* compiler in the Prologue, where he says he has undertaken the work

> in order that the glory and praise gained by those who have gone before us be ... kept in the memory as an example to the noble and virtuous men of the present.[13]

There is nothing novel about this idea; much chivalric literature was seen in exactly this light. The opening lines, for example, of Jehan Wauquelin's superb version of the *Romance of Alexander*, produced for the Burgundian court in the 1440s, articulate the idea perfectly:

12 Graeme Small has well expressed how important a figure Lefèvre was: 'The [Order of the] Golden Fleece, of which Lefèvre was the principal officer, was a central plank of ducal power. Philip the Good used the institution as a means of lending cohesion to his disparate dominions, by recruiting to it members of the most influential families under his lordship, and of cementing relations with other principalities and kingdoms, by offering the [Order's] collar to his peers and superiors among Europe's ruling elite. Lefèvre himself did far more than officiate at the chapters of the Order ... He maintained its records, kept track of the activities of its members at home and further afield, and in its service became one of the most widely-travelled and high-ranking diplomats at Philip the Good's disposal ... [His] seasoned understanding of the finer details of ducal policy with regard to the king of France, and of the workings and membership of the Order of the Golden Fleece, few – if any – could match.' Small, *op. cit.*, pp. 74–5.
13 Below, p. 37.

> The glorious exploits, the deeds of arms, conquests and feats of courage performed by the valiant, mighty, noble men of ancient and former times are an inspiration. Recalling and recounting them rouses the hearts of their counterparts in the present day who yearn to scale the heights of prowess and fame ... The hearts of young knights and squires, especially, are sure to be stirred and filled with thoughts of glory and prowess when they hear such deeds recalled, and be ever fixed upon winning high renown.[14]

This idea is not always voiced in earlier chivalric biographies. The earliest surviving biography of a medieval knight, the 13th-century *History of William Marshal*, makes no mention of Marshal's life being a model for others – its object is to consolidate and celebrate his personal reputation and the pleasure and prestige that it brought his family; and the 14th-century biography of Bertrand du Guesclin presents its subject as an example to knights only by implication, without the idea (important though it is) ever being explicitly stated. But in the early 15th century the biography of Jean le Meingre (Boucicaut) is certainly keen to compare him with the heroes of antiquity (Hector, Alexander, Hannibal and Pompey, not to mention Hercules) and to present him and them as *exempla* of ideal knighthood; and by the 1470s, when *The Book of the Deeds of Jacques de Lalaing* was compiled, the recording and depiction of exceptional chivalry was emphatically intended as a model to be heeded and emulated.

And though the compiler in his Prologue sets up Lalaing as an example of a knight who 'devoted much toil and effort to enhance the honour and prestige of the house of which he was born', he immediately stresses that Jacques was not alone but was part of a tradition – and, importantly, a local one. It is not just a question of him glorifying his own house, but of following in the footsteps of the knights of his home ground of Hainaut, who were 'the flower of chivalry, the finest to be found anywhere' – and not only in the past: having referred to Gillion de Trazegnies, the Hainauter hero of a famous romance, the compiler tells his readers: 'Nor should other valiant knights of Hainaut be forgotten who have been at the forefront since, achieving so much in their time that it will be in eternal memory.'[15] He reminds them of the legendary Hainauter knight Gilles de Chin,[16] and of the more real and recent Jehan de Werchin.

Jacques, then, is about to follow a well-trodden path. And so does the compiler in recounting Jacques's youth. Having presumably been present at no stage of his subject's birth and childhood, he resorts to depicting an absolutely

---

[14] Jehan Wauquelin, *The Medieval Romance of Alexander – The Deeds and Conquests of Alexander the Great*, trans. Bryant (Woodbridge, 2012), p. 29.

[15] Below, p. 38.

[16] 'Virtually reincarnated ... in Jacques de Lalaing, who did his best to repeat Gilles's fictitious adventures in real life.' Vaughan, *op. cit.*, p. 157.

standard, model sequence of events. Firstly, he tells us that Jacques's father Guillaume de Lalaing was 'conceived and born in loyal marriage' – Jacques is of a rightful, legitimate line; his father and grandfather then have a completely stock conversation about a suitable wife; and Jacques's own birth is, in entirely due course,

> a source of mighty joy for [his grandparents] the lord of Lalaing and his lady ... They had lived to see what they desired most in all the world – a legitimate heir apparent to follow their son Sir Guillaume in the lordship of Lalaing, its land, its house.[17]

The descriptions of Jacques's parents' marriage and of his birth might have been assembled from a kit, being a collection of phrases found in any number of romances – and all is one hundred per cent proper. It is, moreover, perfect. Jacques is depicted as a model physical specimen: using further stock phrases, the compiler tells us that 'God and Nature had neglected nothing in his making. He was tall, well built, well formed in every limb'; and he is also a model moral specimen, 'endowed and blessed with such virtues and manners that all who saw him and heard him speak he compelled to act well'; and he is an example to all other knights in being cultured, too, being 'skilled and adept in speaking, understanding and writing Latin and French, surpassed by no one of his age'.[18]

As for the instructions he receives from his father, these are not merely a stock exposition of the Seven Deadly Sins but are lifted verbatim from Antoine de la Sale's romance *Le Petit Jehan de Saintré* – though 'verbatim' is not strictly accurate, as the compiler judiciously (and, for many modern readers, no doubt mercifully) hard-prunes the lengthy passages in which 'le Petit Jehan' is instructed by the 'Dame des Belles-Cousines', and entirely omits the Ten Commandments to which 'le Petit Jehan' is subjected, as he has Jacques's father say: 'I've not yet reminded you of the ten commandments in due order, for I'm quite sure you know them.'[19]

That is not to say that the compiler was going through the motions and paying lip service to the Deadly Sins or the Commandments. This cautionary instruction may be abridged but it is carefully included and is crucial and heartfelt, as Jacques's father tells his son to 'be assured, [God's] blessings will come to you if you strive to follow my advice ... I pray and command you to do all in your power to keep and fulfil [His commandments].'[20] Zrinka Stahuljak has well observed that the recounting of the seven deadly sins is

[17] pp. 40–1.
[18] p. 41.
[19] p. 49.
[20] *Ibid.*

proof of the doctrine's cultural and educational universality ... *The Book of the Deeds of Jacques de Lalaing* is a product and continuation of a long medieval tradition of cross-pollination of a variety of discourses for the purpose of memory, memorialisation, and establishment of comprehensive truth ... There is a correspondence between the author-compiler who writes to comply with a textual model and the knight-soldier who acts to comply with the chivalric model.[21]

This complying with models, both of text and of chivalry, is interestingly seen in Jacques's early tourneying. The description of his first jousts might once again have come in kit form, being couched in phrases borrowed from numerous romances as the compiler tells of

his mighty blows, delivered with such force that he brought knights and horses crashing to the ground. He bore stout and weighty lances that flattened opponents back on their horses' cruppers, and often dashed off their helms to leave them bare-headed in the lists. Then trumpets would blare and ring so loud that you wouldn't have heard God's thunder, as heralds and pursuivants on all sides roared 'Lalaing!'[22]

But amongst all this there is then something striking and unusual: the compiler stresses that Jacques was always clad, and his horse caparisoned, exactly like the young Duke of Cleves who has taken him under his wing:

The young duke and he loved each other dearly, and it's not to be wondered at, for they were of similar age and in build and height and manner so alike that, seeing them, anyone who hadn't known them would have taken them for brothers.[23]

Jacques was, in short, the mirror image of the Duke of Cleves, and the duke was a perfect figure to mirror, being 'vivacious, modest, courteous and charming – and generous, too, a great giver of alms to the poor. Truly, Jacquet de Lalaing could say for sure that he'd found the lord and master he'd have wished and asked for.'[24] Significantly, in the very same passage, Duke Philip of Burgundy, at whose court Jacques is now residing, is depicted as a perfect, model prince:

There was no prince more generous, modest and courteous anywhere. He was held in awe not for his cruelty but for the charm, largesse, valour and

[21] Zrinka Stahuljak, 'The Long Middle Ages of Jacques de Lalaing: Medieval Genres and the Writing of History', in *A Knight for the Ages* ed. Morrison, pp. 82–3.
[22] Below, p. 53.
[23] *Ibid.*
[24] *Ibid.*

other virtues with which he was endowed. In short, truly, no human tongue, however eloquent, could express or describe his mighty virtues. And let it be said that no prince on record showed more compassion or pity towards the poor: if ever he saw them in need they would never be turned away without relief. And he loved his knights, his nobles and all who served him, and rewarded them most liberally.[25]

Chapter 13, in which an embassy comes to the ducal court from the Emperor of Greece and Constantinople, may initially seem an irrelevant digression from Jacques's story, but it is nothing of the kind. The emperor is appealing for help to resist the Infidels led by the Grand Turk, Murad II, and

he said that if the Duke of Burgundy didn't lend him support and aid he could see no other Christian prince with the will to help him defend Christendom, which the Turk was daily striving with all his might to annihilate and destroy.[26]

Duke Philip, then, in addition to his other model attributes, is also a model crusader. And Jacques de Lalaing, therefore, is being raised at the Burgundian court in the company and context of models of all chivalric virtues, and these conclude with crusading, a point to which I shall return.

Are we really to believe in all this perfection? Jacques is the very model of devotion, too. In cautionary words, a model for all knights present and future, he prays to God to 'give me all due strength: without Him no one can achieve a thing – neither I nor anyone else'.[27] And even more than God, the Virgin is a prominent figure throughout Jacques's life: she is the one 'who has more power over me than anyone in the world'[28] and is a constant object

---

[25] pp. 53–4.

[26] p. 55.

[27] p. 61. This echoes an oft-repeated dictum in the *Livre Charny*, the 14th-century French knight Geoffroi de Charny's guide to others on how to succeed in a career in Arms, in which he gives insistent variations on the phrases: 'without God you can achieve nothing: you'll do nothing of worth except through Him'. The *Livre Charny*, trans. Bryant, in Wilson, I., *The Book of Geoffroi de Charny* (Woodbridge, 2021), p. 111. Evidently an ingrained chivalric notion, it appears also in Jacques's father's advice: he had told young Jacques that 'without God's help, dear son, we can perform no virtuous deed or anything of worth' (below, p. 50).

[28] p. 92. And, continuing the thought of the previous sentence (and previous footnote), in the very first lines of *The Book of the Deeds* prologue, the compiler describes Christ *and his mother* as 'the source and driving force of all good works … without whom nothing of worth can be undertaken or achieved'. Geoffroi de Charny had been similarly devoted to the Virgin: in his *Livre Charny* he calls upon knights to commit themselves 'wholeheartedly to the unstinting service of that glorious and most precious one, the Virgin, God's most gracious mother'; and Ian Wilson has noted

of his prayers; during his journey through Spain he takes a long diversion to visit the 'Black Virgin' at Montserrat; her image presides over the Fountain of Tears and plays a major part in the *entremets* that follows; and at his sudden and dramatic end we are told that, as he lies dying, he hears a friar bidding him remember God and the Virgin, and 'he had loved [the Virgin] so much that for her sake he had adopted the motto and device *La Nonpareille*'.[29] His observance of mass is presented as meticulous, and on the morning of his death we are told he had heard three, following which he 'spoke in confession to an eminent doctor of the Dominican order named Master Guy de Douzy, because the firing of the fortress at Oudenhove, carried out by order of the duke, was weighing on his conscience'.[30] Indeed, we are earlier assured that:

> the fine instruction given by his father Sir Guillaume de Lalaing at his departure, when he'd first set out for the court of good Duke Philip of Burgundy, he had well observed; for since his death I've heard from a noble man, a most credible source, that Jacquet de Lalaing would never go to bed without having made confession if he'd thought he might have been in mortal sin.[31]

It may all sound too good to be true, but it is interesting to note the stress on the 'most credible' testimony of 'a noble man'.

Young Jacques is presented as perfect also in terms of courtesy: his conduct continues to be exemplary in his behaviour towards two ladies who become besotted with him and secret rivals for his affections; he bobs and weaves his way through their advances with aplomb:

> Jacquet was well aware of their love for him: they sent secret messages daily! He went regularly to pass the time in talk with them, one day with one and next day with the other, but behaved with all propriety and honour: he did nothing to earn the reproach of God or of the world ... He handled things so perfectly that he was loved and adored by both. It was down to him that it went no further: fearing for his person and for his soul's salvation he had no wish to venture beyond propriety.[32]

---

that the order of chivalry to which Charny belonged, King John II's illustrious but short-lived Company of the Star, had as 'its official title *Chevaliers de Nostre Dame de la Noble Maison* – "Knights of Our Lady of the Noble House", therefore dedicated to the Virgin Mary alone and with no soldier or other saint as her companion'. *The Book of Geoffroi de Charny*, pp. 110, 145.

[29] p. 227.
[30] p. 226.
[31] p. 70.
[32] p. 64.

A reader might be inclined to assume that this elaborate story is an instructive, cautionary fiction; but it does involve two specific, named ladies – the duchesses of Orléans and Calabria – so that, however invented the actual dialogue may doubtless be in their private conversations, it would be surprising if the story of Jacques's behaviour was not in essence true. Likewise, during Jacques's jousting before these ladies at the King of France's court, much of the description may once again be couched in stock phrases of romance, but as soon as we reach an account of a specific joust it begins to sound like an accurate record. Precise details start to appear:

> The fallen knight … was helped back to his house with great difficulty, for in his fall he had injured his knee, and was unable to complete his three courses … [Another knight] shattered his lance while Jacquet, aiming for his visor, found his target with such force and might that he swept the knight's helm fully eight yards away on the end of his lance.[33]

This may of course be merely lively writing; but we should perhaps beware of being too sceptical: the same passage includes reported conversations between Jacques and the counts of Maine and Saint-Pol, a detailed description of the return from captivity of the Count of Angoulême and a curious little episode which has a distinct ring of truth:

> While Jacquet continued to hold his pass, into the lists rode the king and the lord of La Varenne, amid such a mighty blare of trumpets that it seemed the very earth and sky were about to do battle – not that the king and Varenne wished to joust with the holder of the pass: it was purely for the joy of it! They ran four courses against one another and each broke two lances. Then they went off to disarm and returned to the stand and rejoined the ladies, thinking they'd gone unrecognised.[34]

This does seem to be genuine reportage.

It is immediately after this sequence, recounting his dealings with the two duchesses and his virtuous response to their besotted admiration, that the name 'Jacquet' becomes consistently 'Jacques' when he confronts 'a Sicilian knight from the household of King Alfonso of Aragon – Sir Jehan Boniface by name, a man of high renown and most expert and valiant in arms'.[35] Elisabeth Gaucher has viewed the change of name as marking a progression in Jacques from youth to knighthood.[36] This is not really the case. 'Jacquet' changes to 'Jacques' before he has fought Boniface and been knighted by Duke

---

[33] pp. 67, 69.
[34] pp. 73–4.
[35] p. 75.
[36] Elisabeth Gaucher, *La Biographie Chevaleresque* (Paris, 1994), p. 349.

Philip, and there is a far simpler explanation: the name changes because the compiler, interfering with his sources as little as ever, is incorporating text from a different source. As well as the change in name, there is a fairly marked change in prose style. The source is now Jehan Lefèvre's letter to Jacques's father (in which he always calls him 'Jacques'), and it is noticeable that Lefèvre ('Golden-Fleece') himself appears in the narrative for the first time here, advising Jacques on how to proceed with taking up Boniface's challenge.

Apart from converting Lefèvre's reported speech into dialogue and changing first person to third (and inserting glowing compliments about Golden-Fleece's qualities and authority), the compiler has to a large extent quoted the letter verbatim, with only minor interpolations. These interpolations often show a good deal of skill in terms of creating narrative flow. For example, having listed Boniface's 'Chapters' (i.e. the terms and conditions for combat) exactly as recorded in Lefèvre's letter, the compiler has inserted:

> These Chapters, having been shown and presented to Jacques de Lalaing, were perused at length by him and his advisers; he accepted and approved them point by point and, without objection or modification to any, he promised, with the grace of Our Lord and his most worthy Mother, to uphold them.[37]

These lines would have been unnecessary in the context of a letter, but they are a wise addition when telling a fluent story. And there is no reason at all to assume that they are an invention or guesswork; they may also suggest that the compiler had – along with Lefèvre – been present himself, had been an eyewitness. There is a similar possibility with the interpolated description of Jacques making his way to the combat in Ghent:

> Through the streets he rode, and truly, the windows and doorways of the houses along his way were filled with ladies, damsels, townswomen and girls, all of them praying to God to send him back having won high honour. And you can be sure he was much desired by many ...[38]

Is this – an image found in many a romance – a fanciful, glamourised version of events? Or had the compiler been present, and seen it to be exactly as described? And had he seen (and heard) Jacques' return from the combat, which he describes in the following interpolated lines, not found in Lefèvre's letter?

[37] Below, p. 83.
[38] p. 84.

He returned to his house with a grand escort, and with trumpets and clarions sounding before him, a wondrous joy to hear.[39]

Jacques's Journeys

The next section of *The Book of the Deeds* does not appear in Lefèvre's letter at all. It tells how Jacques, copying the Sicilian knight Boniface's example of venturing from land to land in knight-errant fashion in search of noble challengers to single combat, now sets off on just such a journey through France and into Spain and Portugal. This part of the book is clearly drawn from heralds' records. In all probability these included (or were entirely) those of the herald Charolais, given that Lefèvre in his letter had said not only that Charolais had 'witnessed the majority of [Jacques's] noble exploits' but also that:

> I shall refrain from speaking of the high and laudable deeds Lalaing intended to undertake in the kingdom of France, on the isle of Notre Dame at Paris and elsewhere, as appear … in the records made by the aforementioned Charolais.

A further clue that Charolais was the writer of these records lies in the fact that Lalaing's challenge to combat and his 'Chapters' (the terms and conditions) were relayed to foreign parts ahead of him not by Charolais but by 'a herald of arms named Luxembourg',[40] so Charolais may well have been free and available to accompany Lalaing on his travels.

In any event, it is interesting to see what Charolais and/or other heralds deemed worthy of record. When, before setting out on his grand mission, Jacques feels compelled to visit his kinswoman the Countess of Ligny, the reported episode seems a bit of a damp squib, of little consequence: he is given, we are told, a warm and joyous welcome with much feasting and entertainment, but none of it is described in the slightest detail, and then he takes his leave. The episode's only purpose seems to be to record the countess's view that Jacques deserved to be fêted 'more than any man for his fine and noble ambition to increase and enhance the honour of his house, from which he was now setting out on his journey'.[41]

And the degree to which Jacques is fêted at each stage of his journey is precisely the focal point of every 'entry' in what are surely heraldic records. When he comes to English-held Bordeaux, for example, the herald spends no time describing anything except that the mayor, archbishop and others

---

[39] p. 87.
[40] pp. 98, 122.
[41] p. 89.

received him and his company most honourably, as if he had been of the King of England's household. Sir Jacques was delighted, and with good cause: since leaving his homeland he had not been so fêted and honoured as he was then in the city of Bordeaux. He thanked the mayor, the archbishop and the lords, along with the burghers and the commoners of the city who covered their expenses, excusing them all payment, both him and all his men.[42]

This reception by implication (diplomatically, he doesn't overtly say so) compares favourably with that encountered earlier at the French king's court, and is duly logged by the herald, ready to report to the Duke of Burgundy on their return. For it should be noted that Jacques's journey is not just a piece of personal knight-errantry: on one level it is a quasi-diplomatic mission. The duke has given Jacques money as well as his blessing before leaving Burgundy, and the heralds' reports of how this representative of Burgundian chivalry is received in various realms are evidently going to be of key importance. The herald writes respectfully of the King of France, but now logs that 'since leaving his homeland [Jacques de Lalaing] had not been so fêted and honoured as he was then in the [English] city of Bordeaux'.

That Jacques is a representative of Burgundy and of the duke is underlined when, warmly received by the Prince and Princess of Navarre (to whom he 'delivered the greetings of his lord the Duke of Burgundy as he had been charged to do'),[43] the herald records Jacques saying:

> 'The honour my lord and lady show me I take not to be on my account but for the sake of my redoubted sovereign lord the Duke of Burgundy, to whom, God willing, I shall report the great honour they have paid me, for which I humbly thank them.'[44]

This is one of many occasions when honour is deferred to the duke. And if Jacques is frustrated to find his challenges to combat blocked, it is for the very good reason – as the herald carefully records – that the Prince of Navarre

> 'does not deem it appropriate for men of the houses of Burgundy and Navarre to engage with each other in combat or challenge ... The bonds of love and alliance between the houses are so strong that it is quite impossible to sunder them.'[45]

Once again the herald gives not the slightest attention to the unfamiliar sights and sounds of a foreign land or court. What he logs are the greeting given, the

---

[42] p. 94.
[43] p. 96.
[44] p. 97.
[45] p. 98.

presents bestowed, the expenses defrayed and the status accorded the Duke of Burgundy's knight:

> When mass had been said and sung they left the chapel and came to a rich chamber, splendidly hung with tapestry, where the Prince and Princess, the noble barons, lords and council all sat down; and Sir Jacques de Lalaing, at the Prince's command, was seated above them all.[46]

The description may be terse – it is a 'rich' chamber 'splendidly hung with tapestry' (no mention of what the tapestries depicted) – but descriptive detail has no relevance in an almost bureaucratic record: what matters to the herald is to report where Jacques was seated.

The list of hostings, gifts, feasts and receptions continues as Jacques makes his way through Castile and into Portugal, where once again the herald records that the warmth and generosity he encounters

> he attributed not to himself but took to be for the sake of his sovereign lord the Duke of Burgundy, to whom, on his return by the grace of Our Lord, he would relay his deep gratitude. Then the king replied, saying:
>
> 'Be assured, Sir Jacques, that for love of our dear uncle the Duke of Burgundy and our aunt his wife the duchess, we and our people wish to do all in our power to please, serve and honour any who come here in their name.'[47]

This is certainly no travelogue, and a long way from a biography. It's a court official's log, heavy-laden with formality and protocol, and is sometimes not an easy read – though the care and attention devoted to recording the protocol observed, and the status and honour involved, in, for example, Jacques's dealings with the Queen of Aragon, are in themselves interesting to see. But as Jacques journeys on through these foreign lands, unfamiliar though they may be, there is still no description at all of place, people or customs (even the Spanish sport of bull-running is mentioned in detail-less passing), and at one point the herald even writes that 'they encountered nothing worthy of record'.[48] The clear implication is that the only thing that *is* worthy of record is the aforementioned honour shown to Jacques and, by extension, to Burgundy. No wonder, then, that particular time and space are devoted on his return journey to recording the lavish welcome he receives at Montpellier from no less a figure than Jacques Coeur, the merchant whose colossal wealth had funded the King of France's reconquest of Normandy. 'This treasurer,' we are told, 'showed great respect and honour to Sir Jacques de Lalaing, saying:

---

[46] p. 97.
[47] p. 110.
[48] p. 111.

"Sir Jacques, all my wealth counts for nothing if you don't help me! I've been longing for you to come this way!"' And following this surprising greeting he entertains him magnificently and offers him fabulously generous financial aid, 'as if Sir Jacques had been a son or brother'.[49] To show Jacques de Lalaing accorded such a welcome and respect by a figure of crucial financial import for the French king and kingdom borders on Burgundian point-scoring.[50]

Combat in Castile and Scotland

On his journey through Iberia he is refused permission to do combat in Navarre, Portugal and Aragon, but in Castile he has better luck: the King of Castile gives him leave to fight the Castilian knight Diego de Guzmán in Valladolid. The account of this contest is very different in style from what has preceded, for the simple reason that the compiler of *The Book of the Deeds* is now inserting different source material: it is copied, almost verbatim, from Jehan Lefèvre's letter to Jacques's father, and it should be further noted that Lefèvre acknowledges that he in turn is quoting 'what I've seen in a copy of a letter sent by a Navarrese gentleman to my lord the Duke of Burgundy'.

This description of the combat in Valladolid, derived ultimately from the Navarrese gentleman, is very detailed, and does in fact suggest a clear reason for the reluctance of other rulers to allow such contests in the lists; for when it happens it is public in the extreme, attracting

> a large number of knights and great lords, not only from Castile but from Portugal, Navarre and Aragon, and ambassadors from France; all were there that day in response to the news that had spread abroad: everyone was eager to see the event, so orders had been given for several stands to be built so that all could watch in comfort.[51]

The intense formality of the occasion and its presentation all adds to its status and significance; so that, in addition to the declared unwillingness of other rulers to have their subjects fight Lalaing because he was the knight of a cherished ally, there is a distinct possibility that they were nervous also

---

[49] p. 127.

[50] And note that Burgundian Jacques doesn't need Coeur's proffered financial help: 'when I first set out with [the Duke's] leave and approval he provided me with all I needed' (*ibid*). But the exact realities of gift-giving and the fabulous expense involved in Jacques de Lalaing's exploits are interestingly discussed by Rosalind Brown-Grant and Mario Damen in *A Chivalric Life* pp. 27–33. It is clear that 'sixteen years after Jacques's death, the entire Lalaing family was still unable to settle his outstanding debts, his expensive life of chivalry having proved to be one that was well beyond his actual means' (*ibid*, p. 34).

[51] Below, p. 112.

because 'national' honour was at stake. Not that we can be scornful or feel that we've moved on: in much modern sport – the Olympics and tennis grand slams spring instantly to mind – individual prowess is still seen by many (somewhat bizarrely, others might say) as a cause for national pride and a reflection of national worth. Would the chivalry of Burgundy, they might have been worrying, prove superior to their own?[52] It is certainly worthy of note that Jacques is later refused permission to joust with anyone in Aragon despite the fact that Sir Jehan Boniface had previously carried just such a challenge to other lands, including Burgundy, 'by the leave and licence of the King of Aragon'. Having earlier been happy to permit such contests, were they now too worried that Jacques would win? It may also be the case, of course, that Duke Philip in turn would not have encouraged (or allowed) just *any* of his knights to venture across Europe as a representative of Burgundian chivalry: it had to be one who was likely to win – there was, perhaps, a good deal of prestige at stake.

Typically, in the account of the combat at Valladolid the compiler reproduces his source (in this instance Lefèvre's letter) almost exactly. He has good reason to, as the 'Navarrese gentleman' on whose letter it is based appears to give a fine eyewitness report. He carefully records, for instance, how Guzmán attempts to use a non-regulation weapon and then angers the arbiter – the King of Castile – by making not just one false start but two, leaping to the attack before the requisite number of fanfares has been blown. But interestingly, the account does not appear to be the Navarrese gentleman's alone: as in the description of Jacques's combat with Boniface at Ghent, the compiler interpolates certain very particular visual details, such as the 'white silk'[53] of Lalaing's pavilion, which strongly suggest that he or his herald-source, too, had been present at the combat; and the formal exchange which follows the contest, in which Guzmán effectively apologises for any offence he may have caused by his behaviour towards Jacques, does not appear in Lefèvre's letter (i.e. the Navarrese gentleman's account) at all, and may well be the recollection of the compiler or his herald-source.

As discussed above, the likeliest candidate for the herald-source is Charolais; and Charolais must certainly be the source of much of the material for the next episode, in which Lalaing, having returned from Iberia to Burgundy, sends

---

[52] And a challenge to single combat was a serious matter – there was little sense of sport. Note how, when Jacques later arrives in Scotland after challenging James Douglas, Douglas's followers are distinctly uneasy: 'in the exchange of words that followed they wanted to know why he'd challenged master James to combat, and it was clear from their manner of asking that they were far from happy'. They need to be assured that 'it wasn't prompted by hatred, envy or any ill will' (p. 133).

[53] p. 113.

a letter to Scotland challenging the noble James Douglas to combat.[54] The compiler says that 'This letter, I understand, contained the Chapters he'd been sending everywhere';[55] and though the words 'I understand' strongly suggest that Charolais was not himself the compiler, he was the key communicator: it was Charolais to whom the letter was entrusted and who 'instructed in his mission by Sir Jacques, set off with the duke's consent',[56] sailed to Scotland and delivered the letter in person. His return to Sluis with Douglas's reply is described in detail. The compiler, although not Charolais himself, is surely working from Charolais's records here.

When we come to the combat itself, in which Jacques de Lalaing, his uncle Sir Simon and the Breton squire Hervé de Mériadec do battle with three Scotsmen at Stirling (a contest as public as the one at Valladolid: 'four or five thousand', we are told, were present),[57] the account is once again taken largely verbatim from Lefèvre's letter but adds a number of details which certainly suggest that the compiler was himself an eyewitness. He does after all say in his prologue that 'I, the author of this present work, have witnessed some of his illustrious deeds'; and here at Stirling he notes, as Lefèvre does not, that 'at the Scots' request the throwing of lances was forbidden',[58] that a certain blow from his Scottish opponent caught Mériadec 'on the left sleeve of his coat of arms', and that Mériadec in return 'laid him flat out, face down, stunned'.[59] This may of course be simply a desire by the compiler to insert invented colour, but that is not usually his way; and phrases such as 'a fine and splendid sight it was' and 'as became clear when the king threw down his baton and they opened Sir James's visor',[60] phrases which do not appear in Lefèvre's account, do suggest that the compiler had been there and seen it. If this was so, the fact that he is otherwise essentially happy to copy Lefèvre's version almost verbatim is a strong indicator of its accuracy, an endorsement

---

[54] There was nothing random about Lalaing travelling to Spain, Portugal and then to Scotland. The focus of Duke Philip's marital policy had changed markedly from France to Iberia: in 1430 he took Isabella of Portugal as his third wife – 'his first two wives had represented close relations with France, while this third implied independence' – and he arranged the marriages of nearly all his nephews and nieces to Iberian princely houses; and at the same time 'the relations of Burgundy and Scotland ... were carefully maintained and developed by Philip the Good ... For Burgundy they formed part of a system of protective alliances and commercial connections ... [and] helped to display the status of Burgundy as a European power.' Vaughan, *op. cit.*, pp. 55, 290, 110.

[55] p. 129.

[56] p. 131.

[57] p. 134.

[58] *Ibid.*

[59] p. 136.

[60] *Ibid.*

of Lefèvre's reliability as a witness of all the events he describes – not least the Fountain of Tears.

The Fountain of Tears

The exploit for which Lalaing is probably most famous, the passage of arms of 'the Fountain of Tears' at Chalon-sur-Saône in Burgundy, is recorded in abundant detail in *The Book of the Deeds*. It is once again copied almost verbatim from Lefèvre's letter, and, again, there is good reason to trust the reliability of his account. Not only is it typically sober and businesslike in tone – Lefèvre was, after all, King of Arms of the Order of the Golden Fleece and wrote accordingly – but there is striking consistency of detail to be found, for example, in the record of the event written by the chronicler Olivier de la Marche.

And if we can trust the account of the event, we have probably no reason to doubt the event's stated purpose. Lalaing's Chapters (his terms and conditions for combat) declare that 'his aim in undertaking this is to do all in his power to elevate and enhance the noble estate of chivalry',[61] just as, in his earlier combat with an English squire at Bruges, he had been 'yearning to ensure that he and his illustrious deeds might be remembered and stand as an example for all noble men'.[62] The compiler then reports that Duke Philip, giving his blessing for the passage of arms, prays that Jacques will 'acquire renown that will redound to the glory of yourself and all your friends and kin'.[63] It will, by extension, redound to the glory of Burgundy, and it is noticeable that the majority of those who come to compete at the Fountain of Tears are Burgundians,[64] and that the outcome of each combat – the winning or losing – is of far less importance than the taking part (and thereby being trained, equipped, fit and ready, if needed, for war in their lord's service).[65] Jacques clearly makes short work, for example, of the squire Guillaume d'Amange, but the (brief)

[61] p. 147.
[62] p. 139.
[63] p. 149.
[64] A notable exception is 'a knight from the kingdom of Sicily, Sir Jehan de Boniface by name'. The use of the indefinite article – 'a knight' – when Boniface has already appeared prominently in *The Book of the Deeds*, is a sign of just how much the work is a compilation of existing records rather than the composition of a single hand. There are several other instances of this: when, for example, the compiler later turns to a chronicle for the account of the Ghent War, he directly copies its reference to 'a gentle knight named Sir Simon de Lalaing', despite the fact that this is Jacques's uncle, a figure who has already featured many times in the book.
[65] See Lois Forster, *Chevaliers et hommes d'armes dans l'espace bourguignon au XVe siècle* (Université Charles de Gaulle – Lille III, 2018), p. 632.

account avoids saying so: what matters is that yet another Burgundian has had the courage to participate and take up the illustrious challenge; what matters is the glorification of chivalry, especially if it's Burgundian. The descriptions of display and apparel vastly outweigh in most cases the descriptions of the combats themselves – spectacularly so in the case of Jacques's contest with the lord of Épiry, in which paragraphs describing Épiry's crêpe, silk, damask, satin, velvet, his horse's caparison and his fabulous pavilion are followed by a single sentence recounting the fight. And most, if not all, of the combats at the Fountain of Tears, although undertaken in earnest, have a decidedly ritualistic air with the unfailingly repeated and near-identical accounts of the entries, acknowledgements, presentations, announcements and etiquette involved in each case – and those involving combat with swords sound somewhat akin to a highly regulated, almost choreographed ballet.

This elaborate, gloriously glamorous event did not have to wait for memorialisation in any written account: it was memorialised as soon as it had finished, in the stunning *entremets* presented by Lalaing at the 'splendid supper' that he gives after the final day. The centrepiece of the supper is a gigantic model 'some eight feet long and six or seven feet wide'[66] depicting the city of Chalon and the passage of arms at the Fountain of Tears, complete with precisely detailed figurines of all who had taken part. Judging by the account given in *The Book of the Deeds*, which again is copied almost verbatim from Lefèvre's letter to Jacques's father, some of these figurines in the *entremets* appear to have been used in fascinating fashion in the manner of a kind of puppet play, with scripted speeches delivered on their behalf as they are moved around the model. There had been nothing novel about Jacques de Lalaing's *pas d'armes* at the Fountain of Tears – Pierre de Bauffremont, for example, had already staged the *pas d'armes* of the 'Tree of Charlemagne' on the road from Dijon to Auxonne in 1443, and René d'Anjou had staged the *pas* of the 'Shepherdess' at Tarascon in 1449 – but Lalaing seems to have been set on making his own event supremely memorable. The chivalry of Burgundy, in an event staged with Duke Philip's blessing on the Saône where the county and duchy of Burgundy met, was to be shown to be exceptional.

Chivalry and Status

And, as Wim Blockmans has written, 'chivalry in all its permutations was key to Burgundian prestige and served as the main structuring agent of both the lives of individual knights and the society of the court as a whole'.[67] This had been the case since early in Duke Philip's reign; indeed, in 1425 the

---

[66] Below, p. 170.

[67] Wim Blockmans, 'Jacques de Lalaing: The Vitality of the Chivalric Ideal in the Burgundian Netherlands' in *A Knight for the Ages* ed. Morrison, p. 53.

duke himself had challenged Duke Humphrey of Gloucester to single combat, 'pompously hinting that young knights like themselves should settle their differences by personal combat rather than by waging public war, with all the slaughter it entailed',[68] and Jehan Lefèvre recorded in his *Chronique* how Duke Philip withdrew to his castle of Hesdin and went into strict training for the duel, which was finally banned by the pope and blocked by the efforts of the English Parliament and the Duke of Bedford. But the Burgundian chivalrous spirit was undampened, and Philip's founding of the chivalric Order of the Golden Fleece in 1430 with its 'glittering ceremonial' was designed not least 'to proclaim the new-found greatness of Burgundy throughout Europe'.[69] The bibliophile duke's library, rich in chivalric literature (not least works on all-conquering Alexander), is evidence of the cultural importance of chivalry at his court and in the mind of a duke intent on expanding his dominions and enhancing Burgundy's prestige and status in Europe's eyes.

Status is of manifest importance throughout *The Book of the Deeds*. No one is even allowed to take up Lalaing's challenge to combat unless he can qualify by demonstrating sufficiently pure and illustrious ancestry. Jacques is certainly keen to display his own: his pavilion for his contest against an Englishman at Bruges is 'superb: adorned with thirty-two banners bearing the coats of arms of the lords from whom he was descended on both his father's and his mother's side, a glorious sight to behold'.[70] As Graeme Small has written, 'in a century preoccupied with status, respect for blue blood and hierarchy were particular obsessions at the Burgundian court ... [where] lesser social origins were an embarrassment'.[71] And status is proclaimed through dress in no uncertain manner – though a manner which may flit past the modern eye: at Stirling, for example, in the combat with James Douglas, it is carefully recorded that 'Sir Jacques and Sir Simon were dressed in robes of black velvet, long and lined with sable, while Hervé was clad in a short robe of black satin, sable-trimmed';[72] the distinction between long and short, velvet and satin, and being lined as opposed to trimmed, should not be overlooked.[73] It was a time when, in the words of Margaret Scott, 'clothing was bound up with hierarchical ideas beyond anything we can experience today, with complex rules, both written

---

[68] Vaughan, *op. cit.*, p. 38.

[69] *Ibid.*, p. 54.

[70] Below, p. 140.

[71] Small, *op. cit.*, pp. 49, 33.

[72] Below, p. 133.

[73] The same may well apply regarding gifts exchanged. Is there a projection of status involved when, in return for Diego de Guzmán's gift of 'a courser caparisoned in crimson satin', Jacques responds by sending him 'a destrier, caparisoned in rich blue velvet laden with orfrey, its saddle covered in violet velvet'? (Below, p. 118).

and unwritten, governing who could wear what'.[74] The meticulous recording, time and again, of the quality of apparel worn and of the fabrics used, speaks volumes about the attention given to displaying wealth and status.

The Ghent War

The status of individuals and the status of chivalry itself are to the fore in the final section of *The Book of the Deeds*: the Ghent War narrative which, as discussed above, was copied from a chronicle – probably an otherwise lost section of Lefèvre's *Chronique*. Like many chronicles, this is a patchwork of recorded incidents and episodes: it is finely written, but is very much an official record, not a florid or dramatised account. The compiler has incorporated this long extract from a chronicle because the Ghent War was a significant event, Jacques's participation in it was a memorable part of his life (and death), and in the chronicler's account Jacques at times figures notably – he was, quite clearly, a genuinely prominent and valuable participant in Duke Philip's campaigns against the Ghenters. But some of the episodes do not involve Jacques at all. The compiler omits or compresses passages detailing non-military activity – the negotiations of truces and diplomatic efforts to secure peace[75] – but he fully retains passages which involve not Jacques but his uncle Simon, and some passages involving neither of them, because the work is a celebration of Burgundian chivalry and not just the Lalaings.[76] In the same way, a good deal of the 14th-century biography of Bertrand du Guesclin is not about Guesclin at all but about French chivalry as a whole, often digressing from Bertrand's heroics to show other valiant French knights and their fine example of fighting for the God-given fleur-de-lis.[77]

---

[74] Margaret Scott, 'Clad in Crimson and Gold: Dress in the *Book of Deeds of Jacques de Lalaing*' in *A Knight for the Ages* ed. Morrison, p. 121.

[75] These are printed in the full version of the chronicle fragment published by Lettenhove in Volume II of his *Oeuvres de Chastellain*.

[76] Elisabeth Gaucher has written that 'it is incontestable that the author wished to point the spotlight on Jacques de Lalaing to the detriment of the other lords partici-pating with him in the suppression of the Ghentish revolt' (Gaucher, *op. cit.*, p. 204, my translation). This does not seem to me to be the case at all, and it overlooks the fact that this section of *The Book of the Deeds* is not 'the author''s but the work of a chronicler, whose professional objectivity is probably to be trusted. A reader may on occasion suspect that the compiler has indeed inserted a phrase or two to emphasise Jacques's involvement, but this is to the detriment of no one; and his use of Lefèvre's chronicle as the base of his narrative, and the frequency of references in it to Jacques's feats, are surely a confirmation of Jacques de Lalaing's genuine prominence and valiant contribution, showing the extent to which he had made an impression on all involved.

[77] See Cuvelier, *The Song of Bertrand du Guesclin*, trans. Bryant (Woodbridge, 2019), pp. 6–16.

The Ghent War was a war fought by Burgundy's duke and his nobility against 'the most powerful town in the duke's territories, exceedingly wealthy in every respect, incredibly large, and with an exceptionally numerous population'.[78] The conflict was the culmination of long-standing tensions which finally reached a head when the city resisted the duke's attempt to impose onerous taxes on staple commodities, not least salt. It may have been arguably a squalid affair, fought across miles of the region's scrub and befouling marshland cut by ditch and dyke, wholly unsuited to mounted, chivalric combat; but it is reported by the chronicler in noble terms. Any official chronicler would of course be likely to be biased in his view of the conflict; but if he was Lefèvre (which is probably the case judging by his prominent presence on a number of occasions, not least at Lalaing's death), then, being King of Arms of the Order of the Golden Fleece, it is no surprise to see him take every opportunity to show his lord the duke's sober fair-mindedness towards Ghentish ambassadors (they were lucky, he says, not to be 'dealing with a prince of unbridled fury'),[79] and to defend and justify the duke's wrath when confronted with the Ghenters' repeatedly stressed 'disloyal and damnable actions, their faithlessness and disobedience … their bad faith: it was constant'.[80] And while the noble Burgundian knights and squires are shown as displaying chivalric valour and prowess in every encounter, we are usually told that the citizen armies (supported by local peasants) do nothing but flee. At Overmere, for example,

> the attack upon the Ghenters was ferocious, and at the very forefront was Sir Jacques de Lalaing. And as soon as the Ghenters saw the might of the assault, they broke and took to flight.[81]

This is typical; time after time we are told the oiks take to their heels the moment the brave nobles show they mean business. At Hulst

> Sir Jacques and Sir Simon ordered their archers to dismount. They marched straight to engage with the Ghenters who, seeing them advance so near, began to flee.[82]

Even when entrenched and fortified, packed commoners, we are told, are no match for a valiant noble with a mere handful of troops:

---

[78] Mathieu d'Escouchy, *Chronique*, i. pp. 368–9.

[79] Below, p. 183.

[80] pp. 178, 216.

[81] p. 199.

[82] p. 213.

That day the good knight Sir Jacques de Lalaing, by his mighty courage and prowess, conquered and won from the Ghenters seven or eight great bulwarks, and went through two villages, one of them well entrenched and having a fine and fortified church, and with his small company of troops routed the enemy and sent them fleeing all the way to Axel.[83]

Honour, courage and prowess among the Ghenters are reported to be in short supply, but the bravery and daring of the duke's forces are said to be in splendid form at the city of Ghent itself, where they are measured by how close they venture to the walls:

If some of the duke's men and horses were killed and wounded it's no wonder; for that day, I believe, there were three standards borne closer to the city of Ghent in battle than had ever been in the time of emperor, king or prince. The first of the three, and the one borne nearest, was the standard of the lord of Rubempré: three or four times it was carried right to the barriers at the Saint Bavo gate. The second was the standard of Sir Jehan de Croÿ, who had a great body of men at his command as he led the vanguard that day; as in all engagements, he was accompanied by the Count of Saint-Pol. The third was the Duke of Burgundy's standard, guarded by the Duke of Cleves, who had it carried so near that if it were not within range of the cannon fire it could hardly have been closer.[84]

By comparison, while 'brave knights and squires skirmished constantly, trying to draw the enemy away from the city and out beyond the range of their fire', the chronicler records that 'the Ghenters wouldn't venture far, so the army had to withdraw'.[85]

Those knights and squires, clearly, are the models to be emulated. And, says the chronicler, there are many of them: not infrequently he gives detailed lists of who was supporting the duke.

The Marshal of Burgundy was stationed at Courtrai with a great body of knights and squires and excellent troops from Burgundy, Flanders and Artois. At Oudenaarde was Sir Jacques de Lalaing with a very fine company. Sir Anthoine bastard of Burgundy was at Dendermonde, likewise well accompanied by knights and squires. In the town of Aalst were Sir Anthoine de Wissocq and Sir Louis de la Viefville with a large body of troops. Elsewhere, the lord of Gruuthuse was in the city of Bruges with a strong contingent, and in Sluis was Sir Simon de Lalaing with the captain of the Franc of Bruges. As for the nobility of Flanders, they all sided with their prince in waging war against the Ghenters, both in their own immediate areas and in

[83] pp. 213–14.
[84] p. 220.
[85] *Ibid.*

the cities loyal to the duke. At Ath in Hainaut and in the marches thereabouts was Sir Jehan de Croÿ, lord of Chimay, grand bailiff and governor of Hainaut, with a very fine company of knights and squires and other troops from Hainaut and Picardy.[86]

In the context of the chronicle this passage may have been largely a matter of bureaucratic record; in the context of its inclusion by the compiler of *The Book of the Deeds* it is a list of models: just as Bertrand du Guesclin and his fellows had in his biography been shown as paragons of loyalty to the French monarchy, so Jacques de Lalaing is here in a fine company of models of loyalty to the duke. And what admirable exemplars they are compared to the Ghenters who, we are told,

> continued waging war, burning villages and farms, inflicting all manner of harm in Flanders and Hainaut upon the obedient subjects of the duke their lord.[87]

The chronicler emphasises that 'all [Duke Philip] wanted from the Ghenters was that they behave towards him as good subjects should to their good and natural lord and prince'. But the enemies of their 'good and natural' lord included

> a great horde of Ghentish lowlifes, a company calling themselves the Green Tent, a host of outlaws, brigands and arsonists: two or three thousand kept banding together.[88]

Rebellion, however, is recorded as getting its just reward: the numbers of Ghentish dead, in clash after clash, are reported by the chronicler to be chillingly great. While, for instance, at Nevele 'three of the count's men were slain, two of them being noblemen',[89] Ghentish losses are always in the hundreds and not infrequently the thousands.

Relevance

The chronicler's stressing of the chivalrous virtues – courage, loyalty and prowess – displayed by lords, knights and squires in the context of a campaign against a citizen and peasant army might suggest an element of wishful thinking, and a fantasy that those virtues and values are still relevant in a rapidly changing world in which lance and sword are no match for gunpowder.

---

[86] p. 222.
[87] *Ibid.*
[88] *Ibid.*
[89] p. 204.

Indeed, the death of 'the good knight Jacques de Lalaing', inflicted as it is by
a cannonball fired by a commoner, has been seen by some as an ironic and
iconic image of the end of the age of chivalry, rather like the miserable end
of the great swordsman in Kurosawa's film *The Seven Samurai*, wretchedly
shot by a musket. Elisabeth Gaucher refers to it as 'the most shameful of
deaths (*la plus honteuse des morts*)'.[90] But is it? There is no hint of shame
in the account of Jacques's death. It is very noticeable that in *The Book of
the Deeds* there is no disdain whatever of artillery. The duke's army happily
deploys it in conjunction with chivalrous daring:

> The Count of Étampes, following the duke's command, now led his forces
> towards the bridge at Espierres, with a great train of artillery including
> culverins and veuglaires ... As soon as the count drew near, he deployed
> his force and in fine order launched an assault on the bridge and crossing.
> The artillery opened fire, the archers and the crossbowmen advanced, and
> some noble men leapt into the river: Sir Jacques de Lalaing and a number
> of others went in up to their necks to take and secure the crossing.[91]

There is no suggestion at any point that artillery is somehow base, ignoble.
True, the verse epitaph for Jacques says that

> ... in sudden fashion, without skill,
> The Ghenters brought [him] down with a cannon shot.[92]

But, 'skill-less' though it may have been compared to work with lance or
sword, there is nothing unworthy about artillery, nothing backward-looking
about the Burgundian approach to warfare. After all, when Jacques is killed by
the cannonball, he's enjoying himself watching the duke's artillery bombard
the walls of Poeke Castle. The chronicler makes no comment whatever on
the long-range death of the master of hand-to-hand combat: he gets on with
giving a detailed, sober, accurate account of exactly what happened, and
exactly how – perhaps by way of future warning to others – the absence of
the required protection had caused his death:

> On each side of a bombard and mantlet it is usual to dig trenches and
> earthworks to provide cover while observing the damage done by the
> bombard and while the gunner is taking aim. But at this bombard such
> earthworks had yet to be made ...[93]

---

[90] Gaucher, *op. cit.*, p. 378.
[91] Below, pp. 185–6.
[92] p. 230.
[93] p. 227.

The tone is regretful and cautionary, but there is no disdain for gun or gunner.

Nor is there anything backward-looking about the respect for chivalry and the extolling of its virtues throughout *The Book of the Deeds*. Chivalry was not an antiquated, nostalgic notion; it was still very much alive, not only when the book was compiled in the 15th century but well into the next. Even in the 16th century, as Tobias Capwell has written,

> fully armoured mounted knights still played an important role in warfare as well as in lavish courtly spectacles and tournaments. Not only did the skills of the knight still need to be honed over years of intense training, but the ideology of chivalry remained an essential part of the education of young noblemen. Medieval books of knighthood and chivalric romances written in the fourteenth and fifteenth centuries (or even earlier) remained wildly popular ... with new printed editions ... appearing for the first time, vastly increasing their readership.[94]

When, therefore, a lavishly illuminated manuscript of *The Book of the Deeds* was produced around 1530, fully six decades after the compiler had first assembled the work, it was

> not merely a historical record. It was a prize object intended to inspire and instruct.[95]

Capwell has noted how the production of this exquisite manuscript copy coincided with renewed tension between the Duke of Burgundy and the citizens of Ghent,[96] so the example of the Lalaings' loyal service in the earlier war was relevant in the extreme.

It had always been so. At the moment of the compilation's first creation, around 1470, Jacques's father Guillaume de Lalaing had by that time lost three of his four sons, all of whom had died without legitimate male offspring, and this may well have been a significant motive for the memorialisation of the most noted of the three;[97] but again, it was not a matter of sentiment and nostalgia or purely personal concerns: the celebration of the achievements

[94] Tobias Capwell, 'Armor, Weapons and Combat in the Getty *Lalaing*', in *A Knight for the Ages* ed. Morrison, p. 135.

[95] *Ibid.*

[96] *Ibid.*, p. 148.

[97] Rosalind Brown-Grant and Mario Damen have drawn attention to 'the threat of extinction that the main branch of the Lalaing dynasty was facing in this period... The very honour and continuity of [the Lalaing] lineage, not to mention the possession of the eponymous lordship, were at stake... [and Guillaume de Lalaing may well have been] responsible for commissioning the *Livre* due to his regret at his lack of male offspring in general and his famous son's death in particular'. Brown-Grant

of ancestors was central to the nobility's sense of itself – and not only in terms of the family but of court society as a whole. Such a work was of crucial importance for Burgundy. 'Under Philip the Good,' Zrinka Stahuljak has written,

> Burgundy had become a composite, multilingual state-in-becoming. For that it needed a literature with symbolic power. This literature was not a spectacle of luxury, a theatre of decline, or a solipsistic celebration of one's own fossilized grandeur but a literature with agency, promoting a shared culture and productive of social practices, such as perfect service to one's lord, the head of a state.[98]

Commemorating a Burgundian knight who had demonstrated outstanding prowess, courtesy, courage and loyalty to the duke was vital.

And – remarkably perhaps, given Burgundy's pressing problems internally and on its immediate borders – the final didactic element in the commemoration of the good knight Jacques de Lalaing is an appeal to remember the crusades. A few months after Lalaing's death, at the astonishingly elaborate Feast of the Pheasant at Lille, Duke Philip and the knights of the Order of the Golden Fleece made solemn vows to mount a crusade against the Turks who had just captured Constantinople. The crusade never took place, but the vows made on the pheasant – inspired by Jacques de Longuyon's chivalric Alexander romance *The Vows of the Peacock* – were a sign of how enduring the notion of chivalry's ultimate purpose was. The ideal ascending trajectory of a knight's career – first gaining experience in tournaments, then venturing into war close to home,[99] then further afield, and then devoting his service to battling God's enemies in the East – is traced in the French knight Geoffroi de Charny's semi-autobiographical poem of about 1350, his *Livre Charny*:

> If you've achieved success in your own land, and frequently in war, it should rightly earn you credit ... but I declare that when you achieve more

---

and Damen, *A Chivalric Life*, pp. 37, 40. The fourth son, although still living, was a committed cleric, unable to inherit.

[98] Stahuljak, *op. cit.*, p. 87. Graeme Small similarly points to the importance of historiography for Burgundy in building a sense of its own past and promoting cultural and political cohesion. See Small, *op. cit.*, pp. 104–5, 129.

[99] Combat in the lists is hugely admired, but does not compare with acts of valour in war; note how two Portuguese nobles, having seen Jacques's brave action in the battle at Lokeren, are reported as saying that 'they'd heard that this Sir Jacques had fought eighteen combats in the lists, and emerged with honour all eighteen times, but in their view he'd fought as honourably that day, and won as much honour, as he'd done in his whole life previously – though it was a fine thing that so young a knight, only thirty or so, had fought eighteen contests in the lists'. Below, p. 196.

in countries other than your own, you can safely say that no more can be asked: for me that's the ultimate ... So where will you go? To Granada or the Holy Land, to put down the enemies of God? That's a fine course to take in life.[100]

Even the biography of the hard-nosed, rough-hewn Breton hero, Bertrand du Guesclin, does its best to suggest that, during the chaos that followed the disastrous French defeat at Poitiers, he took charge of the Free Companies, 'the mercenary riff-raff ... the most bloodthirsty freebooters'[101] who were pillaging and stripping great swathes of France, so that he could lead them on a sin-absolving crusade:

'My heart is set on going to Cyprus to fight the infidels, or to Granada, to bear my whetted sword against the worshippers of Tervagant!'[102]

The Book of the Deeds, as noted previously, records how the Emperor of Greece sends an ambassador to Duke Philip appealing for troops to help him resist 'the Infidels led by the Grand Turk' Murad II, and the duke is presented as a paragon of the crusading spirit by having the ambassador say that 'if the Duke of Burgundy didn't lend him support and aid he could see no other Christian prince with the will to help him defend Christendom'. Indeed, when he is first introduced in *The Book of the Deeds*, three of the four epithets applied to Duke Philip are 'the most Christian champion of the faith, the honour of Christendom, the quaking terror of infidels'.[103] Later, in an account of the assembly of the Order of the Golden Fleece at Mons, we are told that

it was decided that a great and distinguished embassy should be sent to our holy father the Pope with a view to countering the designs of Mahomet [Mehmed], the grand emperor of Turkey, so that plans might be made in good time, urgently.[104]

Interestingly, the purpose of this embassy is not explained in Lefèvre's letter to Jacques's father – there he simply says it was 'on great matters' – but the compiler of *The Book of the Deeds* (who tells us that 'I, the author of this book, was present [at Mons] and witnessed all the solemnities')[105] clearly

---

[100] The *Livre Charny*, trans. Bryant, in *The Book of Geoffroi de Charny* (Woodbridge, 2021), pp. 117, 115.

[101] Maurice Keen, *Chivalry* (London and New Haven, 1984), p. 232.

[102] Cuvelier, *op. cit.*, pp. 162–3.

[103] p. 38.

[104] p. 177.

[105] *Ibid.*

thought it important to make plain that countering the designs of the Infidel was at stake in a mission of which Jacques de Lalaing was at the forefront.

Most striking of all in this respect is the closing passage of *The Book of the Deeds*, where Jacques's ultimate aim in life is revealed. He had resolved, the compiler tells us,[106] that

> once the wars in Flanders were over, out of love for his brother he would pass to Philippe all rights and responsibilities that would fall to him on his father's death – in other words, the lordship of Lalaing. For his own part, he was intent on devoting his body and his life to the service of Our Lord, to go to the lands that bordered the infidels and never return, keeping only a pension sufficient to support him, such as his father and close family and friends together deemed fit.[107]

Jacques's career, then, was following the model trajectory. With the blessing and support of his lord the Duke of Burgundy, he had first devoted himself to splendid feats of chivalry in the lists. He had then given his lord exemplary, valiant service in his war. Once that local war was done, he had planned to follow the ideal progression of a knight's career and commit himself to venturing East to face the infidel. In hindsight, knowing as we do that the crusades were over and done, this might appear a romantic fantasy. But judging by the vows made at the Feast of the Pheasant, his fellows of the Order of the Golden Fleece would have seen him as 'the good knight Jacques de Lalaing' indeed – a complete model of chivalry, and a model which was real, attainable and still absolutely relevant.

The Book of the Deeds of the Good Knight Jacques de Lalaing, compiled as it is from a variety of sources whose prime purpose had not been to entertain but to record, may not always be the easiest of reads; but it holds rich seams of information to be mined, offering invaluable insights into the behaviour and thinking of the nobility in the late Middle Ages.

---

[106] And it is the compiler who tells us, not the chronicler. The final paragraphs of *The Book of the Deeds* (from 'Just a short while later, the good knight ended his days', p. 227), are not part of the Ghent War narrative borrowed from the chronicle. Since these closing paragraphs are much concerned with the Lalaing family's response to Jacques's death, and with his burial, it might be reasonable to speculate that they are the compiler's own encomium for Jacques followed by his record of what he witnessed at the funeral and what the family told him about their son, brother, nephew.

[107] p. 228.

THE TEXT TRANSLATED

*T*he *Book of the Deeds of Jacques de Lalaing* has survived in thirteen manuscripts.[1] This is a translation of the text as it appears in the earliest complete copy, dating from the late 1470s or early 1480s: Paris, Bibliothèque nationale, MS fr. 16830. Beautifully illuminated – though less sophisticated in style than the magnificent manuscript of c. 1530, now in the Getty Museum in Los Angeles[2] – and copied with great care, it has few obvious errors or accidental omissions; on the rare occasions when these occur (all indicated in footnotes), I have referred to the text of Lettenhove's edition (Volume VIII of his *Oeuvres de Chastellain*, Brussels, 1866), which was based on a late 15th century manuscript belonging to the comte de Lalaing and another from the late 15th or early 16th century: Valenciennes, Bibliothèque municipale, MS 665. The Paris MS 16830 is accessible on line: https://gallica.bnf.fr/ark:/12148/btv1b10537591f/f11.item. Chastellain's edition is also accessible on line: https://archive.org/details/oeuvrespubparleb08chasuoft/page/n5/mode/2up.

---

[1] Listed and described by Anne-Marie Legaré in 'A Family Text: *Book of the Deeds of Jacques de Lalaing*' in *A Knight for the Ages* ed. Morrison, pp. 151–2.

[2] The central subject of Morrison's *A Knight for the Ages.*

FURTHER READING

Barber, Richard and Barker, Juliet, *Tournaments* (Woodbridge, 1989)

Barker, Juliet, *The Tournament in England 1100–1400* (new edition Woodbridge, 2020)

Boulton, D'Arcy, and Veenstra, Jan, eds, *The Ideology of Burgundy: The Promotion of National Consciousness* (Leiden, 2006)

Brown-Grant, Rosalind, 'Commemorating the Chivalric Hero: Text, Image, Violence, and Memory in the *Livre des faits de messire Jacques de Lalaing'*, in *Violence and the Writing of History in the Francophone Middle Ages,* ed. Guynn, N. and Stahuljak, Z. (Cambridge, 2013), pp. 169–86

Brown-Grant, Rosalind and Damen, Mario, *A Chivalric Life: The Book of the Deeds of Messire Jacques de Lalaing* (Woodbridge, 2022)

Charny, Geoffroi de, *Livre Charny*, trans. Bryant, in Wilson, Ian, *The Book of Geoffroi de Charny* (Woodbridge, 2021)

Cuvelier, *The Song of Bertrand du Guesclin*, trans. Bryant (Woodbridge, 2019)

Forster, Lois, *Chevaliers et hommes d'armes dans l'espace bourguignon au XVe siècle* (Université Charles de Gaulle – Lille III, 2018)

Gaucher, Elisabeth, *La Biographie Chevaleresque* (Paris, 1994)

——, 'Le vrai et le faux dans l'écriture de quelques biographies du XVe siècle: "Écrire la vie, une autre histoire"', in *Écritures de l'histoire (XIVe–XVIe siècle): Actes du colloque du Centre Montaigne, Bordeaux, 19–21 septembre 2002,* eds Bohler, D. and Magnien-Simonin, C. (Geneva, 2005), pp. 205–17

History of William Marshal, The, trans. Bryant (Woodbridge, 2016)

Kaeuper, Richard, *Chivalry and Violence in Medieval Europe* (Oxford, 1999)

Keen, Maurice, *Chivalry* (London and New Haven, 1984)

——, *Nobles, Knights and Men-at-Arms in the Middle Ages* (London, 1996)

Kreuger, Roberta and Taylor, Jane (trans.), *Jean de Saintré: A Late Medieval Education in Love and Chivalry* (Philadelphia, 2014)

Morand, François (ed.), 'Épître de Jean Le Fèvre, seigneur de Saint Remy, contenant le récit des faits d'armes, en champ clos, de Jacques de Lalain, et publiée, pour faire suite à sa *Chronique,* d'après un manuscrit de la Bibliothèque nationale', *Annuaire-bulletin de la Société de l'histoire de France,* 21: 2 (1884), pp. 177–239

Morrison, Elizabeth (ed.), *A Knight for the Ages – Jacques de Lalaing and the Art of Chivalry* (Los Angeles, 2018)

Morse, Ruth, 'Medieval Biography: History as a Branch of Literature', in *Modern Language Review,* 80: 2 (1985), pp. 257–68

Nadot, Sébastien, *Le spectacle des joutes: Sport et courtoisie à la fin du Moyen Âge* (Rennes, 2012)

Planche, Alice, 'Du tournoi au théâtre en Bourgogne: Le Pas de la Fontaine des Pleurs à Chalon-sur-Saône, 1449–1450', in *Le Moyen Âge, 80* (1975), pp. 97–128

Riquer, Martin, 'Les Chevaleries de Jacques de Lalaing en Espagne', in *Comptes rendus des séances de l'Académie des Inscriptions et Belles-Lettres 135* (1991), pp. 351–65

Small, Graeme, *George Chastelain and the Shaping of Valois Burgundy* (Woodbridge, 1997)

Stanesco, Michel, 'Le héraut d'armes et la tradition littéraire chevaleresque', *Romania* 106 (1985), pp. 233–53

——, *Jeux d'errance du chevalier médiéval: aspects ludiques de la fonction guerrière dans la littérature du Moyen Âge flamboyant* (Leiden, 1988)

Szkilnik, Michelle, 'Mise en mots, mise en images: *Le Livre des Fais du bon chevalier Jacques de Lalain*', *Ateliers de l'Université de Lille III, 30* (2003), pp. 75–87

Taylor, Craig and Taylor, Jane (trans.), *The Chivalric Biography of Boucicaut, Jean II le Meingre* (Woodbridge, 2016)

Vale, Malcolm, *War and Chivalry: Warfare and Aristocratic Culture in England, France and Burgundy at the End of the Middle Ages* (London, 1981)

Vaughan, Richard, *Philip the Good* (revised edition Woodbridge, 2002)

——, *Valois Burgundy* (London, 1975)

THE BOOK OF THE DEEDS
OF THE GOOD KNIGHT
JACQUES DE LALAING

Translated by
Nigel Bryant

I write this in joyous praise and honour of our saviour Jesus Christ and his glorious mother, who are the cause and driving force of all good works and without whom nothing of worth can be undertaken or achieved. I write it also because the remembrance of men fades and passes with their lives' end, and all things are forgotten and neglected unless set down in written record.

So, in order that the glory and praise gained by those who have gone before us be not extinguished but enhanced and kept in the memory as an example to the noble and virtuous men of the present, I wish to record the high deeds and valiant ventures accomplished in his day by Sir Jacques de Lalaing, eldest son of the lord of Lalaing.[1] In his time, in the quest for immortal glory, he devoted much toil and effort to enhance the honour and prestige of the house of which he was born. And because I, the author of this present work, have witnessed some of his illustrious deeds – and also to avoid idleness, the mother of all vices! – I have been pleased to undertake their recollection. And I ask those who read this work to forgive my dim and limited skill and judgement, and pray that Our Lord will give me grace to perform my task in a manner pleasing to those who read it and who hear it read. [*folio 1v*]

It's an established fact that in the past the land of Hainaut and the surrounding region possessed the flower of chivalry, the finest to be found anywhere at that time; for it was then the custom that once noblemen reached the age fit to bear arms they wouldn't cease – regardless of bodily danger and the trials and struggles they might face – to go in search of illustrious deeds of arms and fine ventures overseas[2] and elsewhere, where they would achieve so much with their mighty feats of prowess that their renown would flourish and spread to every realm. And so it does still today, as you can hear in what follows. Their eminence I have found recorded in books and histories, especially in relation to a knight of outstanding valour in his day named

---

1   Jacques was born (in 1420 or 1421) to a prominent family in the county of Hainaut – Lalaing (now Lallaing) is just to the east of Douai, some 20 miles south of Lille. Wim Blockmans notes that 'the most recurrent name among the [Duke of Burgundy's] courtiers from Hainaut was that of Lalaing as early as 1385'; Jacques's father Guillaume became grand bailiff of Hainaut in 1427 and governor of Holland and Zeeland in 1440. However, in 1445 he was dismissed from the post in some disgrace and, unlike his brother Simon and son Jacques, was never made a member of the Order of the Golden Fleece. 'We might hypothesize,' writes Blockmans, 'that Guillaume's disgrace gave a strong impetus to his eldest son, Jacques, to enhance his family's honour.' Blockmans, 'Jacques de Lalaing: The Vitality of the Chivalric Ideal in the Burgundian Netherlands', in *A Knight for the Ages*, ed. Morrison (Los Angeles, 2018), pp. 53–4. It might also, perhaps, have given some of the impetus for the commissioning of the book itself.
2   '*voyages d'outremer*', frequently implying pilgrimage/crusade to the Holy Land.

Gillion de Trazegnies,[3] a native of the noble land of Hainaut who, as is told in his story, performed so many deeds of high prowess that he won immortal glory. Nor should other valiant knights of Hainaut be forgotten who have been at the forefront since, achieving so much in their time that it will be in eternal memory. One was named Sir Gilles de Chin[4] and another Sir Jehan de Werchin, seneschal of Hainaut.[5]

But truly, were I to name them all and recount all the high deeds and worthy feats of prowess they accomplished, it would greatly extend this work that I've begun, which – if Our Lord grants me grace – I mean to carry on and complete. For things worthy of praise should never be suppressed or concealed; and as I've said, in the land and territory of Hainaut there were hitherto great houses from which have sprung noble and valiant knights, as you're about to hear. [f. 2r]

In the land of Hainaut, while its prince and lord was the glorious Duke Philip of Burgundy[6] – the most Christian champion of the faith, the patron and model of all virtues, the honour of Christendom, the quaking terror of infidels, who by his great and soaring courage has won immortal fame among all living men – there was a baron named Sir Othon, lord of Lalaing,[7] who had three fine knights as sons by the lady Yolande de Barbançon, conceived and born in lawful marriage: that is to say, Sir Guillaume, his first and eldest son, the second Sir Sanche and the third Sir Simon.[8] This Sir Othon, lord of Lalaing, engaged in martial action far and wide[9] and undertook many fine missions over the sea and elsewhere, first in the service of his sovereign lord Guillaume, Count of Hainaut,[10] and then of the aforesaid good Duke Philip.

This lord of Lalaing, seeing clearly that his eldest son Sir Guillaume was of fitting age, summoned him one day and said:

'Guillaume, you know and have long heard tell that in this house and lordship of Lalaing there has always been a legitimate heir, of noble lineage

---

3   The subject of a 15th-century prose romance, dedicated to Philip the Good, Duke of Burgundy, in which the central character was an almagam of several members of an illustrious Hainauter family: *Le roman de Gillion de Trazegnies*, ed. Stéphanie Vincent, Turnhout, 2011.

4   '*Gyon de Chin*'. Gilles de Chin was a legendary knight of Hainaut, killed at the siege of Rollecourt in 1133.

5   Jean III de Werchin, 1374–1415, a much-praised knight (and esteemed poet) from Hainaut.

6   Philip the Good, r. 1419–67.

7   '*messire Othes*'; Othon de Lalaing, 1365–1441.

8   Guillaume de Lalaing's date of birth is unclear – he died in 1475; Sanche's date of birth is also uncertain – he died in 1460; Simon was born in 1405 and died in 1476.

9   Literally 'pursued and frequented [deeds of] arms'.

10   Count William IV, r. 1404–17.

on both sides and descending in proper line from father to son. So before I die, as your father I would like to see that it did not end with you – albeit you have two brothers, Sanche and Simon. As you are the eldest, it is only right that you should marry first. So, if you love me and wish to please me, I bid you turn your thoughts and efforts to finding a fitting woman of good lineage to take to wife. I promise to help you and give of my wealth to your full satisfaction, for I desire with all my heart that before my passing I see you have legitimate children to succeed you in this lordship of Lalaing.'

Sir Guillaume, hearing his father's will and bidding, replied with all humility, saying: 'My dear and most respected father, I am ready to obey all your good commands and have no wish to go against them; but if it please you, I am still quite young, and hope you will be content to wait awhile till I have seen and experienced more in Arms, and crossed the sea or embarked on some fine mission to gain praise and renown as our forebears have done, including my grandfather and you. That said, sir, I shall obey all your good instructions.'

Then the lord of Lalaing, delighted by his son's response, said: 'Guillaume, the reply you have given will serve you well! I shall do all I can to find a marriage pleasing to me, to your mother and to you.'

The lord and his son said no more about the matter; but the lord of Lalaing, ever mindful of Sir Guillaume's humble and pleasing response, did all he could, searching far and wide for an honourable match for his son, personally asking his closest friends and kinsmen, telling them his intentions and praying them to find a young lady or damsel of good extraction whom they deemed a fitting wife for his eldest son Guillaume. A number of these friends replied, one of whom said:

'My lord of Lalaing, I and other kinsmen of yours have striven for a good while now to find such a lady or damsel as you desire. I know a lady of high and noble birth, surpassingly beautiful and of the finest character: intelligent, courteous, charming, abounding in all virtues. In my view, truly, if a match with her could be secured – as I hope it would – she is much to be commended. Before going further you could send someone to make an initial approach, to see if so early a remarriage would be welcomed: her husband was only lately slain at the piteous battle of Agincourt – the lady had been married and with him for a mere six weeks.' [*f. 3 v*]

1

*Concerning the marriage of the lord of Créquy's daughter to
Sir Guillaume de Lalaing*

Hearing this gentleman's words, the lord of Lalaing reflected a moment and then replied, saying:

'Tell me, I pray you, who is this lady you praise so highly, and of what family? And who was her husband?'

The gentleman replied that the damsel was the daughter of the lord of Créquy, and had been married to the only son of the lord of Wavrin who, along with his father, had been killed on the day of the battle of Agincourt.[11] 'She is fifteen or sixteen or thereabouts, tall for her age and shapely in every limb: no one could wish for a greater beauty.'

The lord of Lalaing, delighted by the squire's fine advice, thanked him deeply and said he would investigate as soon as he could and learn the wishes of her friends and kin. And so he did: by diligent procedure he secured the match, and the young lady and his son Sir Guillaume were betrothed and duly married.

Most nobly accompanied by her two brothers Jehan and Raoul de Créquy, young squires both, together with their mother the lady of Créquy and a host of knights and squires, she was escorted to the castle of Lalaing where she was received by the lord and lady of Lalaing and a great company of knights, squires, ladies and damsels, their relations and neighbours. They welcomed the noble lady with much joy and happiness. Gorgeously dressed and adorned, she was led up to the hall by her two brothers-in-law Sanche and Simon de Lalaing, young squires as they then were, tall and handsome and well built in every limb. Then the celebration and feasting began in the great hall of the castle of Lalaing. The supper tables were set and spread, the water brought, and they washed and took their seats at table. Of their order of seating and the dishes they were served and the entremets presented[12] I've no wish to give a long account; suffice to say that they were served that day with all possible lavishness and plenty.

When supper was done and the tables were cleared, trumpeters and minstrels struck up and dancing began there in the hall. Music was played on all manner of dulcet instruments, the players performing at the peak of their skill.

And when the dancing and celebration were finally over, it was time for all to take to their beds. The young bride was escorted to her chamber where she lay that night with her lord and husband. And it was only a short while later that they conceived a most handsome son, whose birth was a source of mighty joy for the lord of Lalaing and his lady. They proffered humble thanks to our lord Jesus Christ: they had lived to see what they desired most

---

[11] Jeanne de Créquy had been in her early teens when she had married Robert de Wavrin, who had indeed died at Agincourt with his father (also Robert).

[12] In the later Middle Ages entremets evolved from being delicacies between courses to become dishes of increasingly elaborate decoration and display, to the point where 'they do not involve the cook at all, but are the work of artisans: carpenters, smiths and painters... The next step...was to introduce stage scenery and props. These stage-set pieces soon gave way to actual dumb shows in the late fourteenth century, and even to spoken interludes in the next.' Richard Barber, *Magnificence* (Woodbridge, 2020), p. 240.

in all the world – a legitimate heir apparent to follow their son Sir Guillaume in the lordship of Lalaing, its land, its house. And in that house it prompted soaring celebration, as it did among their men, their subjects, their friends and all their kin. And when the young lady was happily delivered and the child had come into this world, he was taken to be baptised and was given the name Jacques – or Jacquet as he was always called till he reached the age to be knighted, as you can hear more fully in what follows. [*f. 5r*]

2

How the young Duke of Cleves asked leave of the lord and lady of Lalaing to take their eldest son Jacquet with him to the court of good Duke Philip of Burgundy

After the child had been nursed and raised with all possible care to the age of seven, he was taken from the hands of the women to whom he had been entrusted. His wise and prudent father saw he was old enough for tutoring and training, so the child was given to a [clerk][13] for his instruction; and before long he had made him skilled and adept in speaking, understanding and writing Latin and French, surpassed by no one of his age.

Jacquet de Lalaing grew and developed splendidly – none so handsome was then to be found. In all truth, God and Nature had neglected nothing in his making. He was tall, well built, well formed in every limb, and endowed and blessed with such virtues and manners that all who saw him and heard him speak he inspired to act well: such pleasure they took in his fine example, giving every sign as he did of being bound for great prowess and high renown.

The lord and lady of Lalaing, and the child's father Sir Guillaume and the young lady his mother, gave thanks and praise to Our Lord for having sent them a legitimate heir apparent who would hold their lands and lordships after their passing; and this was ensured when, shortly after, Sir Guillaume and the good lady his wife had another fine son named Jehan de Lalaing, later to be provost of Saint Lambert at Liège,[14] an eminent and most learned cleric. They then had two fair daughters, the elder named Yoland and the second Isabel, both of whom were placed at the court of Duke Philip of Burgundy, with the duchess his wife. Their beauty and modesty could not be overpraised; and for their goodness and humility and adorning virtues one was married to the lord of Brederode, a great baron of Holland,[15] and the other was given as wife to

---

13 Word accidentally omitted in MS 16830.

14 Saint-Lambert is Liège's cathedral; provost (*prévôt*) usually refers to the head of a cathedral or collegiate church.

15 Reinoud II van Brederode (1415–73); Brederode is just north of Haarlem.

the lord of Bossu, a great baron of Hainaut;[16] from both of them came fine issue indeed. Thereafter Sir Guillaume, named lord of Bugnicourt,[17] had two more fine sons, one named Philippe after the good Duke of Burgundy who raised him from the baptismal font,[18] and the other named Anthoine. Both became valiant knights, courageous in arms, as you may hear at the end of this history. But for the present we shall say no more of them; we shall return to tell of Jacquet de Lalaing, the subject of this work.

When his childhood was behind him he delighted, amongst other pastimes, in hunting and hawking which he conducted in fine fashion, with restraint. In backgammon[19] and chess, and in wise and gracious conversation, he surpassed all others of his age. And truly, he had a natural inclination and aptitude for all that the heart of a noble man should rightly desire – except that he had never yet borne arms or heard tell of such matters or seen any jousting or tournament. But as the saying goes, 'a good bird preens naturally'![20] And so it was to be with this fine squire.

For one day, while Jacquet was there in his father's house, the young Duke of Cleves,[21] nephew of the most glorious and good Duke Philip of Burgundy, came to Lalaing where he was grandly received and fêted by the lord of Lalaing and his son Sir Guillaume and by the two ladies their wives, nobly accompanied by ladies and damsels that day: they gave him and all his company a joyful welcome. At the castle of Lalaing the celebration was great indeed for the visit of the young Duke of Cleves: the lord and lady of Lalaing, who were now of very great age, did all in their power to feast and entertain him, as did their son Sir Guillaume and his wife the lady of Bugnicourt. Now, she had with her their eldest son, Jacquet de Lalaing; and the Duke of Cleves, seeing Jacquet – the same age as himself – so tall and well built and so assured in his bearing and demeanour, was most pleasantly struck by him, as was everyone around him, so much so that he couldn't resist asking Sir Guillaume and his wife the lady of Bugnicourt to give and entrust Jacquet to him.[22] This request Sir Guillaume freely granted, as did the lady his wife, and the duke thanked them very courteously. When Jacquet heard of the promise they'd made he was happier than he'd ever been: he couldn't wait to go! But

[16] Pierre I de Hénin, lord of Bossu (d. 1490); Boussu is east of Lallaing, near Mons.

[17] 10 miles south of Lalaing.

[18] i.e. he was his godfather.

[19] '*tables*', a dice game related to backgammon.

[20] i.e. birds don't need to be taught to preen, and young Jacques would take to Arms instinctively.

[21] John I, 1419–81 (r. 1448–81).

[22] i.e. to complete his training and education as a member of the young duke's socially superior household.

he couldn't be gone so soon, not before gowns and clothes were arranged, along with horses and harness and all he would need to accompany such an illustrious prince at the court of good Duke Philip of Burgundy.

The young Duke of Cleves stayed there a day and a night, and then took leave of the aged lord of Lalaing, his son Sir Guillaume and the ladies and damsels, thanking them most graciously for the reception they had given him. And he took Jacquet by the hand and said:

'Jacquet de Lalaing, my friend, I pray you join me as soon as you can at the court of my uncle the duke. I promise you a joyous welcome and we'll have the finest time you could wish.'

And Jacquet replied: 'Sir, whenever it please my father and my lady my mother to send me to you – would it were this instant! – I shall be ready.'

Then the young Duke of Cleves departed and headed for Brussels. There he found his uncle the duke who received him with great cheer and, smiling, said:

'Dear nephew, where have you been? I've not seen you for the last four days.'

'Sir,' the young duke replied, 'I've been to see the lord of Lalaing, where my company and I were made most welcome. And I arranged for him to give me his eldest son to come and join me here.'

'I'm very grateful to you, nephew,' said the duke. 'That's well done: from the house of Lalaing have come many fine knights and squires who've been of great service to us and our forebears. I'm sure the one who is to come and serve you won't let down his line but follow in their footsteps.'

With that their conversation ended. [f. 7v]

3

How Sir Guillaume and the lady of Bugnicourt, father and mother of Jacquet de Lalaing, instilled in him a number of fine principles before he left

You've heard now how the young Duke of Cleves came to the castle of Lalaing in Hainaut, and how on his departure he asked Sir Guillaume to entrust to him his eldest son Jacquet, which he granted, promising to send him. And so he did. The day at last came when all the clothes made for his son and the necessary servants, horses and equipment were ready. Sir Guillaume gave him four fine rounceys,[23] a gentleman to serve him, a learned clerk to continue tutoring him so that he wouldn't forget his Latin, and a boy to groom the horses.

---

[23] Rouncey ('*roncin*') tends to imply a good, multipurpose horse, lacking the cachet of the very best warhorse (the '*destrier*') but still a fine mount, ridden in combat by squires or less wealthy knights.

Then, when Sir Guillaume de Lalaing and his wife the lady of Bugnicourt saw that he was ready and set to depart the following day, they called him and took him to a chamber. There were only four present: the lord and lady his parents, Jacquet who was their eldest, and his brother Philippe who was very young. As for Yoland and Isabel, they remained with the damsels of the house. Once inside the chamber, the lord and lady called for the doors to be closed and then sat down on a bench. The lord then began to address and caution his son, saying:

'Jacquet, you are my eldest son, in line to succeed as the rightful heir to this house of Lalaing. I desire with all my heart to enhance and elevate the house, and to see it in my lifetime maintained and undiminished, our forebears having striven to raise it to immortal fame. That is why I swear by the One who made me that I would rather see you dead than any failing in you which would debase the house in any way. I expect no such thing, unless it be through sins which lead and draw men and women to damnation. And so that you understand what vices are, and that you beware of falling into such peril, I shall tell you, Jacquet my dear son, their nature and how you may avoid them.

'Strive with all your might and power to obey God's commandments; and with regard to our souls, know that whoever resists committing mortal sins is saved. For be assured, my son, that the other venial sins are redeemed and annulled with very little penance. So in protecting yourself from mortal sins, if you're willing to do as I say, you cannot fail to be saved. [*f. 8v*]

4

Concerning the sin of Pride

'So, my son, to win glory and high renown, now that you're going to reside at the court of so illustrious a prince, you must follow the example of those you perceive to be of good morals. First and foremost, you must avoid the sin of Pride if you wish to come good and win the favour of the lady you desire – for know this: few noble men have achieved the heights of prowess and renown without being in love with a lady or damsel. And listen, my son: so that you understand the kind of love I mean, I shall tell you.

'If, in all honour, you come to feel love for a lady or damsel unrelated to you, and you're inclined towards amorous liaison, then take care – if you wish to attain the high virtue of prowess – that it proves not to be a reckless, lustful love, for it would be much to your discredit and earn you lasting reproach. Moreover, dear son, if you'll follow my advice and guidance, you must be kind, modest, courteous and gracious, so that no unseemly word is ever said of you. For know this: if you had the wealth and wisdom of Solomon, the nobility of King Priam of Troy and were endowed with all physical perfection, pride alone, if it dwelt in you, would obliterate all your virtues. Wise Socrates says in this regard: "*Quantumcumque potes, fili, non esto superbus*",[24] and many other authorities say the like. It would take too long to cite them all, so I'll leave it for the present! But to return to the point, I tell you, my son, that the true lover I'm referring to, who has the virtue of humility rather than that sole sin of pride, cannot fail to gain the favour of the lady he desires. So put to flight and banish the vile and abominable sin of pride and all it entails, and you cannot fail to achieve salvation in your longed-for lady's favour, with all honour. [*f. 9r*]

5

Concerning the sin of Wrath

'As for the second sin, called Wrath, no true lover, I tell you, was ever wrathful. I've often heard tell of Love inflicting various trials on people to test them, but they never gave way to anger unless stricken with something other than love! So do all you can to avoid it and follow the philosopher's words:[25] "*Tristiciam mentis caveas plus quam mala dentis. Se[g]niciem fugias. Nunquam piger ad bona fyas*;" which is to say: avoid dark thoughts more than toothache! And if you wish to avoid heartache, shun Sloth: strive always to do good deeds. Flee anger and wrath, so that you're not infected by their dire disease: they'll lead you astray from the right path; they nurture all schism and division. Bear anger and hatred to no one; live at peace with all, for whoever hates his neighbour is a murderer, as the Gospel says[26] – and Saint Augustine says of this in one of his letters that, just as bad wine taints and ruins the vessel it's in if it's stored there very long, so anger pollutes and corrupts the person who harbours it. So be sure of this truth, my son: that wrath and ire so block and blind a person's heart that he cannot see the truth.

'The true lover, as I see it, is and must always be of joyful spirit, hoping that by serving well and loyally he'll have merciful reward from Love and from the lady he so desires. So he sings, dances and makes merry, following the words of the philosopher who says: "*Bene vivere et l[a]etari*", which is to say, live well and joyfully. But good living doesn't mean simply eating fine food and drinking fine wines, lying in fine beds all morning long and indulging in endless pleasure! First and foremost it means living well in relation to God, behaving with honesty and sincerity and finding joy in doing so.

'So I say that all true lovers, to win the longed-for favour of their fair ladies,

---

[24] 'As far as you possibly can, son, avoid being proud.'

[25] Medieval references to 'the philosopher' would almost always be understood as being to Aristotle, much translated and viewed as pre-eminently important.

[26] Not strictly speaking a gospel but the first epistle of John, 3:15: 'Whosoever hateth his brother is a murderer...'

must strive with all their might to avoid the sin of Wrath, most displeasing to God and to the world, and keep company with the loving virtue of Patience. They will thus be free of that most unpleasant and inimical of sins. [*f. 10r*]

6

Concerning the sin of Envy

' **A**s for the third sin, Envy, I say that a true lover will be envious of no man, for if his lady knew he was envious he would lose her, truly. No lady of honour has ever been able to love an envious man – except, that is, if he envies virtues and is striving to be the best: the most devout in church, the most refined in manners at table, the most gracious and pleasant in the company of ladies, the most valiant in arms. There's no envy in striving to excel in virtues – that's not the mortal sin of Envy as I understand it.

'I forbid you furthermore, dear son, to frequent taverns and to follow those who haunt them: drinking and gambling and the company of loose women will make you ever poor, mean and wretched, despised by all good people. Again, of the vile sin of Envy Plato speaks, saying: "Train yourself to shun Envy, for envy is loveless, it drains the body and makes the heart hard and cruel." So, my beloved son, flee all vices and all those guilty of them: Love and ladies of honour command all true lovers so to do.

'As a final word on the sin of Envy, be mindful of the maxim: "I would rather starve to death than lose my good name." And know this: in being more nobly born than another, you must be nobler in virtue, for nobility of conduct is worth more than nobility of parentage – and noble birth, no matter how high and mighty, cannot overcome death. So, as I say, in being a true lover, you will avoid the most unworthy sin of Envy and espouse the noble virtue of Charity, the daughter of God and much commended to us by Him; then you'll be free and clear and unsullied in respect of that sin.

7

Concerning the sin of Avarice

' **I**'ve now set forth my thoughts on the sins of Pride and Wrath and Envy. Now I must expound on the sin of Avarice. Truly, my son, avarice and true love cannot dwell together in one heart. If a miserly man should by some chance feel love, it's bound to be for some base, unworthy reason if it means he has to spend anything! But the true and loyal lover will wish only to serve Love and his lady honourably, with proper largesse, keeping himself well dressed and mounted, and all his retinue likewise, in a manner befitting his rank.

'On the other hand, a man who spends beyond his means will be foolish –
and unhappy, for Love and ladies of honour don't approve of extravagance
in lovers. They love those who present themselves in jousts and tourneys
and grand assemblies in as fine a manner as they can afford, without reckless
expense – and who give of their wealth to those most in need, out of love
for God, following Our Lord's words in the gospel, in the fifth chapter of
Matthew: *"Beati misericordes, quoniam ipsi misericordiam consequentur."*[27]
This means in short, my son, that to keep yourself clean and pure you must
avoid being covetous and avaricious, regardless of how much wealth you
have; a man so inclined will be loved by no one but universally despised.
The philosopher concurs who says: "Friend, avarice is the cause of theft,
robbery, usury, fraud, simony, trickery, perjury and conflict – in short, of all
ills." And Saint Augustine says that the avaricious heart is comparable to Hell;
for Hell, no matter how many souls it swallows down, will never say "That's
enough!" So it is with the avaricious man: if all the world's treasures were
in his clutches he would still not say "Enough!" That's why the true lover, to
win the longed-for favour of his fair lady, and of all ladies, must spurn that
contemptible sin of Avarice and keep company with the sweet and gracious
virtue Largesse, loved by God and admired by the world. In so doing he will
be saved. [*f. 11r*]

8

Concerning the sin of Sloth

'As for the fifth sin, Sloth, no true lover was ever idle; for the sweet
and amorous thoughts that occupy him night and day in the hope of
winning the longed-for favour of his lady can't allow it. Whether in singing
or in dancing he's more committed and keen than any. He'll rise early and
say his Hours, hear mass with all devotion, and go hunting or hawking while
shiftless[28] lovers are still abed!

'So, dear son, avoid idleness and excessive food and wine so that you're
not sullied with lust – for the lazy and the overfed will struggle to stay chaste.
Of this wretched sin of Sloth Saint Bernard says: "Friend, I've known some
fools who blame their state on Fortune. You'll rarely find a hard-working man
who's saddled with bad luck, but if you're idle you'll find misfortune's always
at your side!" In Saint Bernard's words, *"Revidere qu[a]e sua sunt, summa
prudencia est,"* which is to say: "Reviewing what you have is the height of

---

27 'Blessed are the merciful, for they will be shown mercy.'
28 Literally 'gout-ridden', a metaphor for being useless, unable to move themselves!

good sense." He doesn't say simply "see" it but "review" it, by which he means you can never consider too often what you have.[29]

'Idleness is frequently the toxin that poisons young people's thoughts: their indolence is a particular cause of vice. So cast out laziness, my son – it brings great trouble in life. Flee all that opposes virtuous qualities. True lovers are saved by such virtues, as they abandon the vile and wretched sin of Sloth and seek the company of the shining virtue Diligence; so I pray and command you to strive to join their ranks – then you'll be free of the miserable sin of Sloth, and rid of it you'll be saved. [f. 12r]

9

Concerning the sin of Gluttony

'As for the sixth sin, Gluttony, the true lover hasn't the slightest trace of it! He eats and drinks only for sustenance: in the philosopher's words he doesn't live to eat and drink, but drinks and eats to live – unlike some folk who live like pigs. So, my son, keep a rein on your mouth so that it doesn't have you drink too copiously; and an excess of ill-digested food is very harmful to the body, so avoid it. Never drink your fill of wine, lest you lose control – you'll be deemed a lout if you're immoderate with wine and wine becomes your master. On this subject Saint Gregory says in his *Morals*[30] that when Gluttony gains mastery over someone, all the good that person has ever done is lost. When the stomach is unrestrained by abstinence, all that person's virtues are engulfed. Saint Paul says of this that those consumed by worldly delights, who make their bellies their God, are doomed: their glorying in it will be the ruin of their soul, their honour, their body.

'So I beg you, my son – and command you – do not be one of them, but heed the words of Avicenna[31] on avoiding the sin of Gluttony; he says: "*Sic semper comedas, ut surgas esuriendo; sic etiam sumas moderate vina bibendo*", which is to say, always eat so that you rise from the table with your appetite unsated, and drink in moderation. That way, my son, you'll naturally live a long life, and be in God's grace with regard to that sin, and in the good graces of Love and your lady, too. You'll have shunned the base and shameful sin of Gluttony, and kept company with the sweet virtue Abstinence, the flower of all virtues. You'll be free and safe from that sin, and close to attaining the salvation of true and faithful lovers from the seven deadly sins. [f. 12v]

[29] These sayings cannot in fact be found in any known work of Bernard of Clairvaux.

[30] His *Moralia* – a commentary on the Book of Job.

[31] The 11th-century Persian polymath, a leading figure in medicine.

10

Concerning the sin of Lust

' So now, my son, we must come to speak of the seventh sin, Lust. Be sure of this: this sin must be quashed utterly in the true lover's heart, so great is the risk of his lady's dismay if he harbours a single unworthy thought. Hence the words of the holy apostle who says: "Flee lust, friend, lest you be sullied with a base reputation. Don't give in to the flesh, lest you offend Jesus Christ with your sin."

'So I urge and pray and command you, my son, to abstain from carnal pleasures, for they battle night and day against the soul. And I say this furthermore: the man who frequents loose women loses six things, the first being his soul, the second his wits, the third his morals, the fourth his strength, the fifth his sight and the sixth his voice. So flee this sin, my son, and all it entails. As Cassiodorus says,[32] vanity turned the angel into a devil, and brought death to the first man and stripped him of the blissful state bestowed on him. And vanity nurtures all evils; it's the wellspring of vice and stream of iniquity that bears a man away from glory and the grace of God.

'If I wished to tell you all that the philosophers and poets and sages of the pagan past said about that reviled sin – and they had yet to have any knowledge of the holy, loving grace of our true God, of the Holy Spirit – their writings would be too lengthy to recite! So I'll move on. But I tell you, my son, lust burns in congress, stinks at separation, brings fleeting pleasure, and ruin to the soul. This sin is so contemptible that the true lover flees it, for fear of displeasing his lady and losing her favour – and losing too, the grace of God, the bestower of all blessings. But be assured, those blessings will come to you if you strive to follow my advice.

'Let that suffice – though I've not yet reminded you of the ten command-ments in due order, for I'm quite sure you know them. But I pray and command you to do all in your power to keep and fulfil them. Love and fear God above all else; and in word and deed treat others as you would have them treat you. Beyond this I leave it to you and to the discretion of your confessor, who'll give you better guidance than I. But I've explained to you the seven deadly sins and the good that will accrue from avoiding them – and the woes in store if you fall in.

'Dear son, I'm sending you to the court of my sovereign lord Duke Philip of Burgundy, to serve and be companion to the young Duke of Cleves, who's done you and us such honour in asking for you. It's up to you, but I'm sure you'll achieve great success, without fail. If you do, you'll give me and your mother much pleasure. I promise to provide for you so worthily that, if you're

---

[32] In his 6th-century commentary (*Expositio*) on the Psalms.

deserving, you'll be able to present yourself among the sons of the other knights and barons and keep company with the highest.

'Above all, my son, I forbid you to mix with the serving boys – pay them no heed except in relation to the service they're there to provide. And trust those of them who're good. I'm not suggesting that none of them will be, but I'm thinking of those who might contemplate or do something which could bring you dishonour. So listen to the good and ignore the bad or mischievous. But don't beat or mistreat your servants: if they do something inappropriate, courteously point out their faults and, if they refuse to amend or correct them, pay them what they're owed and then dismiss them. It's unbefitting of a worthy man to beat or hit his boys or servants. Beat and correct your children when you have them, but beating and hitting others has sometimes led to grave trouble!

'Avoid bad men like poison, and seek the company of the good: spend all the time you can with those who can enhance your worth. Above all, my son, my wish and command is that you be always present at your master's retiring to bed and at his rising, and be diligent in serving him and doing his will – it's always said that diligence is better than prudence! Observe and strive to recognise the good and emulate them: you'll benefit very greatly.' [f. 14r]

11

How Jacquet de Lalaing left his father's house and came to the court of the Duke of Burgundy

After the lord of Lalaing had given this cautionary guidance to Jacquet his son, expounding his advice and beliefs at length as he saw fit, Jacquet humbly went down on one knee before Sir Guillaume and said:

'My dearly respected lord and father, my intention and heart are wholly set on following the fine instruction you've laid before me: by Our Lord's grace I'll strive earnestly to follow it.'

Then Sir Guillaume looked at his son and said: 'God grant that you do: without His help, dear son, we can perform no virtuous deed or anything of worth.'

And he took Jacquet by the hand and bade him rise. They left the chamber all together, the lord and lady hand in hand with their son, and came to the hall where the tables were laid and sat down to dine.

When dinner was over and the tables were cleared, Jacquet de Lalaing, eager to be gone and on his way, ordered his servants to make ready and to have the horses brought from the stables. Then he took leave of his father Sir Guillaume and his mother the lady of Bugnicourt, who kissed him, sighing deeply, as he departed, for of all her children he was dearest to her, though she loved them all.

After taking leave of his brothers and sisters, he went down the steps from the hall to the courtyard below, where he found his horse ready for mounting, and without stepping in stirrup leapt into the saddle. Seeing his servants and escort ready he thrust in his spurs and rode from the castle of Lalaing and on to the road for Brussels. Once he'd ridden about a league[33] he gave leave to those who'd seen him on his way, save a number of gentlemen appointed by Sir Guillaume to guide and present him to the young Duke of Cleves.

They pressed on in fine fashion till they came to Halle.[34] The morning after their arrival Jacquet de Lalaing had a mass sung before the image of the Virgin Mary, where he made humble prayers and appeals, prompted by the devotion that he felt.

After hearing mass, and having eaten, he and his retinue mounted and set off, pressing on till they entered the city of Brussels. As Jacquet approached the palace where the Duke of Burgundy held court[35] he saw his lord and master the young Duke of Cleves, who was on his way to join his uncle the duke and accompany him to mass. The Duke of Cleves was about to enter the gate when he caught sight of the approaching Jacquet and stopped and said to his gentlemen:

'I do believe I see Jacquet de Lalaing coming! Let's wait and see if it is!'

Jacquet, who'd been looking that way, recognised his master the duke immediately. He stepped down with a number of his closest attendants and walked towards the duke his master, who proffered his hand, saying:

'Well met indeed, Jacquet!'

Jacquet, his honourable manners well instilled, knelt and gave most humble greeting to the young Duke of Cleves, who received him with great courtesy, bidding him very welcome. Then he took him by the hand and bade him rise, and said his arrival was most timely and he would take him to the duke his uncle to pay his respects. Holding him by the hand, the young Duke of Cleves entered the palace courtyard, climbed the steps and arrived at the very moment when the Duke of Burgundy was coming to hear mass. He came before him, hand in hand with Jacquet, and presented him to the duke his uncle, saying:

'My lord, this is Jacquet de Lalaing, entrusted to me by his father Sir Guillaume to serve you and to be my companion, if it please you.'

The duke looked at Jacquet, smiling, and said: 'We bid you welcome, Jacquet. My dear nephew of Cleves has been eagerly awaiting your arrival.'

And he took him by the hand and bade him rise. Jacquet, having bowed the knee to the Duke of Burgundy, then went aside with the Duke of Cleves till the time arrived when the Duke of Burgundy came to make the offering as

---

[33] A notoriously vague unit of land distance as it varied from region to region and period to period; at this time, in France, it should be understood as about three miles.

[34] '*Haules*': presumably Halle, 20 miles south-west of Brussels.

[35] The Coudenberg Palace.

was his custom. The offering made and complete, the young Duke of Cleves left the chapel, taking Jacquet by the hand and conversing with him till he reached his lodging. There he took his seat at table, and Jacquet attended to his cup throughout dinner.

Once dinner was over the duke rose from table and all engaged in gracious conversation; and so gracious indeed were Jacquet's conversation and behaviour with the duke, in company with the young knights and squires of their age, that all delighted to hear him speak, and praised and esteemed him above all the others there at court, his assurance in speech and conduct such that everyone marvelled and sought to please him and hung on his every word. For he surpassed all others in his knowledge of the art of hunting and hawking; and in chess and backgammon and other pastimes in which noble men should be adept, he was more skilled and accomplished than any of his years. So well did he conduct himself with the young duke that he won the love and praise of all, of every degree. And when he found himself with his lord the duke in the company of ladies and damsels, no one knew better how to behave and speak, conversing with them so charmingly that they were all eager to hear his gracious words. It earned him such credit that they all declared they'd never met his equal: many of them desired him, attracted by his handsome looks and modesty.

So fine was his conduct in every respect that the young duke his master held him as the closest of his household; they were the same age, the same height and build and bearing, and the young duke loved him dearly, treating him almost as if he were his own brother. If one day the young Duke of Cleves wore a new outfit – be it a gown or other garment, no matter how rich – Jacquet de Lalaing was dressed and clad in the same or very like. In the end, the young duke loved him so dearly that if Jacquet wasn't with him he felt he was alone, accompanied though he always was by many a knight and squire. [*f. 16v*]

12

Of the jousts and entertainments at which the young Duke of Cleves and Jacquet de Lalaing found themselves together

As you've heard, Jacquet de Lalaing strove so admirably to serve and please the young Duke of Cleves that nothing was done or undertaken without Jacquet being the first to be summoned. For in council and many other affairs he behaved with such maturity that he won great praise and admiration at the Duke of Burgundy's court, where he was much esteemed and loved.

And he never missed a joust or tournament, where he always performed so impressively, with such success, that the prize was awarded to him as the finest on either side.[36] He and his destrier[37] were always clad and caparisoned exactly like the young duke his master. And truly, as soon as he appeared in the lists he was recognised in an instant by his mighty blows, delivered with such force that he brought knights and horses crashing to the ground. He bore stout and weighty lances that flattened opponents back on their horses' cruppers, and often dashed off their helms to leave them bare-headed in the lists. Then trumpets would blare and ring so loud that you wouldn't have heard God's thunder, as heralds and pursuivants[38] on all sides roared 'Lalaing!'

The Duke of Burgundy and the ladies in the stands watched him with delight. A good many were wishing their husbands and lovers had been like him! And truly, when the Duke of Cleves was jousting in person, accompanied by Jacquet de Lalaing and other gentlemen of his household, they made the lists tremble: the opposing side to a man feared facing them, for they were all outstanding jousters. Many jousts, many courses[39] were run in the city of Brussels before the duke and duchess, along with all the ladies and damsels in the stands and at the windows, watching to see who would excel.

When the jousting was done they returned to their lodgings to disarm and then came to the banquets, in the presence of the duke surrounded by ladies accompanied by many a knight and squire, engaging in all manner of gracious conversation. You may be sure that the young Duke of Cleves did his utmost to enhance the joy of these occasions: in the days of his youth there was no one to equal him in raising the spirits of all, men and women alike. He was young, vivacious, shapely in every limb, tall in stature, modest, courteous and charming – and generous, too, a great giver of alms to the poor. Truly, Jacquet de Lalaing could say for sure that he'd found the lord and master he'd have wished and asked for. The young duke and he loved each other dearly, and it's not to be wondered at, for they were of similar age and in build and height and manner so alike that, seeing them, anyone who hadn't known them would have taken them for brothers.

Returning to the feasts held daily with their dances and entertainments, at that time there was no high prince's court to match the court of the noble Duke of Burgundy. Nor did the feasts and entertainments stop on account of any war he might be waging: there was no prince more generous, modest and courteous anywhere. He was held in awe not for his cruelty but for the charm, largesse, valour and other virtues with which he was endowed. In short, truly, no human tongue, however eloquent, could express or describe his mighty virtues. And let it be said that no prince on record showed more compassion

---

[36] Literally 'both insiders and outsiders': i.e. those on the hosting side and opponents from further afield.

[37] The finest of all warhorses, very costly and by no means common.

[38] Officers of arms, ranking below heralds but with similar duties.

[39] '*courses de lances*', a course being each individual charge by a jousting knight.

or pity towards the poor: if ever he saw them in need they would never be turned away without relief. And he loved his knights, his nobles and all who served him, and rewarded them most liberally.

But returning to the story we've begun, we'll say no more about the noble duke till later: we'll continue with our theme and tell of the deeds of Jacquet de Lalaing. [*f. 18r*]

13

Of an embassy that came to Chalon on the Saône, sent from the Emperor of Greece to the Duke of Burgundy

You've now heard how Jacquet de Lalaing came to court to serve and be companion to the young Duke of Cleves, and how his qualities earned him the young duke's love and close confidence: he became his constant companion. And as mentioned above, the duke wore no garments, jewels or rich accoutrements but Jacquet would have the same, and be provided equally with horses, harness, trappings, be it in combat, tourneys, jousts or other sport. And he behaved with such refinement and discernment that by princes, lords and ladies he was commended above all others. Nor did he leave any festival or joust without carrying off the prize as the best competitor from either side. As for ladies and damsels, he knew better than any of his age how to behave in their company.

Now, while he was there with his master the Duke of Cleves at the court of Duke Philip of Burgundy, news reached Duke Philip that certain matters required his presence in his lands of Burgundy.[40] His brother-in-law Duke Charles of Bourbon and a number of other knights and nobles gathered there, and he met them along with his nephews the Duke of Cleves and Count Charles of Nevers and many barons, knights and squires from Burgundy, Flanders and Artois. They came to Dijon, where the duke feasted them with great honour before leading them to Chalon-sur-Saône where he richly enter- tained them likewise. Duke Philip held a great court, being joined by a host of barons and knights from Burgundy, Savoy and more distant parts.

Among them was a knight ambassador from the Emperor of Greece and Constantinople,[41] accompanied by some dozen persons dressed and arrayed in Greek fashion. As the two dukes were leaving the Oratory where they'd been hearing mass, this ambassador began to set forth and explain his mission on behalf of his lord the Emperor. It would take too long to recount in full, but to come to the point he was appealing for troops; they would be sent by

---

[40] i.e. the duchy of Burgundy and county of Burgundy (Franche-Comté).
[41] The Byzantine Emperor John VIII Palaiologos, r. 1425–48.

galleys and warships to confront the Infidels led by the Grand Turk,[42] who was mounting constant attacks and wreaking destruction upon the Christians of the Greek Empire. He said that if the Duke of Burgundy didn't lend him support and aid he could see no other Christian prince with the will to help him defend Christendom, which the Turk was daily striving with all his might to annihilate and destroy.

When the ambassador had conveyed his message from the Byzantine Emperor, the duke replied that he fully understood and promised he would have a quick response – which he did, for after conferring with his council the duke resolved to send the Emperor, for the defence of Christendom, a certain number of men at arms and archers and crossbowmen.

Chosen to lead this army was the lord of Wavrin.[43] With his troops he boarded galleys at Venice, accompanied by a Spanish knight named Pedro Vásquez[44] and a most valiant and accomplished knight named Sir Gauvain Quiéret,[45] a native of Picardy. They sailed on swiftly till they reached Modon,[46] where they found the cardinal of Sainte-Croix, legate of our Holy Father the pope, and with him four galleys armed at the Holy Father's expense. But of their army and what they did I've no wish to give a long account: as I understand it, they were of little help to Christendom then and achieved nothing of profit to themselves, so I'll say no more about them but will speak of what happened next. [f. 19v]

14

How Duke Philip of Burgundy conquered the city and land of Luxembourg

As you've heard, following great deliberation in council, good Duke Philip of Burgundy ordered troops to be sent to the aid of Christendom, and sent the Emperor's ambassador away with lavish gifts.

Then he left his city of Chalon and headed for Dijon. With him were the Duke of Bourbon, his nephew the Duke of Cleves and his cousins the

---

[42] Murad II, sultan of the Ottoman Empire from 1421–44 and again from 1446–51.

[43] This is Waleran de Berlettes, lord of Wavrin, nephew of the notable chronicler Jehan de Wavrin. He was a member of a noble family of Artois into which Jacques de Lalaing's mother had first been married (see above, p. 40).

[44] 'Messire Vaascq'. This is Pedro Vásquez de Saavedra (c. 1410–77), a chamberlain of Duke Philip from 1443 to 1457. He is to reappear later (below, pp. 152, 155, 161, 195, 200–1), in passages taken from a different source, with his name rendered as 'Pierre Vasque'.

[45] Lord of Dreuil, near Amiens, a member of an old and prominent Picard family.

[46] 'Mondon'. Modon was the Venetian name for their fortress at Methoni, substantial remains of which survive, on the south-western tip of the Peloponnese.

brother counts of Nevers and Étampes.[47] On his arrival there, great feasts and entertainments were arranged, especially jousts, in which Jacquet de Lalaing, along with his lord and master the young Duke of Cleves, performed so well that, no matter which team he was in,[48] the prize was awarded by the ladies to him. The best of the opposing side was judged to be the lord of Wavrin, considered at the time a most valiant jouster, and when those two met in a joust there was no question of them parting till they'd broken a stack of lances! They would often stay so long in the lists that they'd have to be led away by torchlight! And they never failed to win the prize, one as the best from the host side and one from the visitors. And after the jousting, as is the custom, banqueting followed, and then dancing and entertainment, where Jacquet de Lalaing behaved with such surpassing charm and manners that he was loved and admired by all the ladies and damsels.

So impressive was he in every place and circumstance that he won the favour of the Duke of Burgundy and his nephew the Duke of Cleves to the point where he was often invited to private councils along with many barons and knights much older than himself. And whenever his opinion was sought on any question, he replied so astutely that his view was often adopted and concluded the matter – much to the wonder of many in light of his age, for he was then only twenty years old.

It was at this time that Duke Philip of Burgundy was threatened with the loss and denial of major rights he had in the duchy of Luxembourg.[49] This he would never tolerate. To counter it he mustered a mighty force of men at arms and archers and crossbowmen from Burgundy, Artois and Picardy, and marched from Dijon accompanied by his nephew the Duke of Cleves and his kinsmen the counts of Nevers and Étampes and many knights and squires from his lands.

He headed for Luxembourg and the country thereabouts. He had sent ahead the Count of Vernembourg,[50] his lieutenant there, and Sir Simon de Lalaing with many noble knights and squires and a great number of men at arms; they had secured the obedience of several cities in the region, and also of a number of knights and squires of those parts. This prepared the way for the good Count of Étampes, the duke's cousin, to leave the duke and go

---

[47] Charles I, count of Nevers (1414–64), and Jehan II, count of Étampes (1415–91).

[48] i.e. whether competing for the 'insiders' or the 'outsiders': see note 36 above, p. 53.

[49] The thrice-widowed duchess of Luxembourg, Elisabeth of Görlitz, had appointed Duke Philip as regent in 1441.

[50] Virneburg in Germany north-east of Luxembourg. The count was a member of the Order of the Golden Fleece and had been governor of Luxembourg for thirty years.

with them along with a great host of knights and squires, including the lord of Saveuse,[51] Sir Simon de Lalaing (lord of Montignies),[52] his brother-in-law the lord of Créquy[53] and many more, well equipped with ladders and other gear of war. They advanced in force and raised the ladders as secretly as they could, about three hours before dawn,[54] and without being seen they scaled the wall and entered in. With a mighty roar, crying 'Our Lady! Burgundy!', they swept on as far as the city square, right outside the castle. Townsmen from several streets and squares assembled; armed with weapons and cudgels, they were planning to resist and drive them back outside. But the Count of Étampes and his company repulsed them forcefully, in the course of which Jacquet de Lalaing performed many splendid feats of arms with lance and sword alike: the sight of him striking to right and left filled all who saw him with wonder. The Count of Étampes and his company were finally victorious and the citizens forced to flee. There were a good many killed and captured, and some even leapt over the walls to save themselves. The city was pillaged and ransacked.

Next morning the Duke of Burgundy entered the city of Luxembourg in triumph. He came before the castle where the Count of Gleichen,[55] appointed captain there in the Duke of Saxony's name, had retreated. It was only a few days after the city's capture that he slipped over the castle wall and away where he thought best.[56] Those left behind in the castle surrendered it to the Duke of Burgundy, and so it was that, with hardly any loss, he was lord of the city and castle of Luxembourg. Having installed a garrison and left his bastard son Corneille[57] as governor, he departed in great triumph and glory and returned to his city of Brussels, where he was joyously received by the burghers and the commons of the town. [f. 21v]

---

51 Philippe de Saveuse (1392–1468), councillor-chamberlain of Duke Philip and a prominent commander in a number of campaigns: he will appear several times later in *The Book of the Deeds* in the account of the Ghent War. Saveuse is just west of Amiens.

52 Montignies-Saint-Christophe, in Hainaut; Simon was Jacques's paternal uncle (see above, p. 38).

53 Jehan de Créquy (1395–1474) from Artois, one of the first of Duke Philip's Order of the Golden Fleece, and Jacques de Lalaing's maternal uncle (see above, p. 40).

54 It was 22 November 1443.

55 '*Clicq*'. Ernst, count of Gleichen (in Lower Saxony near Göttingen).

56 The chronicler Monstrelet records that he fled to the castle of Thionville, which was then besieged by the Burgundians for three weeks before he surrendered and 'returned to his land of Germany having suffered great loss, shame and confusion'.

57 Corneille de Beveren (1420–52), the duke's first and favourite illegitimate son.

15

How mighty jousts were staged in the city of Nancy, in the presence of
the kings of France and Sicily and the queens their wives

It then happened that, after this conquest of Luxembourg, King Charles
of France[58] and his son the Dauphin[59] mustered a great and mighty army
which the Dauphin led into Germany[60] where he achieved next to nothing and
returned with little gain. Passing through Burgundy on the way back, some of
his captains were given a hiding and plundered by the Marshal of Burgundy.
The Dauphin was much aggrieved by this, but there was nothing he could do
about it; and he made his way, with such men as he had, to the King of France
his father, who at that point was returning from Metz in Lorraine, where the
people had come to terms with him on payment of 100,000 Rhenish mailles.[61]
It was to Nancy that the king returned, and there his son the Dauphin found
him. He told him how he'd fared, and when the king heard the news he was
less than pleased, seeing he'd achieved so little. But for the moment there
was nothing he could do: he would have to be patient.

There in the city of Nancy were the King of France, the King of Sicily,[62]
the Dauphin, the queens of France and Sicily,[63] my lady the Dauphine,[64] the
Duchess of Orléans,[65] the Duchess of Calabria[66] and with them all the high

---

[58]   Charles VII (r. 1422–61).

[59]   '*le Dauphin de Viennois*', the full and formal title of the heir apparent to the
French crown, in this case Louis (b. 1423), later to be Louis XI (r. 1461–83).

[60]   '*vers les Allemagnes*'. This is a reference to the Dauphin Louis's expedition
of 1444, leading a huge army of '*écorcheurs*' – ('flayers'), mercenaries who were
a troublesome presence in France, being idle during a break in hostilities in the
Hundred Years War and 'skinning' people of everything they could lay their hands
on – to support his future brother-in-law, Sigismund of Austria-Tyrol, against the Swiss
Confederacy. In the Upper Rhineland he defeated the Swiss in battle at St Jakob an
der Birs, but suffered very heavy losses against much smaller numbers, and quickly
agreed to a peace treaty with the Confederacy, failing wholly in his original aim.

[61]   Amid continuous confrontations between magnates in the region – and partly
to counter Burgundian expansion – in 1444–5 Charles VII supported his brother-in-
law René of Anjou, who was the Duke of Bar, in besieging Metz. The exact value
of the sum paid by the citizens is hard to evaluate, but probably equates to the very
substantial 200,000 French écus.

[62]   i.e. René of Anjou, who was king of '*Sicilia citra*', otherwise known as the
kingdom of Naples.

[63]   Marie of Anjou and Isabelle of Lorraine (René of Anjou's first wife).

[64]   Margaret Stewart, daughter of James I of Scotland.

[65]   Marie of Cleves (1426–87), the third wife of Charles, duke of Orléans (1394–
1465). The youngest sister of John 'the young Duke' of Cleves, at this point she was
eighteen years old.

[66]   The title given to the wife of the heir apparent to the kingdom of Naples (in this

princes, princesses, counts, barons, knights, countesses, baronesses, ladies and damsels of the French royal court and from the duchy of Bar and from Lorraine, of which there were a great many. You may well imagine that such a great gathering of nobles wouldn't part without first engaging in some display of arms; and that was the case as you're about to hear, according to the accounts I've heard from those who were present – knights and squires and other credible sources.

The truth is this: on the tenth day of June in the year 1445[67] the King of France was residing in the city of Nancy in the duchy of Bar together with the King of Sicily and the Dauphin and a number of dukes, counts, barons and knights and the queens of France and Sicily, the Dauphine, the duchesses of Orléans and Calabria and other duchesses, countesses, baronesses and ladies and damsels in great numbers. And one day after supper, the kings of France and Sicily went to relax in the fields and green meadows, gathering herbs and flowers and engaging in gracious conversation. To join them came my lord Charles of Anjou, Count of Maine and Perche,[68] along with the Count of Saint-Pol[69] and a good many knights and squires. They began to converse with the ladies and damsels and to tell them their news; and among other matters they spoke of the splendours of the Duke of Burgundy's court, with its jousts and tourneys and entertainments daily staged. Some of the French said:

'Truly, there is no prince in France to compare with the Duke of Burgundy; there is none more courtly. He is great-hearted, wise and generous above all others.'

In the course of this the counts of Maine and Saint-Pol drew aside and said to one another: 'We must do something worthy of note! You've heard the ladies being told how, day after day, jousts, tournaments and dances are held in the court of the Duke of Burgundy, and look around us: here we all are in vast numbers at the king's court, and we do nothing but sleep and eat and drink! We never engage in arms! It's unbecoming of us all to spend our time so idly!'

And the Count of Saint-Pol, wanting to remedy this, said privately: 'My lord of Maine, let the two of us proclaim at once, in the presence of the king and the ladies, jousting to take place between all comers. And you and I, or in our stead some knight or squire of note, will hold the pass[70] and take on

---

case René's son, Jean of Anjou). This is Marie de Bourbon (1428–48), Duke Philip of Burgundy's niece, now about 16.

  67 The MS accidentally omits the final digit of the date.

  68 René of Anjou's brother, Charles (1414–72); the reference to Perche is puzzling: he was count of Maine and Guise.

  69 Louis of Luxembourg (1418–75), a close friend of the Dauphin.

  70 'tiendrons le pas'. The phrase refers to its origins: the term pas d'armes – 'passage of arms' – 'seems to have originated in a challenger proclaiming his intention to defend a pass or narrow defile, which could be a natural one, or alternatively an

all challengers for a full week – beginning in a fortnight, for we need time to make arrangements and prepare.'

The Count of Maine, hearing these words from his brother-in-law Saint-Pol,[71] began to smile, and said he couldn't be more pleased: they should see it done. With little more ado they found a herald and bade him announce the jousts in the presence of the kings, queens, princesses and ladies. There was a delighted, joyous reaction from the ladies and damsels. Among the gathering was Jacquet de Lalaing; he was seated near my lady of Orléans and the Duchess of Calabria, who said, smiling:

'Jacquet de Lalaing, you've heard the counts of Maine and Saint-Pol proclaim a jousting contest: I'm sure you won't fail to be there!'

'No,' said the Duchess of Orléans, 'he wouldn't miss it for the world! He's quite an expert! My dear brother of Cleves and he are well practised and used to jousts and tourneys: in the house of my dear uncle of Burgundy all manner of sport occurs daily!'

Then Jacquet de Lalaing, who was thrilled by the news, replied: 'Most noble ladies, if for the duration of these jousts it pleased you to retain me as your squire and servant, I'd be delighted to accomplish something to your honour and your pleasure.'

My lady of Orléans answered, saying: 'Jacquet de Lalaing, my friend, I've seen you with my dear brother of Cleves for quite some time, so I feel entitled to engage you as my squire in these contests!'

'My lady,' Jacquet said, 'as servant to my lord your brother, I wouldn't wish to refuse or disobey your fair commands: a brother's servant should be his sister's!'

When the second lady heard the offer made by Jacquet to the first, she started to flush and burn red! She turned aside and began talking to the princes there, giving no sign of agitation or rage. She got through the day as best she could – there was nothing else she could do – but Jacquet, having committed to the first lady, instantly realised that the second had left in high dudgeon! This troubled him and he became rather subdued. The first lady said to him:

'Don't worry about it, Jacquet – you'll be fine!'

'What, my lady?' he said. 'I was thinking about the day to come – it bothers me that it's so far off!'

'Stop that, Jacquet!' said the lady. 'That's not what's on your mind! I could see at once what was going on, but I'll say no more about it for now!'

'My lady,' Jacquet said, 'I don't know what you're getting at or what this is about! But I've no wish to press you on the point!'

---

artificial one created solely for the purposes of the hastilude'. Juliet Barker, *The Tournament in England, 1100–1400* (Woodbridge, 1986, reissued 2020), p. 156.

[71] Charles of Anjou (the Count of Maine) had married Saint-Pol's sister Isabelle of Luxembourg.

'No, Jacquet,' said the lady, 'be content for the present. Let it suffice that I've engaged you as my squire for the duration of the festival – indeed for evermore if you deserve it: if you perform as you should!'

'My lady,' he replied, 'may God give me all due strength: without Him no one can achieve a thing – neither I nor anyone else.' [*f. 24r*]

16

Of the stir at the King of France's court following the proclamation of the jousts, and of the request made by Jacquet de Lalaing to the counts of Maine and Saint-Pol

A fter this exchange between the Duchess of Orléans and Jacquet de Lalaing, the kings and queens, princes and princesses, in a great stir of excitement, returned to the king's residence. Wines and cordials[72] were served, and afterwards all went their separate ways to rest. Jacquet de Lalaing, escorting the lady to her lodging, took leave of her right at the entrance to her chamber. The lady, smiling, bade him a courteous goodnight and said as they parted:

'Jacquet, we only ever see you on special days! I don't know how it'll be henceforth, but you've been at court a fair while with my dear kinsman Saint-Pol and have never come to see us!'

'Better late than never, my lady!' he replied. 'You have chosen to engage me as your squire. I thank you for that honour, and pray to God that I may perform such a service as will be pleasing to you.'

'Amen,' said the lady. 'It is well within you.'

In taking leave she took Jacquet by the hand and gave him a golden ring mounted with a gorgeous ruby, saying: 'Go with God, Jacquet.'

With that the lady turned and entered her chamber with a number of ladies and damsels, while Jacquet set off with a group of knights and squires in excited conversation about the jousts to come. Amid their lively talk they came to the lodgings of my lord Charles of Anjou. There they found the Count of Saint-Pol who called to Jacquet de Lalaing and said:

'Jacquet, my friend, you must come and help us in this contest – the men of the king's household are bragging and exchanging oaths that they'll batter us out of the lists!'

Jacquet replied: 'Let them say so, my lord! When the time comes I hope they'll be worthy competition! But if I were sure, my lords, that the two of you who've proclaimed the jousts would grant me a request I'd like to make, I shall be ever bound to you.'

---

[72] '*espices*': spiced wines such as hippocras, often served heated, were extremely popular as digestive cordials.

The two princes, hearing that he had a request of them, said: 'Tell us, then, what it is you wish.'

'My lords,' he said, 'promise me, both, that you'll grant my request and I'll tell you.'

The two lords, smiling, looked at one another and said: 'Come, let's accept! We'll at least hear what he has to say – let's go along with it for now!'

Having thus conferred, but still not knowing the request he wished to make, the Count of Saint-Pol called to him and said: 'Jacquet, my friend: my lord of Maine and I have discussed this, and since you've come with me and in my company, I've persuaded my lord here that your request should be granted. So ask what you wish: for my part, I grant it.'

Then Jacquet de Lalaing, hearing the Count of Saint-Pol's reply, went down on one knee and, smiling, said: 'Most honoured and respected lords, I thank you both.'

The Count of Saint-Pol stepped forward and took Jacquet by the hand and bade him rise. But Jacquet wouldn't do so; he said: 'Most noble lords, before I rise I'll reveal what I would have you grant me.'

They accepted this and bade him speak. Delighted by the lords' response, he replied, saying: 'Most honoured and respected lords, the truth is that you have had Maine Herald[73] proclaim to the king's household a noble festival of arms[74] – that is to say, jousting – to begin in a fortnight's time. I humbly beg and request, my lords, that it may please you to forgo your own part in this, and let me undertake it in your place. With Our Lord's grace I shall perform in such a way as to preserve both your honour and my own. In agreeing to this you'll do me greater honour than has long been shown to any man of my line, and in return I and my kin shall be bound to serve you evermore.'

The two lords, hearing Jacquet's fine, grand aspiration, were quite astonished in view of his youth. They drew aside and conferred with those they thought could advise them. They replied that it could be legitimately done, so they agreed to Jacquet's request. He was overjoyed. He thanked the lords deeply, and they promised to accompany him to the lists and wherever they saw was needed.

Having thanked the two counts, Jacquet took his leave and went to his lodgings to prepare and discuss matters with the gentlemen who'd accompanied him there; he had great faith in them, and they were well informed and knowledgeable in how to proceed. They assembled all that was necessary, and when the time came they were equipped and supplied with everything one could think of.

---

[73] i.e. the herald engaged by the Count of Maine.

[74] The phrase used here is 'pardon d'armes', which elsewhere – in, for example, René d'Anjou's Livre des tournois – tends to imply an event at which indulgences may be granted.

News of what was planned created a mighty stir in the king's court and in the city of Nancy and all the surrounding towns. Knights and squires made busy preparations, ensuring they were ready for the appointed day. There was all manner of talk among the king's men; they were saying to each other:

'Now we'll see who comes out on top! It would be a deep disgrace to us all if a squire from Hainaut, from the household of the Duke of Burgundy, won the honour and acclaim ahead of everyone in the king's court! We would earn grave reproach if he wasn't properly met and dealt with!'

'Truly,' some replied, 'he will be!'

And others said: 'He's pretty young: he hasn't yet learned how Frenchmen handle lances!'

Such was the talk among the king's men, in the presence of the ladies and wherever they met. News of this reached Jacquet de Lalaing, but all he did was laugh. His only words were:

'No doubt some Frenchman could have me out of my saddle or bring my destrier crashing down. If that happens – God forbid! – I'll just have to tell the ladies: "That's me finished!"'

And so it was that, despite this and similar talk among the French in the royal court, Jacquet de Lalaing and his companions took little notice. [*f. 26v*]

17

How Jacquet de Lalaing was welcomed to the King of France's court,
and how he then fared

When Jacquet saw he was ready and there was nothing now but to wait for the day he so desired to come, he joined the counts of Maine and Saint-Pol and went with them to the king's court. The king was then in the ladies' chamber; present were the queens of France and Sicily, my lady the Dauphine, the duchesses of Orléans and Calabria and several other duchesses, countesses, baronesses and ladies and damsels in great numbers. On their arrival they greeted the king, the queens and ladies and joined them in conversation; and Jacquet de Lalaing behaved and spoke in their company so charmingly that all, of every degree, delighted to listen and hear him speak. They said to each other:

'Truly, this young squire shows in every way that he's been raised in a place of the highest class and is born of noble line.'

Such and similar thoughts were expressed by all. And among them were two eminent ladies I've mentioned before[75] who were particularly keen to converse with him; he'd charmed them both exceedingly, though they gave each other no sign of it. They hung on his every word, wishing their husbands were like

---

[75] i.e. the duchesses of Orléans and Calabria.

him! And they had good reason: he was so handsome, so finely built in every limb, that God and Nature had neglected nothing in creating him. And truly, he was also good-natured and courteous in word and deed, devout towards God and generous to the poor. As for his conversation, it was so pleasant that all who met him were eager for his company. It's no wonder he was viewed by the ladies as he was; but let me tell you, those two were in such a state that they were fixated night and day on finding a seemly way to meet and converse with him! Jacquet was well aware of their love for him: they sent secret messages daily! He went regularly to pass the time in talk with them – one day with one and next day with the other – but behaved with all propriety and honour: he did nothing to earn the reproach of God or of the world. He loved and feared God above all things, ever mindful of the fine advice and principles instilled by his father Guillaume de Lalaing when he'd left home. But messages from these two ladies kept on coming – unbeknown to each other! – and he handled things so perfectly that he was loved and adored by both. It was down to him that it went no further: fearing for his person and for his soul's salvation he had no wish to venture beyond propriety.

So, as you've heard, Jacquet de Lalaing was stuck at the king's court, eager to be done with his business there; for as everyone knows – or certainly should – the Devil seeks only to lead men and women to perdition, to have possession of their souls. That's why every day before leaving his lodging Jacquet had mass sung and heard it most devoutly, praying to God and the Virgin Mary His mother to protect him from all trouble. After hearing mass he would order his affairs before leaving his house and heading for the king's court with the counts of Maine and Saint-Pol. When they arrived the king would often give him audience; indeed, he was so much in the king's favour that he engaged him in his household.

And so it was that Jacquet de Lalaing, through his modest conduct, had earned high standing at the royal court: he was well acquainted with every duke, count, baron, knight, squire, lady and damsel, and was especially admired by the queens and princesses, who held him in higher esteem than all others there. And the king above all, and my lord the Dauphin and the Duke of Orléans[76] and the other dukes, counts, barons, knights and squires – indeed, everyone at court – had the highest regard for him, all declaring that he couldn't fail to achieve great things provided Death didn't intervene. Jacquet de Lalaing, then, was most welcome at the court of the King of France; but for the moment we'll say no more about him, and will tell of the busy preparations for the coming jousts. [*f. 28r*]

[76] Charles d'Orléans (1394–1465), famous for the poetry and songs he wrote during his long imprisonment in England following his capture at Agincourt.

18

How Jacquet de Lalaing made ready, and came and rode past the ladies' stand, accompanied by the counts of Maine and Saint-Pol

When the knights and squires of the king's household saw the day of the jousts draw near, they all of course began acquiring and preparing all they needed. If you'd been at Nancy then, you'd have seen a mighty stir and heard such a din of horses neighing and armourers, saddlers and farriers busy putting heads on lances and shoeing chargers that you'd have thought it an army about to do battle. Men of France,[77] Champagne and other lands[78] were striving to be the best equipped. And some were full of talk of how they meant to beat Jacquet de Lalaing out of the lists. Some of the French were saying it was great pride and presumption that had driven him to such a lofty challenge as to meet and see off all comers for four whole days, and to break three lances on each.

The day came at last, so eagerly awaited by Jacquet de Lalaing. He'd paid the utmost care and attention to ensuring that all he needed was prepared, and so it was, for he had men at hand – nobles and servants alike – experienced and adept at the task. He had himself fully armed and arrayed, and his roan destrier was brought from the stables, its caparison adorned with richest gold. As for his helm, atop it he sported a gorgeous wimple bordered and garnished with pearls and with golden fringes trailing to the ground: it had been sent to him by one of the two ladies. And on his left arm he wore a beautiful sleeve heavily decked with pearls and jewels, sent to him by the second lady through a secret messenger. Truly, when he was mounted on his destrier, armed and arrayed as you've just heard, he cut an impressive figure indeed: his manner and bearing were quite awesome. Those present couldn't take their eyes off him, such a joy was he to behold.

At last the time arrived for setting forth: word was sent that he should come – for it was he who was to hold the pass[79] – and that the kings and queens of France and Sicily and the noble princesses, ladies and damsels were already seated in the stands. He was raring to go, awaiting only the arrival of the counts of Maine and Saint-Pol who had promised the previous evening to accompany him and serve him with his first three lances. And so they did; as soon as they heard he was ready they rode from their lodgings and came to join him. They found him astride his destrier, ready to depart.

---

[77] i.e. the French royal domain – more or less what is still referred to as the Île de France – as opposed to the counties and duchies such as Champagne or Normandy (or, of course, Burgundy).

[78] '*nations*', with its etymological sense of 'land of birth'.

[79] '*tenir le pas*'. See note 70 above, p. 59.

They greeted him with beaming smiles. Then trumpets and clarions blared and heralds cried, a joyous and mighty sound, and with the counts of Maine and Saint-Pol at either side he set off with a splendid company of knights and squires. Together they rode to the jousting ground. Arriving there he passed before the stands and hailed the king and all the ladies, whose eyes were firmly on him – especially the eyes of the two ladies by whom he was dearly loved! Not that either of them realised it was so – each of them thought she loved alone, and both were startled, to say the least, to see the wimple and the sleeve! They were troubled and downcast! But they didn't show any sign of this and started talking about all manner of things concerning the festivities and the jousts to come without mentioning Jacquet de Lalaing! But the first lady[80] did say this:

'Truly, it seems to me that this young squire who's taken on such a mighty challenge will have his work cut out today! He'll have a hard time, being so very young. I don't think he's thought it through – I'd have thought he'd realise that from the king's court there'll be a host of knights and barons and men of high worth all raring to take him on and drive him from the lists!' [*f. 29v*]

19

Of the two ladies' exchange about Jacquet de Lalaing

The second lady,[81] hearing these words of the first and desperate to know who it could have been who'd given Jacquet the wimple he was wearing on his helm, spoke up, saying:

'I tell you, madam, the young squire you speak of, with amazement that he should undertake such a daunting feat, you needn't worry on his account. It's often observed that a gale can be stilled by a little rain. I'm well aware that in my lord the king's household there are plenty of men eager to take him on and oust him from the lists, but unless I'm much mistaken, madam, I do believe you'll see him make so fine a show today that before they get the better of him, before he's thrown or driven from the lists, there'll be some of them given a very hard time! You may be sure, madam, that if the young squire didn't trust in his valour and prowess he would never have dared undertake such an awesome challenge. So relax and enjoy the entertainment! For my own part, I'd venture to suggest he's in love with some noble lady who perchance is here at court – and she may count herself the happiest present! But one thing puzzles me: he's wearing a gorgeous wimple on his helm, and on his left arm a rich sleeve adorned with jewels and embroidered with letters of gold – though I can't make out what's written: but I shan't enquire more for the moment.' [*f. 30v*]

80 The Duchess of Orléans, sister of the young Duke of Cleves.
81 The Duchess of Calabria.

20

More about the ladies' exchange

The first lady heard every word the second had said. Flushing somewhat she replied: 'I'm surprised, dear cousin, that you praise and admire this squire from Hainaut when he's only lately arrived at court and you'd never seen him before! In the words of the old adage: "Act in haste, repent at leisure"! You're rushing to conclusions, being so effusive about the squire! Wait till this evening when you've seen how he holds the pass and if he's judged to have prevailed. Then if he's proved to be as you imagine you'll be able to declare him worthy of praise and acclaim above all the rest.'

The second lady was delighted to hear this from the first, thinking now that she wasn't the one who'd sent the wimple to Jacquet as she'd suspected.

But for her part the first lady was far from pleased with the second! She was convinced it was she and she alone who'd sent the sleeve he was wearing on his arm! But she gave no sign of her displeasure, and saying no more on the subject the two ladies walked together to the queens' stand, where all the ladies began discussing the jousts and entertainment to come. And that's what we'll turn to now, and leave the ladies to their gracious conversation! [*f. 31r*]

21

How Jacquet de Lalaing performed wonders in the joust

When it was announced to the opposing knights and squires that Jacquet de Lalaing was in the lists, ready and waiting to fulfil his challenge, they started coming from all sides, amid such a clamour throughout the city that you wouldn't have heard God's thunder, as trumpets, clarions and minstrels filled the air with a glorious din. The one appointed to run the first courses entered the park and hailed the king and ladies; then he drew aside to his mark, lance propped upright on thigh, ready to charge. Jacquet de Lalaing, not waiting another instant, lowered his lance and thrust in his spurs. His roan destrier charged like lightning, with such power that the two brave jousters shattered their lances, the splinters flying over the ladies' stand, earning both of them much acclaim and praise for their very first joust. Turning back from their charge, they lowered lances once again and charged with such fury that the opponent broke his lance; but Jacquet de Lalaing, supremely skilled in arms, landed a lance-blow right in the middle of his shield, and as they met in a mighty collision Jacquet brought man and horse together crashing to earth so fearsomely that mount and rider were utterly stunned. On rode Jacquet to finish his charge, while from all sides people rushed to pick up the fallen knight. He was helped back to his house with great difficulty, for in his fall he had injured his knee, and was unable to complete his three courses.

This joust now done, another knight entered the lists. Seeing Jacquet de Lalaing was ready he lowered his lance and let his horse go full tilt. For his part Jacquet spurred his fine roan steed and it charged with such force that the ground beneath it thundered. They struck each other on their visors and smashed their lances, such were the power and might of their blows; but Jacquet dealt the Frenchman such a brilliant blow that, without inflicting hurt, he whipped the helm clean from his head! The knight was left bare-headed and bewildered before the ladies' stand, struggling to make sense of what had happened! The blow earned Jacquet thunderous acclaim: trumpets blared, and heralds, pursuivants and many more roared 'Lalaing!' And the kings of France and Sicily and the queens, princesses and ladies started praising him most highly, filled with wonder, in view of his youth, that he'd withstood and survived two such valiant opponents: no one who hadn't seen it would have believed it.

There were numerous jousters awaiting their turn, all determined to avenge their fellows. But it's often observed that 'In setting out to avenge a shame, a man can be mired more deeply!' And that's what happened to some of them, as you're about to hear.

So the first two knights had run their courses against Jacquet de Lalaing: the first having been unhorsed, and the second with his helm being whipped from his head leaving him so dazed that he did nothing more of note, so I'll move swiftly on to those who are worthy of mention. Jacquet de Lalaing steeled himself next to face the challenge of a knight from Auvergne who at the time was deemed one of the strongest and fiercest knights to be found. The counts of Maine and Saint-Pol came to Jacquet, smiling, and said:

'Jacquet my friend, let's see how you fare now! You've made a fine start: God grant you the honour to go from strength to strength!'

'Thank you, my lords,' he replied. 'With God's grace I've every intention of seeing your honour and my own preserved.'

Then the Count of Saint-Pol took a lance and handed it to Jacquet, who couched it and thrust his spurs into his fine roan steed. The Auvergnat knight came storming towards him, lance lowered, and they struck each other on their shields with such might that they shattered their lances down to their fists, the splinters flying skyward. They galloped on past to complete their charge, then took fresh lances, set themselves firm in their stirrups and levelled their lances again. This time they landed blows full on their visors, sending sparks flying and smashing their lances to bits. The blows were so fierce that both struggled to see, but they carried on through and completed their charge. From all sides came a mighty clamour of trumpets to add to the joyous excitement, and the course the knights had run earned the praise and acclamation of the kings, queens, ladies and all those watching: they said they'd never seen such fearsome jousts in all their lives.

Back at their marks the two jousters paused an instant, each of them eyeing his adversary. It was time for the third and final course. Then Count Louis of Saint-Pol came to Jacquet and said:

'I pray you, my friend, in this last course show whether Hainauters know how to joust!'

'My lord,' replied Jacquet, 'we'll see which of us God grants the better of the clash. For my part I'll give it all I've got!'

Without more delay or ado Jacquet called for his lance. It was handed to him, while at the other end the knight from Auvergne grasped his. Then they let their destriers go with such furious power that, seeing them charge to meet, it seemed the ground they ran on would crumble beneath their hooves. With their great, stout lances they exchanged such terrible, awesome blows that all who watched were filled with dread that they would kill each other. The Auvergnat struck Jacquet in the middle of his shield and broke his lance, while Jacquet, using all his strength and skill to aim his blow, landed it full on the knight's visor, so immense a blow that sparks flew and the knight bent back over his horse's crupper. He was so stunned by this colossal blow that if people hadn't rushed to hold him up he would have pitched into the sand. As it was, he had to be taken back to his house, and it was an hour before he recovered his senses – there were some who'd thought he never would! He'd taken such a massive blow that bright blood was pouring from his mouth, his nose, his ears.

But let's leave him and return to Jacquet de Lalaing. He was very concerned to see the knight depart in such a state, but when he heard he was unhurt and only stunned he felt easier, and returned to his mark and awaited another knight who was preparing to run his courses. When he saw he was ready Jacquet called for his lance; it was handed to him, and they let their horses go full tilt. They met each other with their strong, stout lances full on their shields, such fearsome blows that the lances of both jousters smashed to pieces. They rode on past and made ready to run the second course, and without a word they let their horses go, levelled their lances and struck each other on the shield again, sparing nothing. The knight was flattened back over his horse's crupper, but he righted himself and they rode on past and completed their charge. Back they came for their third course and exchanged tremendous blows: the knight shattered his lance while Jacquet, aiming for the visor, found his target with such force and might that he swept the knight's helm fully eight yards[82] away on the end of his lance. The knight, finding himself disarmed, bare-headed, turned his eyes to the ladies' stand. On all sides laughter erupted, trumpets rang and men, heralds and pursuivants cried: 'Lalaing!'

---

[82] 'more than four *toises*', a *toise* being a measure of six feet.

The clamour in the stands and around the lists was wondrous to hear, and every word was to the praise and glory of Jacquet de Lalaing, especially from the ladies in the stand. And you may be sure that the two ladies mentioned earlier were overjoyed, elated, each of them believing that she alone was his beloved! All the same, the first lady[83] was a little suspicious of the second: she saw she was as jubilant as could be, and noticed that her eyes were fixed on Jacquet.

For his part, his mind was fixed on winning praise and high renown, which he did that day with the wonders he performed. Were I to record what happened with each opponent he faced I think it might be wearisome for those who read this or hear it read, so I'll move on. But this much I dare say for sure: the fine way he began the day he continued to the end, and all the princes, knights, squires, princesses, ladies and damsels were amazed, filled with wonder that so young a man – only twenty-two years of age as he was then[84] – could have withstood and endured so much, for that day he'd faced some of the mightiest and most renowned nobles in the King of France's household. The princes declared that if he carried on and lived to fullest manhood he would surpass all others of his time, and that the house of which he was born was fortunate indeed; he couldn't fail to achieve the heights of prowess and renown.

Such was the talk throughout the city of Nancy in acclaiming Jacquet de Lalaing, who was still in the lists, waiting to see if anyone else would come to joust with him that day. But by now it was late and he left it at that; seeing no one else come forward, the counts of Maine and Saint-Pol told him he'd done enough and it was time to go, which he did: he had his helm removed and then set off, riding past the stands and saluting the kings, queens, princes and princesses, ladies and damsels, who acknowledged him most courteously in return. You may be sure he was the object of the admiration of many and the avid desire of some, and little wonder: a more handsome young squire was nowhere to be found, and as well as being handsome he was modest, courteous and charming. And truly, the fine instruction given by his father Sir Guillaume de Lalaing at his departure, when he'd first set out for the court of good Duke Philip of Burgundy, he had well observed; for since his death I've heard from a noble man, a most credible source, that Jacquet de Lalaing would never go to bed without having made confession if he'd thought he might have been in mortal sin. So there was every reason to believe he was bound to attain the heights of virtue, prowess and renown for which he strove throughout his life, as you can hear in detail in what follows. [f. 35v]

---

83 The Duchess of Orléans.
84 To be precise, he was probably twenty-four.

22

How Jacquet de Lalaing jousted the following day, and how the Count of Angoulême, brother of the Duke of Orléans, arrived from England where he had long been prisoner

You've now heard how Jacquet de Lalaing, having completed and held his first passage of arms,[85] returned to his lodging accompanied by the counts of Maine and Saint-Pol and a great host of knights and squires – and also, not to be forgotten, by a host of heralds and pursuivants, trumpeters and minstrels who escorted him all the way to his house crying 'Lalaing!', as did a throng of townsfolk and children. As he was about to enter the house he turned to the lords who'd escorted him and thanked them courteously for the honour they'd shown him.

The lords then returned to the king and found him descending from the stand, and with him the queens and my lord the Dauphin and my lady the Dauphine and the other princesses, ladies and damsels, who all made their way to where the banquet was set.

To the banquet soon after came Jacquet de Lalaing, handsomely dressed in a rich red gown reaching down to his feet and embroidered all in gold; how splendidly it became him, tall as he was and with his bright complexion, fresh as a rose. He came forward and greeted the king and the queens, princesses and ladies, who gazed at him admiringly – especially the two aforesaid ladies: he conversed with them a good deal that night, behaving with such modesty and charm that they were both well pleased. He, more than anyone, was able to converse on any subject, with an eloquent response to any question raised. He was such a welcome presence in the king's household that all, of every degree, were eager to enjoy his company. That night good King Charles himself engaged him in lengthy conversation, discussing many matters, to which Jacquet replied with such good sense that the king was charmed and delighted to have heard him speak.

The seating that night of the kings of France and Sicily, and of the queens, princesses and ladies, followed custom. And Jacquet de Lalaing was seated between the two princesses mentioned earlier. He behaved with perfect decorum; but the first lady[86] surreptitiously, without the other noticing, gave him a gorgeous diamond, and then the second likewise gave him a handsome ruby mounted in a golden ring. He took them both, not daring to refuse. Each of them longed for some dalliance with him, but Jacquet was ever mindful in all respects of the fine instruction his father Sir Guillaume had given him at his departure, guiding and constraining his behaviour in such a case. Each

---

[85] See note 70 above, p. 59.
[86] As before, this is the Duchess of Orléans.

was giving him such an eye behind the other's back that he hardly knew how to cope!

But cope with it he had to, and regularly, all the time he was there, finding ways to deflect and avoid them courteously; for throughout his time at Nancy not a day went by without one or other lady sending for him. Sometimes he went to speak with them and sometimes not. Yet for all of this, he might have loved either of them dearly, and had it not been for the fear that this would do him serious harm he wouldn't have left the court so soon, for the king had retained him in his household. But he found a way to make his excuses gracefully, so the king was quite happy.

But we'll return to the joyous feasting at the banquet, rich and splendid, where knights and ladies were deep in talk of arms and love and their closest concerns, as is the custom at such noble, high festivities. And above all others, Jacquet de Lalaing was hailed and acclaimed as the best performer, having nobly held the pass as all had seen. He was accorded the prize that day for having best achieved his end, for which he thanked the king, the queen and all the ladies.

When the banquet was done and everyone rose from table, the hall was filled with dancing. Trumpets sounded and minstrels played all manner of melodious instruments, and ladies on every side began to dance and sing and make merry. Elsewhere knights and squires were planning and proclaiming the order of the next day's jousts, and they awarded a prize to the one who'd performed best against Jacquet de Lalaing. After this, wine and cordials were served and all took their leave and retired to their lodgings.

They rested till next morning, when everyone went to hear mass. Then they made their way to court to attend the king's mass. It was then that word arrived that the Count of Angoulême was to be present at dinner: he was returning from England where he had long been prisoner.[87] All the great lords, knights and squires of the royal household made ready and went to meet him and led him to the king who received him joyously, embracing him and saying:

'Dear cousin, you are welcome indeed! We have longed to see you!'

'My lord,' the count replied, 'I praise the Lord that I see you prospering so!'

Then he was escorted to the queen, the Dauphin, the Dauphine and the other princes and princesses, who greeted him with all possible joy, especially his brother the Duke of Orléans and his sister-in-law the duchess, and so did all the lords and ladies of the court.

So the atmosphere of joyous celebration in Nancy was heightened by the coming of the Count of Angoulême, close kinsman to the king. Dinner was now ready, the water was brought and they washed and sat down at table. Of

---

[87] Jehan d'Orléans, Count of Angoulême (1399–1467) had been a hostage in England since 1412 under the terms of the Treaty of Buzançais. He was not released until 1444.

the arrangement and the dishes and the entremets they were served I'll not give a long account, for you may be sure that of all the fare and produce to be found in the city of Nancy and the surrounding land they were served in the greatest plenty.

Once dinner was over they rose from table and the king took the Count of Angoulême by the hand and spoke with him for a long while. Then all went their separate ways, and those who were to joust made ready.

The queens, ladies and princesses took their places in the stands. Jacquet de Lalaing, his heart set on achieving a feat to be remembered, had himself armed and then mounted his destrier, with new array and caparison not worn the previous day. The counts of Maine and Saint-Pol came to find him and escorted him to the lists. Amid a mighty clamour from trumpeters and minstrels they entered the park and saluted the ladies who were there in the stands awaiting the jousters' arrival. Jacquet de Lalaing took his place at the head of a track, and a short while after a host of other challengers appeared. Among them a knight of splendid bearing, a most impressive figure, made ready, and seeing Jacquet set and waiting to joust, he thrust in his spurs; Jacquet did likewise and they charged full tilt, not holding back, and struck each other on the shield so mightily that their lances flew into pieces. They rode on past and launched into the second course, and exchanged such furious blows that they smashed their lances down to their fists; and Jacquet dealt his opponent so great a blow that he laid him back flat on his horse's crupper, completely stunned: he was beyond any further action that day and had to return to his lodging. But Jacquet stayed fast and erect in the saddle: I assure you he faced eight jousters that day and not one of them found a way to make him bend. All day long he was as bright and fresh as the moment he arrived, which earned him soaring praise and acclaim from the lords and ladies present. And he was declared to have performed the best of everyone that day. [*f. 38r*]

23

More on this; and of the king's departure for Châlons-en-Champagne

Now, while Jacquet continued to hold his pass, into the lists rode the king and the lord of La Varenne,[88] amid such a mighty blare of trumpets that it seemed the very earth and sky were about to do battle – not that the king and Varenne wished to joust with the holder of the pass: it was purely for the joy of it! They ran four courses against one another and each broke two

---

88 Pierre II de Brézé, a major figure at the French court in the 1440s; Georges Chastellain wrote a lament for his death when he was killed at the Battle of Montlhéry in 1465.

lances. Then they went off to disarm and returned to the stand and rejoined the ladies, thinking they'd gone unrecognised.

After holding the pass all day, Jacquet de Lalaing, still helmeted, rode past the stand and left and returned to his lodging. He had himself disarmed, and then mounted a little hackney[89] and rode to join the Count of Saint-Pol and went with him to court, where the king gave him a grand reception. They spoke of the jousts and what had happened there that day. Then it was time for all to sit for the banquet as they had the previous night; and like the night before, the ladies awarded Jacquet the prize. And when the banquet was done everyone began to dance and make merry, the trumpeters and minstrels enhancing the revelry by playing till almost dawn, and all the while knights and ladies sang and danced and conversed with one another. Jacquet kept finding himself with the two ladies mentioned previously, discussing whatever they pleased; he spent equal time with one and with the other, and managed to leave each of them on good terms without either of them knowing about her rival!

So, as you've heard, throughout the time he was there Jacquet won such praise and acclaim from the king and queen and Dauphin and all the other princes, princesses, ladies and damsels, that all were eager for his company and to hear him speak. And he performed so splendidly on each of the days he was holding the pass that he earned renown and recognition as the finest of all who jousted there.

But all festivities must come to an end, and at the end of these days at Nancy the king, who had spent a good while in the marches of Bar and Lorraine dealing with matters of high import, departed and headed to Châlons-en-Champagne accompanied by the queens of France and Sicily, the Dauphin and Dauphine, the duchesses of Orléans and Calabria and other eminent princesses and ladies and the majority of those who had been at the feast at Nancy. He was joined there by many other knights and ladies and damsels from France[90] and Champagne, so even greater festivities now began than had been at Nancy; and they lasted long, with jousts and other entertainments daily, in which Jacquet de Lalaing performed with such aplomb that he won praise and acclaim as the finest of all those present. [f. 39v]

24

Of the arrival of a Sicilian knight from the household of Alfonso, king of Aragon and Sicily, who wore a sign of commitment to a feat of arms[91]

So as you've heard, at this time Jacquet de Lalaing's heart was set on achieving the heights of prowess and renown. Being the first-born, eldest

---

89 A smart, high-stepping horse used for general purposes rather than in combat.
90 See note 77 above, p. 65.
91 *'une emprise pour faire armes'*. An *'emprise'* was a token, a device. Referring

son of the house of Lalaing, he would do all he could in his youth, through mighty deeds and brave exploits, to ensure that the reputation won by the noble and valiant knights his forebears should not diminish or come to an end with him. He offered frequent and heartfelt prayers to God and the Virgin Mary His mother to grant that he succeed in his aims and desires, that the house of his birth should be enhanced and made greater.

It was a short time after the events above that a Sicilian knight from the household of King Alfonso of Aragon – Sir Jehan Boniface by name, a man of high renown and most expert and valiant in arms – left the court of his lord the King of Aragon and, having taken leave of him, passed through Lombardy, Burgundy and Savoy and journeyed on till he came to the city of Antwerp in Brabant. The prince and lord of that land was then the most excellent and victorious Philip, Duke of Burgundy. This Sicilian knight entered the city on the twenty-sixth day of September in the year 1445; and just a few days earlier Jacques de Lalaing had arrived there, knowing nothing about the Sicilian knight.

What happened then was as follows. On the following day, the twenty-seventh of that month, the Sicilian knight left his lodging accompanied by those he'd brought with him, and made his way to the great parish church of Antwerp. On his left leg he was wearing a shackle, one such as is worn by slaves, attached to a golden chain;[92] and behind him was a pursuivant sporting the knight's coat of arms. It was thus that Sir Jehan Boniface heard mass in the church and, mass heard, he returned to his lodging in the same state.

---

to an example mentioned by the chronicler Monstrelet, Juliet Barker writes: '… feats of arms were nominally undertaken for purely chivalric reasons. Often the challengers bore a device which their opponents had to endeavour to win from them. Chivalric terminology posed the wearer of the device as undergoing a penance from which he sought deliverance, as in the case of Michel d'Oris who bore a piece of leg armour until he was "delivered" by an English knight.' Barker, *op. cit.*, p. 157. It was a 'secular version of a religious, pious vow, and its declarer considered himself a captive of his promise … until another knight or knights, by engaging in combat with him, "liberated" him from his self-imposed servitude'. Riquer, Martin de, 'Les chevaleries de Jacques de Lalaing en Espagne', in *Comptes rendus des séances de l'Académie des Inscriptions et Belles-Lettres*, No. 2, 1991, p. 353.

92 This is the knight's '*emprise*' (see previous note). It is reminiscent of the Order of the Fer de Prisonnier founded in 1415 by Jean, Duke of Bourbon, which was 'specifically concerned with the performance of feats of arms in the lists. The sixteen noblemen of name and arms who formed the Order swore together that every Sunday for two years they would each wear an emblem, the iron and chain of a prisoner fashioned in gold, until they found sixteen other gentlemen who would accept their challenge to fight on foot … on condition that they would become prisoners if vanquished … Indeed the device of a prisoner's chain, borne as the outward and visible sign of a binding vow, is one that is encountered often.' Maurice Keen, *Chivalry* (New Haven and London, 1984), pp. 186, 212.

Word of this spread straight through the city and was reported to Jacques de Lalaing – who at this point was still but a squire. When he heard the news he gave humble and devoted thanks to Our Lord and the Virgin Mary His mother, praying with clasped hands that they might aid and guide him in all his deeds and affairs – and it seemed to him then that the prayers he made them every day were being fulfilled, were heard and answered. Pondering the matter, it appeared to him that, to judge from what he was wearing, the knight could have come from so far away with no other aim than to engage in arms. But he wanted to be sure, to know the truth, and to find out he sent for the King of Arms of the Fleece,[93] who was an expert in such matters and other lofty subjects and would be able to say how to proceed. As chance would have it, Golden-Fleece (for so he was called) was in Antwerp on that day; he was ready to come to Jacques de Lalaing and did so, and asked him why he'd been summoned. Jacques took him by the hand and, smiling, said:

'Golden-Fleece, my friend, you're very welcome!' And he took him aside and told him about the Sicilian knight: how he'd heard from his companions and other men of note that in the city's great church they'd seen a knight from foreign parts wearing on his leg a token signalling his wish to engage in arms. 'And since, Fleece my friend,' he said, 'my only wish is to win praise and reputation, I'd like to be able to answer the knight's challenge,[94] if it please my honoured lord and prince the duke. That's the main reason I sent for you, to have your advice and guidance as to how I should proceed.'

Golden-Fleece was delighted but said nothing for a moment; then, considering the young squire's fine and lofty aspiration, answered: 'Jacques de Lalaing, your noble desire and admirable courage fill my heart with joy. But I must warn you that you should in no way respond to the knight's challenge[95] without the approval and leave of your master and lord the duke, who is not in these parts at present: he has gone on a pilgrimage to the church of Our Lady at Boulogne.[96] But I hope, if it please Our Lord, he will soon be back, and the best advice I can give is that you go to his chancellor,[97] who represents him in his absence, and explain to him what you wish and aim to do.'

---

[93] i.e. the chief herald of the chivalric order, the Order of the Golden Fleece, founded by Philip of Burgundy in 1430; this was Jehan Lefèvre de Saint-Remy (c. 1395–1468). As discussed in the Introduction (p. 12), this part of the book is taken from a letter written by Lefèvre to Jacques's father.

[94] Literally 'I'd like to give the knight deliverance', i.e. free him from his oath: see note 91 above.

[95] Literally 'touch the knight's device'; as will become clear, the acceptance of the challenge involves touching the knight's shackle.

[96] Notre-Dame de Boulogne, most notable for the wedding of Edward II and Isabella of France in 1308.

[97] The scribe of MS 16830 accidentally wrote 'knight' ('*chevalier*' instead of '*chancelier*').

To Jacques and the gentlemen in his company this advice of Golden-Fleece seemed sound; so he left his lodging and went to the chancellor[98] who, hearing Jacques express such noble desire and courage, joyously replied that he would gladly give all the aid and advice he could till the duke returned. Jacques de Lalaing, with more respect and understanding of honourable ways than any man of his years, humbly thanked the chancellor, who told him at length how he should proceed. [*f. 41v*]

25

How Jacques de Lalaing sent the King of Arms of the Golden Fleece to the Sicilian knight, to discover his wishes and why he had come wearing a sign of commitment to engage in arms, and how the knight replied

After Jacques de Lalaing and the chancellor had discussed the matter at length, Lalaing called Golden-Fleece and bade him go to Sir Jehan Boniface and tell him on his behalf that a number of gentlemen and others had lately reported that, since his arrival in Antwerp, he had been to the city's great church and returned through the town sporting a device like a slave's shackle and followed by a pursuivant wearing his coat of arms; these were both evident signs that he wished to engage in arms.

'So, Fleece,' said Jacques de Lalaing, 'tell the knight from me that to relieve and free him of his burden I shall be glad to answer his challenge if it please my lord the duke,[99] but he must kindly be patient till the duke's return.'

Having heard Jacques's message to the Sicilian knight, Golden-Fleece said he would happily take it. He set off and came to the knight's lodging and found him in his chamber; he bowed to him in his accomplished fashion and greeted him in the name of Jacques de Lalaing. The knight bade him welcome and Golden-Fleece told him exactly why he'd come. They spoke of this and other matters, and after these exchanges the knight eagerly gave his response to Golden-Fleece, saying:

'Since my arrival I've heard such fine reports of Jacques de Lalaing, who's sent you here, that I praise God and thank you, Golden-Fleece, for the news you bring. From what I've heard of his sagacity, valour and fine reputation, I

---

98 Again, this is accidentally given as '*chevalier*'. The chancellor is Nicolas Rolin (1376–1462), a major figure at the Burgundian court.

99 The scribe's concentration was evidently suffering a temporary lapse and he makes another error, accidentally slipping into the third person in mid-speech ('he will be glad … his lord the duke'). In translating I have corrected this. But the fault may in fact originally have been the compiler's: he may have confused himself in the process of converting phrases in Lefèvre's letter to Jacques's father into a speech by Lalaing.

shall be pleased to engage with him, and will await the arrival and approval of the duke.'

In confirmation he took Fleece by the hand and gave his word.[100] Then Golden-Fleece, having heard the knight's response, took his leave and returned to Jacques de Lalaing and relayed in full what the Sicilian knight had said and promised. Jacques was overjoyed by this, and bade Fleece go to the chancellor and report to him what had been said. He went at once, and told the chancellor exactly how the Sicilian knight had responded to Jacques's message. When Golden-Fleece was done, the chancellor advised that Jacques should gather as many knights and squires as he could find and seek further guidance on how to proceed. Jacques followed this advice, assembling a number of knights and squires and setting forth his intentions, and asking for their direction in the matter. He told them what the chancellor had said and they all agreed it was sound advice. But then Jehan, lord of Arcis,[101] who was one of those present, stepped forward and said to Jacques:

'More than any of the noble men of these parts, you are the one I'd most gladly serve and I wish you every fortune and honour; but truly, knowing nothing of what you'd done I sent the King of Arms of Artois to speak to the Sicilian knight, and he told me he'd promised to engage with no one for the present but myself.'

So saying, he asked the chancellor, who was present there, to defer the matter till the following day. Then Jacques de Lalaing replied:

'My lord of Arcis, I realise you'd like to do me the favour of relieving me of this trouble! But if you please, my lord the chancellor nonetheless will ask the nobles here their opinion of what I should do about the Sicilian knight's reply.'

Then the chancellor, seeing Jacques's determination and ardent desire, asked the noblemen for their advice. And it was the view of all – not least the chancellor – that Golden-Fleece should be sent back to the knight to thank him for the response he'd made to Fleece and to ask him to be patient and await the duke's return, and if the duke so pleased, Jacques de Lalaing would go and answer his challenge.[102] It was decided that two noble and valiant squires, one named Hervé de Mériadec[103] and the other Maillart de Fléchin,[104] should go

---

[100] Again the scribe (or perhaps the compiler) accidentally slips between first person and third and includes some of this sentence in the direct speech; I have again corrected.

[101] '*Arci*'; other MSS name him more fully as 'Jean de Poitiers, lord of Arcis'. This is Arcis-sur-Aube, north of Troyes.

[102] As before, literally 'touch the knight's device'.

[103] Originally from Brittany, Hervé had become a squire of the stables in Duke Philip's household in 1435 and remained so throughout his reign.

[104] '*Fleusin*'. Jehan ('Maillart') de Fléchin (in Artois) was a squire of the stables in the households of both Philip the Good and his successor Charles the Bold.

with Golden-Fleece to meet the knight, and so they did. On arriving, Golden-Fleece spoke to the knight and thanked him for the words and promises he'd given him to relay to Jacques de Lalaing, who was most grateful.

'Sir,' he said, 'Jacques de Lalaing has sent me with these two gentlemen to thank you for the fine reply you gave me when last I came. I delivered your message to Jacques de Lalaing who thanks you likewise.'

Such were his words, and the knight was very pleased and said: 'Fleece, I am very mindful that you came today from Jacques de Lalaing and I'm sure you recall my response. I repeat that from the moment you'd spoken on his behalf, if the greatest prince in the world had sent me a challenge to combat I would have rejected it, for truly, I've heard so many reports of the qualities and virtues of Jacques de Lalaing that I count myself lucky to have come across a man of such renown. I praise God for it, and pray that by His grace we may both emerge with honour from our contest. For the present, Fleece, tell him that I consider him a brother, and thank him for the honour he has done me; and I am very happy to await the duke's return and to hear what he chooses to command.'

After this and further words exchanged between the four, they took their leave of the knight and returned to Jacques; and there, in the presence of the chancellor, they reported word for word what Jehan Boniface had said, which filled Jacques's heart with joy and he thanked Our Lord for the knight's reply. [*f. 44r*]

26

How the Sicilian knight came to the duke's court, where Jacques de Lalaing with the duke's leave and permission answered the knight's challenge to combat both on horseback and on foot

It wasn't long before the Duke of Burgundy returned from his pilgrimage and came to the city of Antwerp. Hearing of the duke's arrival, Jacques de Lalaing went to meet him. The duke had entered the city to a joyous welcome from nobles and the common folk alike, and next morning Jacques gathered a large number of gentlemen, his kinsmen and his friends, to accompany him to the duke's presence, where he made his request which the duke most graciously granted. For his part, Sir Boniface sent to the duke asking permission to come and pay his due respects; the duke agreed and named the day.

When the day came the knight appeared before the duke in the same state in which he'd gone to church and through the town, wearing his shackle, and the duke received him with much honour. Then Jacques de Lalaing, hearing that the knight had arrived, came into the duke's presence and, with leave reaffirmed, approached the Sicilian knight and said:

'Sir Jehan Boniface, I see you bear a device declaring your wish to engage in arms, and I have sought permission of my redoubted lord and prince here present to answer your challenge,[105] if it please you, and with God's aid to engage in combat in accordance with your Chapters,[106] which I believe and have no doubt will be such as are fitting for noble men.'

Then Sir Jehan Boniface replied: 'Jacques de Lalaing, I thank you for the honour you have done me, and am very pleased that you should now touch the shackle I bear, as a sign that you will do battle according to the Chapters I shall offer you in writing.'

Jacques happily declared his satisfaction, and stepped forward and touched the knight's shackle in the presence of the duke, who undertook to be arbiter for Boniface and Lalaing and said he would decide and inform them of the place and day when they could do battle. With matters thus settled, Boniface took his leave of the duke and returned to his lodging, where he made no delay in sending Jacques his Chapters of Arms, which were as follows; firstly: [f. 45r]

27

The Chapters of Arms on horseback

'To the honour and praise of Our Lord Jesus Christ and His most glorious virgin mother, and of my lord Saint George, I, Jehan Boniface, knight, native of the kingdom of Sicily, declare to all princes, barons, knights and gentlemen without reproach,[107] that to serve my fair lady and attain the title of prowess, by the leave and licence of that most excellent, mighty and victorious prince the King of Aragon and Sicily (both island and mainland),[108] of Valencia, Jerusalem, Hungary, Majorca, Minorca, Corsica and Sardinia, Count of Barcelona, Duke of Athens, Count of Roussillon and Cerdanya,[109] I

---

[105] Once again, literally 'touch your device'.

[106] '*chappitres*': as will become clear, 'Chapters of Arms' are the terms and conditions specified for a particular combat.

[107] 'We hear of technical "reproaches" that could entitle the heralds to exclude a knight from the tourney, such as a suspicion of having breached his pledged faith, or of having in one way or another done dishonour to womankind. We are reminded here that the famous phrase *chevalier sans reproche* (a qualification insisted upon as the condition of membership of many chivalrous orders) need not imply a truly stainless character, but simply a record clear of all technical fault ... Lack of hereditary qualification, or marriage below one's estate, were the commonest "reproaches" against would-be jousters ...' Maurice Keen, *Chivalry*, pp. 174, 211.

[108] Literally 'on both sides of the lighthouse': Alfonso V was king of Naples as well as Sicily after his defeat of René of Anjou in 1442–3.

[109] '*Pulsardin*'. Cerdanya was a Catalan county inherited by the counts of Barcelona.

bear a token of my commitment to engage in arms on horseback and on foot, with the condition that whoever first touches the said token will do battle with me in accordance with the following Chapters:

'First: we will do combat on horseback, and the first of us to break the shafts of six lances in striking his opponent will receive a jewel, of a kind and value deemed fitting by the one who has failed to break six; this jewel will be taken and presented by the loser in person to a lady or damsel at the court of that illustrious princess the Duchess of Burgundy and Brabant, as named and directed by the winner. However, if any of the lances are broken only at the head, they will not count as breaks.

'The second Chapter is: if one of us is brought to ground by a clean lance-blow to his armour, he will be obliged to surrender as a prisoner to the one who has unhorsed him; and by way of ransom and acquittal he must give to the lady or damsel to whom he is sent the helmet he has worn in the combat.

'The third Chapter is: we may wear whatever harness we please – double or single[110] – for fighting on horseback, but involving no illicit device, and there must be no addition to the arret:[111] only what is used in war.

'The fourth Chapter is: we will each bear lances of the thickness of our choice, but their length, measured from the arret to the tip of the head, will be such as I shall stipulate; each of us may fit the lance with whatever head or coronal[112] we choose.

---

[110] 'Double harness' was reinforced armour developed in the 15th century specifically for jousting.

[111] '*avantage en l'arrest*'. The arret is a hook attached to the breastplate to support the base of the lance; the word used here is '*avantage*': no advantage must be gained by any adaptation or addition. The sense of this is clarified in a paragraph from Juliet Barker's chapter on tournament armour: 'By the late fourteenth century there was a difference between the war lance and the jousting lance. In place of the *arrêt de la lance*, a leather grip behind the hand grip which prevented the hand slipping down the shaft in the encounter, the jousting lance was fitted with a grate (*agrappe*). This device had a series of cog-like projections which interlocked with the lance-rest on the breastplate (*arrêt de la cuirasse*). The grate and the lance-rest ensured that the jouster took the full weight of his own lance on his chest and increased his chances of breaking his lance by preventing it rebounding backwards on encounter.' Barker, *op. cit.*, p. 178. Since breaking a lance is to be an important score, the Sicilian knight is insisting on the use of lances without adaptations to the *arrêt* which would facilitate this.

[112] A crown-shaped fitting with three or four blunted projections, designed to prevent the piercing of armour and serious injury.

'The fifth Chapter is: we will joust separated by a tilt[113] which shall be five feet high and no more.

'The sixth Chapter is: if this mounted combat cannot be concluded on the first day, we must complete it on the day following, provided neither of us is prevented by infirmity, be it illness or injury, such that he cannot ride or bear arms. [*f. 46r*]

28

*Here follow the Chapters declaring how the combat
on foot is to be fought*

'The first Chapter is: we shall be armed as we choose in armour befitting combat in the lists, without any hook or other illicit device, and without the use of anything forbidden by our Holy Mother Church.[114]

'The second Chapter is: each of us may carry spears or throwing-knives,[115] to be thrown as we see fit; after the exchange of missiles we shall fight with axes,[116] swords and daggers as are customary in combat in the lists, until one of us falls to hand or knee or fully to the ground or surrenders to the other; and the one to whom God grants victory will spare the one defeated in exchange for the sword with which he has fought or which he brought to the lists.

'The third Chapter is: the one who touches my token of commitment to combat will be bound to fulfil the challenge,[117] in accordance with these Chapters, in the presence of the most excellent and mighty prince the Duke of Burgundy and Brabant within a month or six weeks of touching the token.

'The fourth and final Chapter is: to confirm to all that the terms set down above express my own will and that I intend to observe and fulfil them point by point, I, Jehan above-named, have set my seal upon these Chapters and signed them by my own hand, on the first day of April in the year 1445.'[118]

---

[113] '*à la toile*': with a barrier to prevent the horses colliding.

[114] This may well imply the use of magic charms.

[115] I take this to be the meaning of '*espees de get*'.

[116] i.e. pollaxes. The pollax (or pole-axe) was generally about the height of the bearer in length, with a head usually incorporating a spike for stabbing and an axe-blade or hammer on one side and a spike, hammer or barb on the other. There would often be a spike also on the butt of the shaft. The fighting technique was based on the quarterstaff, the pollaxe being used not only for striking and cutting but also for tripping and disarming an opponent and for blocking blows, while thrusts could be delivered with the spikes at both ends.

[117] Literally 'to deliver me': see notes 91 and 94 above, pp. 74–5, 76.

[118] The MS reads '1444' because in the Burgundian dominions, as in many parts

These Chapters, having been shown and presented to Jacques de Lalaing, were perused at length by him and his advisers; he accepted and approved them point by point and, without objection or modification to any, he promised, with the grace of Our Lord and his most worthy Mother, to uphold them. [*f. 47r–48r*][119]

29

How Jacques de Lalaing did battle on horseback against the Sicilian knight

The Duke of Burgundy, seeing matters thus advanced, with both parties eager and determined to fulfil their undertaking, decreed that it should take place in his fine city of Ghent. There the lists were prepared and erected for combat on horse and foot, and very handsome and splendid they were;[120] and the date was set for the contest to be fought there in Ghent on the fifteenth day of December in the aforesaid year.

Sir Jehan Boniface was in the city for a month prior to the combat. For his part Jacques de Lalaing, mindful of the appointed day,[121] arrived at the city of Ghent and entered with a cavalcade five hundred strong, among them the Count of Saint-Pol, his brother the lord of Fiennes[122] and many other great lords, both from the duke's court and of his own blood and lineage. He came and dismounted at the house which he found ready and arranged for his lodging, where he hosted a great dinner and supper that day.

Then, next morning, both combatants made their preparations to accomplish and fulfil their undertaking. The duke appointed two eminent knights of his court to advise Sir Jehan Boniface, one of whom was Sir Guillebert de Lannoy[123] and the other – .[124]

After dinner it was time for the two champions to do battle. The Duke of Burgundy was their arbiter; also present were the Duke of Orléans, the Count

---

of Europe, the start of a new year was determined by the date of Easter.

[119] In the MS there is no missing folio, but the number 'xlviii' was accidentally not used.

[120] According to Ghentish chroniclers it took place in the Friday Market Square.

[121] Lefèvre's letter to Jacques's father simply says 'the night before the combat was to be fought'.

[122] Thibaud de Luxembourg (c. 1420-77), lord of Fiennes.

[123] Guillebert de Lannoy (1386–1462), a knight of the Golden Fleece, was a widely travelled diplomat and a long-standing servant of the Burgundian dukes.

[124] The second name is given in none of the MSS (in MS 16830 a large space is left to enable later insertion); Lefèvre's letter names neither. It was customary to appoint experienced knights to advise a competitor on procedure, especially if, as here, he came from foreign parts where practices might differ.

of Charolais[125] and many other great lords now seated in the stands, which were richly arranged and bedecked for them. Into the lists came the Sicilian knight, armed and mounted, ready to face Jacques de Lalaing who, in good time after, left his house, mounted, armed and in splendid array. Through the streets he rode and, truly, the windows and doorways of the houses along his way were filled with ladies, damsels, townswomen and girls, all of them praying to God to send him back having won high honour. And you can be sure he was avidly desired by many, for indeed, as has been said before, there was no more handsome squire, better built in every limb, to be found anywhere.

Through the great streets rode Jacques de Lalaing, grandly accompanied by counts, barons, knights and squires, till he arrived at the square where the lists had been set. He entered in, and found Sir Jehan Boniface ready to receive him. He rode past the duke's stand and bowed to him before making his way to his station. At the other end of the lists the waiting knight prepared and took his lance. They both lowered their lances and charged to meet, as fast as their horses could go. The Sicilian knight looked every inch a warrior, poised in the saddle, superb in his armour and bearing his lance so expertly that he was praised and admired by all. They dealt one another such almighty blows with their great, stout lances that it seemed they would surely destroy each other! Jacques de Lalaing, strapping and strong and heavy-burdened with armour, looked less fine and elegant than the knight; but each time they clashed he made Boniface rock back violently. Truly, they ran many a fine course and exchanged many mighty blows, rarely missing their target; but most were struck without their lances breaking, for they were stout and very strong.

They kept charging and clashing till darkness fell, when the duke, who was their arbiter, sent word requesting that they agree to stop and saying they'd both performed well and valiantly, and that they still had to do combat on foot so they should be content to halt now and retire. From both champions, Boniface and Lalaing, came gracious replies, saying that the duke should not request or ask: as their arbiter he could and should demand. The duke in conclusion sent word that they should consider their combat on horseback accomplished.

All the same, Jacques de Lalaing wasn't happy: Boniface had broken three lances while he had broken only two and splintered another. But in truth Jacques's lances were a good deal stouter than the knight's, as was clearly seen in the mighty blows he'd dealt, one of which he'd landed on the cheek of Boniface's helm with such force that it had left him stunned for quite a while – he hadn't known where he was. And although Boniface had broken more lances, Jacques had landed as many blows or more – and harder – than

---

[125] Duke Philip of Burgundy's son, the future Duke Charles the Bold. Born in 1433, he was at this point only twelve years old.

Boniface had dealt him. Truly, all who saw them declared they'd never seen better and greater blows struck in so many courses as they had both delivered.

So in the end the two of them were satisfied, and the combat on horseback ended to the honour of both parties. It was now dark and torches were lit, and Boniface and Lalaing returned by the separate ways they'd entered, not together. [*f. 50r*]

30

How the combat on foot was accomplished, and how the Duke of Burgundy knighted Jacques de Lalaing

The following day, with the combat on horseback performed and accomplished, the Duke of Burgundy, the Duke of Orléans, the Count of Charolais and many other great lords took their places in the stand where they'd been the day before. Once they'd arrived, the Sicilian knight, accompanied by two notable knights his advisers, together with his servants, all on foot, came from his lodgings to the lists. Fully armed and clad in his coat of arms, he entered the lists and came and bowed to the duke his arbiter, and then withdrew to his pavilion where he stayed for a long while, waiting for Jacques de Lalaing.

Lalaing was delayed by waiting for the Duke of Cleves, who he knew was to arrive at any time: he'd been told so by a string of messengers. But his arbiter the duke sent word that he must come to the lists as Boniface had done some time ago; so he dared delay no longer, nor wait for the Duke of Cleves. He mounted, and after him three pages, on horses richly harnessed and caparisoned with cloth of gold. With him went a large number of great lords, knights and squires who accompanied and escorted him to the lists. He entered and bowed to the duke, then made his way to his pavilion to arm, for he had come clad in little of his armour. While he was arming, the Duke of Cleves arrived. He came and bowed to the Duke of Burgundy and then went straight to see Jacques in his pavilion: Jacques was overjoyed, and not without cause, as they'd been raised together in their youth.

As soon as he was armed, Jacques de Lalaing left his pavilion with the Duke of Cleves and other great lords, and they accompanied him as he came before the duke's stand. And there he asked him by his grace to bestow on him the order of knighthood. The duke graciously agreed. He came down from the stand, and Jacques de Lalaing drew his sword from its scabbard, went down on one knee and once more asked the duke to make him a knight and bestow on him the order of chivalry. The duke took the sword and gave Jacques de Lalaing the accolade, saying:

'May you be a good knight, in the name of God, of Our Lady and of my lord Saint George!'

Then he kissed him on the lips, and in kissing him hit his forehead against his visor. After this Sir Jacques de Lalaing returned to his pavilion and changed his headgear: he fought in a helmet with only a half-visor, his nose and lower face being uncovered.

Once all this was done, the weapons with which they were to fight were inspected and due announcements and prohibitions proclaimed.[126] Then Sir Jehan Boniface left his pavilion, armed with the weapons he was to use; Sir Jacques de Lalaing did likewise. They came striding fiercely towards each other, and as they drew near they threw their spears[127] at one another, right before the duke's stand. After this exchange of missiles they engaged in fine and valiant style with axes.[128] At one point in their combat Sir Jacques de Lalaing nearly forced the axe from Boniface's grip,[129] but he recovered it and they fought on as before. In the course of this Sir Jacques dealt his opponent a blow that made him reel,[130] but they battled on ferociously once more, exchanging mighty blows. But it wasn't long before Sir Jacques, so strong and powerful, attacked and struck the knight so fearsomely that he dashed the axe from both his hands. The Sicilian knight, finding himself disarmed, aimed to grab Sir Jacques by the visor,[131] but he used all his strength to drive him back with the end of his axe, and Boniface couldn't get near.

Then the Duke of Orléans, seeing the Sicilian knight in a desperate plight and gasping for breath, said to Duke Philip: 'What do you make of this, dear brother? You can see what a state this noble knight's in: unless you wish him to suffer total dishonour it's time to throw down your baton.'

The good Duke of Burgundy, hearing his brother-in-law the Duke of Orléans and recognising the worth of the two fine knights, threw his baton down. Then those guarding the field intervened at once and stopped the fight, and took both knights and led them before the duke's stand. He said to them:

'You have fought well and with great honour, and I deem your feat of arms accomplished. I pray you put your hands together[132] and be henceforth brothers and good friends.'

---

[126] i.e. the rules and regulations applying to the contest.

[127] '*lances*': i.e. the spears (javelins?) – and perhaps also the 'throwing-knives' – mentioned above, p. 82.

[128] Pollaxes: see note 116 above, p. 82.

[129] Literally 'made Boniface lose the axe from one of his hands'.

[130] Literally 'made him turn his body side-on'.

[131] Awkward syntax in the MS's rendering of this sentence, which reads 'aiming' rather than 'aimed', suggests an accidental omission, and the passage in Lefèvre's letter which is being copied here does indeed say that Boniface 'drew his dagger and aimed ...'

[132] Literally 'touch together'. It is nowhere specified in this text, but others suggest that the formalities at the end of a contest involved touching hands – perhaps in the manner of boxers touching gloves.

So the combat was concluded. Boniface returned to his lodgings on foot and his company with him, just as he had come. For his part Sir Jacques de Lalaing mounted his horse, newly caparisoned, and his three pages rode after him, all newly robed, their horses covered in cloth of gold of three different colours.[133] He returned to his house with a grand escort, and with trumpets and clarions sounding before him, a wondrous joy to hear.

The challenges now complete, festivities were held in honour of the foreign knight. The Duke of Burgundy, noble prince that he was, made great and prestigious gifts to Sir Jehan Boniface in gold coin and plate and silks, for which the knight thanked the duke most graciously before taking his leave. Then Sir Jacques de Lalaing feasted him and gave him a most handsome gift. Sir Jehan Boniface thanked him and took leave of him and headed back to King Charles in France. [*f. 52v*]

31

How Sir Jacques de Lalaing sent a herald to France with a challenge to arms, but the king would not allow any of his court to engage

After the completion of this feat of arms Sir Jacques de Lalaing, wishing with all his heart to seek further deeds and through his high and laudable exploits achieve lasting memory of his illustrious feats, that his renown might never wane but ever grow, sent to France, with the aim of doing combat there. The place he chose was in the city of Paris, beside the great church of Notre-Dame. He sent Charolais Herald to King Charles's court with a letter and Chapters to that effect. But for the moment the king would not allow any of his court to step forward in response.

Sir Jacques de Lalaing, seeing no favourable reception in France and no one wishing to fulfil the Chapters he'd sent through Charolais, was nonetheless unwilling to abandon his pursuit of deeds of arms. He'd no wish to see the glory and renown he'd won in his early years die away: he wanted to do all in his power to increase and enhance them.

So one day, in the duke's court, he revealed his thoughts to two noble and valiant knights, his uncles, one being the lord of Créquy[134] and the other Sir Simon de Lalaing.[135] He told them what he yearned to do and showed them the Chapters he had personally dictated to a secretary. The two noble knights, hearing their nephew's fine and lofty ambition, were filled with joy to see

[133] Cloth of gold is any fabric incorporating gold thread, either as the background or (as evidently here) to provide patterning on top of another colour.

[134] As noted above (p. 57), Jehan de Créquy was a member of the Order of the Golden Fleece and a prominent figure in the Burgundian court.

[135] Simon de Lalaing (1405–76), who first appeared above (pp. 40, 56, 57), was Admiral of Flanders and a member of the Order of the Golden Fleece.

the young knight intent on attaining the heights of prowess and renown; they were sure that one day, if he lived long enough, his deeds would be gloriously commended. They praised him for his noble goals, but said he shouldn't think of undertaking the plan without the knowledge and leave of his lord the duke. So to the duke he went, and the duke was delighted when he heard and saw in writing the Chapters describing the feats of arms he aimed to perform. Sir Jacques had a number of private audiences with the duke, who gave him generous gifts to aid him in accomplishing his high and noble venture.

Having told the duke of his plans in full, he took leave of him and his uncles and returned to the house of his father the lord of Lalaing. He was most warmly received, especially by the lady of Lalaing his mother, who loved him very dearly. After he'd been there several days he told his father of his undertaking and showed him the Chapters detailing what he meant to do and achieve. The lord of Lalaing, hearing his son's ambition and mighty courage, was overjoyed and praised him heartily, saying:

'I'll do all in my power to help, my son, though your going will pain me, as it will your mother, my lady of Lalaing. But God forbid I stand in your way or divert you from your fine and noble plan.'

Then the lord of Lalaing gave him much good advice and guidance, such as should be given to a young knight eager and intent on attaining the heights of prowess and renown. Sir Jacques, his heart brimming with joy to see his lord and father so inclined to praise his enterprise, thanked him very humbly. Then they discussed the details of his departure, and who he should take with him. He could not have arranged it better. Once all was in order and he was ready to depart he took leave of his father the lord of Lalaing and of the lady his mother, who wept deeply to see her beloved son go; but being a lady of great virtue she rejoiced, too, at her dear son's noble ambition. She kissed him many times at their parting, weeping heartfelt tears and voicing her regrets and sorrow; but the lord of Lalaing comforted her as best he could with tender and loving words.

But I'll say no more about the lord of Lalaing and the lady his wife; I'll return to Sir Jacques their son. [*f. 54r*]

32

How Sir Jacques de Lalaing came to the good, wise King of France,
who received him very kindly and showed him great favour

After taking leave of the lord of Lalaing his father and of the lady his mother, Sir Jacques mounted along with his company. He rode for some time thinking about the journey on which he was now embarked; his heart was set on accomplishing it, but for all that, he had no wish to leave the lands of his sovereign lord the Duke of Burgundy without visiting the Countess of Ligny, to whom he was related.[136] So he called some of the noble men of his company and bade them head for Paris without delay, and they did as commanded, taking with them horses and arms and the packhorses with all their baggage. Then, keeping with him only one worthy squire named Cornille de la Barre and a number of servants, he set off for Beaurevoir,[137] where he found his kinswoman the countess with a fine company of noble men and women. She greeted him with great joy and courtesy, and kissed him, bidding him most welcome and saying how grateful and pleased she was that he had come to see her before leaving. Sir Jacques, so bright and courteous, replied:

'My lady, I would never have left without seeing you and offering you my service if you've any command to make, as is my duty.'

The countess thanked him, and summoned an elderly and eminent squire of hers and other gentlemen of her household and gave them firm instructions to make Sir Jacques most welcome and to fête and entertain him and his company: he deserved it more than any man for his fine and noble ambition to increase and enhance the honour of his house, from which he was now setting out on his journey. The countess's bidding and command were done and Jacques was fêted by all as he richly deserved.

Having been treated with great honour and joy by the countess, ladies, damsels and noble men there at her house, Sir Jacques de Lalaing took leave of them all and humbly thanked the countess for the honour and welcome she had shown him. She kissed him at his leave-taking, and holding him by the hand she said:

'Sir Jacques, I pray to Our Lord Jesus Christ that He may be your guide and grant that you achieve your goal and return to the honour and advantage of the house of your birth and in the favour of your sovereign lord. I sincerely hope you will.'

The horses were ready, and having taken leave of all he set off and headed for the city of Noyon. There he found a number of noble men who'd left their homes to join his company and to serve him according to his command, namely: Jehan de Monfort, Félix de Ghistelles, Perceval de Belleforière, Galléran de Landas, Othe de Marquette, Guillaume d'Auberchicourt, Jehan

---

[136] Rather than Jeanne de Bar who was Countess of Ligny at this time (the wife of Louis of Luxembourg who has appeared above under his other title the Count of Saint-Pol), this is probably Jeanne de Béthune, whose husband Jean II of Luxembourg, Count of Ligny, had died a few years earlier in 1441. Whichever countess is referred to here, Jacques de Lalaing was related via his mother, who was of the house of Béthune on her mother's side. If it is Jeanne de Béthune, she was famously one of the guardians of Joan of Arc during her imprisonment at the castle of Beaurevoir, where Jacques is about to visit the countess.

[137] Between Cambrai and Saint-Quentin, about 40 miles south of his home at Lalaing.

Rasoir, the aforementioned Cornille de la Barre, Jehan du Fresnoy, Yollin de Villers,[138] and with them a herald of arms named Luxembourg and a pursuivant from Lalaing who went by the name of Loyal.[139]

Arriving in the city of Noyon, he sent the herald and pursuivant to the court of the most Christian king Charles of France, the seventh of that name, to proclaim and publicise his Chapters, so that if any noble men were willing to take up his challenge to engage in arms[140] according to the terms laid down in the Chapters, they might be informed and ready to fulfil what he required when he arrived. But for the moment, for certain reasons of his own, the King of France would not permit any noble men of his court to do so.

When he heard news of this refusal, the noble Sir Jacques was nonetheless set on visiting the most Christian and noble King of France to pay his respects to his royal majesty. So he left Noyon and went by way of Compiègne, Senlis, Paris and other cities and towns in the kingdom of France,[141] being highly honoured and welcomed everywhere, and all the while seeking news of the king's whereabouts. He finally had word that he was in residence at Bois-Sire-Amé;[142] delighted by this, he and his company headed there and arrived to find the king accompanied by a great number of princes, knights and noble men.

King Charles, informed of Sir Jacques de Lalaing's coming and the purpose of his visit, received him with great cheer and honour, as did all the princes, barons and knights then in his household: all greeted him with the highest respect. As well as discussing other matters, the knight told the king exactly why he'd come, giving full details of the form and manner of combat offered in his Chapters, and saying:

'Sire, of all realms, the most noble and Christian house and kingdom of France should not be forgotten: it is the first place, before any other, that I should have my Chapters of Arms proclaimed.'

The most noble King of France, hearing Sir Jacques voice such admirable ambition, looked at the princes around him; then he joyously said:

'Sir Jacques de Lalaing, you are welcome! Your deeds and works have started splendidly! God grant you bring them to glorious fruition – and you cannot fail, it seems to us: we have known of your deeds and qualities for a good while now, ever since we were in Nancy; there we clearly saw that you are bound to attain the heights of prowess and renown if you continue as you have begun and Fortune does not turn against you.'

---

[138] The fiefs of these men are mostly in Hainaut, some of them (Landas, Auberchicourt) close neighbours of Lalaing. Marquette is near Lille; Jehan Rasoir was lord of Beuvrages, near Valenciennes.

[139] 'Léal'.

[140] Once again, the phrase is 'touch his device'.

[141] As noted previously, this refers to the French royal domain, more or less what is still referred to as the Île de France.

[142] The castle of Bois-Sire-Amé is at Vorly, some 12 miles south of Bourges.

When Sir Jacques heard the King of France honour him so, he went down on his knees, thanking him with all humility and saying:

'Sire, may God in His mercy grant it.'

The king, deemed at that time to be the wisest prince in his kingdom, stepped forward and, taking Sir Jacques de Lalaing by the hand and bidding him rise, said:

'Sir Jacques, we consider you a member of our household, and to pass the time, wish you to rest and enjoy the company of our court.'

And he commanded the lord of Brézé, seneschal of Poitou,[143] and Sir Jehan de Hangest, lord of Genlis and several others to fête him and show him all possible honour, and the king's bidding was duly done.

But for all the celebratory welcome, Sir Jacques saw no one come forward to touch the device he wore on his right arm – a golden bracelet to which was attached a fine veil – which he'd worn in numerous places signalling his aim to accomplish feats of arms set forth in his Chapters. These were as follows. [*f. 57r*]

33

The Chapters of Arms sent by Sir Jacques de Lalaing to many kingdoms

B eginning with the first:

'The first Chapter states that whoever touches my device will be bound to answer my challenge[144] according to the terms laid down in these Chapters, provided he be of noble stock in all lines of descent and without reproach.[145]

'The second Chapter is: that each of us will be armed as is customary for combat on foot, and each will provide his own arms.

'The third Chapter is: we shall fight with axe or sword until one of us is brought fully[146] to the ground.

'The fourth Chapter is: if, God forbid, I am brought to the ground, I shall be bound to surrender to the lady or damsel to whom the one who has felled me chooses to send me; and to her I shall be bound to give by way of ransom a diamond to the value of five hundred écus.

---

[143] Pierre de Brézé (c. 1410–65), a notable soldier to whom Georges Chastellain was at this time secretary. He appeared above (p. 73) as lord of La Varenne.

[144] Literally 'deliver me': see note 91 above, pp. 74–5.

[145] See note 107 above, p. 80.

[146] Literally 'whole body', i.e. not just forced down on one knee, for example.

'The fifth Chapter is: in the event that God and she who has more power over me than anyone in the world[147] grant me the fortune to bring a knight or squire to the ground, he will be bound to send his gauntlet where I command, by an officer of arms, who will be obliged to testify to the feat of arms involved.

'The sixth Chapter is: if in the course of the combat one of us should lose his axe, the first to be so disarmed will be bound to give his opponent a diamond.

'The seventh Chapter is: we each shall fight with whatever axe and sword we choose such as are customary in combat on foot, without a hook or any other illicit device whatever.

'The eighth Chapter is: the said combat on foot being performed and accomplished, if my opponent's wish is to do combat on horseback and he so requests, I shall be ready on the third day following to run as many courses as he pleases in the manner set out below, provided I have no physical injury preventing me from bearing arms, or any other reasonable excuse.

'The ninth Chapter is: we shall fight in armour customary in combat on horseback, double or single,[148] without targe[149] or shield, and neither party shall have any addition to the arret or extra girth for the saddle.[150]

'The tenth Chapter is: we shall joust with a tilt[151] and bear similar lances, and use each until they are broken in the shaft, or at the head by at least a finger's breadth.[152]

---

[147] Although this cryptic phrase has the potential to refer to some unknown sweetheart, the likelihood is that it refers to the Virgin Mary. See below, p. 116.

[148] See note 110, above, p. 81.

[149] From the 15th century, the word was used quite often for a shield designed for jousting.

[150] *'sans arrest avantageux et sans attacher longne à la selle'*. On the arret, see note 111 above, p. 81. I take the *'longne'* to be additional strapping; Juliet Barker notes: 'The only obvious difference between saddles for hastiludes and for other purposes was that the former required much stronger means of attachment. Double girths were usually issued for all such saddles to ensure that they did not slip off backwards in the shock of the encounter.' Barker, *op. cit.*, pp. 172–3. However, in his edition of Lefèvre's letter to Jacques's father, Morand gives the reading 'sans actaichier *l'omme* à la selle' ('without attaching *the man* to the saddle'), and this may be correct, as one of the Chapters for the later passage of arms at the Fountain of Tears stipulates that 'they will joust in saddles of war, without being strapped in the saddle' (below, p. 145).

[151] *'toile'*: see note 113 above, p. 82.

[152] Interestingly, Jacques's Chapter here does not assume the possible fitting of a

'The eleventh Chapter is: to engage in the aforesaid feats of arms and accomplish them in every point according to the terms of these my Chapters, I have chosen as arbiter the most excellent and mighty prince the King of Castile,[153] whom I humbly pray by his kindly grace to do me the honour of granting my request.

'The twelfth Chapter is: to attest to all that the above expresses my own will, and that I wish and intend to accomplish it, I the aforenamed Jacques de Lalaing have attached my seal of arms to these Chapters and signed them by my own hand, on the twentieth day of July in the year 1446.' [*f. 58r*]

34

How Sir Jacques de Lalaing left the court of France and came to Navarre, where he was well received and fêted by the king and prince and princess, the Princess of Navarre being sister of the Duke of Cleves

As you've heard in this true history, these – in detail and word for word – were the Chapters of Arms declared by Jacques de Lalaing, at this point twenty-three years old.[154] But he saw that at the King of France's court, honourably received though he had been, no one was coming forward to touch his device; so he decided to set out and search all Christian realms, one after another, intending after France to head first for Spain where there are several kingdoms – which is why he'd chosen as arbiter, before all others, the King of Castile. His heart was set on achieving his quest and accomplishing what he'd undertaken, and realised that lingering there was delaying matters, so he took leave of the King of France and the princes and barons of his court and set off.

He and his company journeyed on till he came to the city of Bordeaux, which at that time was English, obedient to the King of England.[155] When Sir Jacques arrived there, the mayor of the city, Sir William Clifton[156] by name, Sir Guillotin de Lansac[157] and Mondon de Lansac his brother, together with the

---

coronal as Boniface's had done (above, p. 81), so the jousting now is potentially more dangerous.

[153] Juan II, king of Castile and León (r. 1406–54).

[154] He was probably twenty-five. In the course of this work – perhaps because it is a compilation of different writings – the stated age of Jacques de Lalaing in relation to given dates does not consistently tally. When he is killed in 1453, we are told (below, p. 228) that 'when Death took him he was only about thirty-two'.

[155] Bordeaux was not taken by the French until 1451.

[156] '*Guillaume de Chisecon*'; presumably related to Robert Clifton, Constable of Bordeaux 1439–42.

[157] In the 1420s he appears as captain of Louviers, the English stronghold in Normandy.

archbishop of Bordeaux, received him and his company most honourably, as if he had been of the King of England's household. Sir Jacques was delighted, and with good cause: since leaving his homeland he had not been so fêted and honoured as he was then in the city of Bordeaux. He thanked the mayor, the archbishop and the lords, along with the burghers and the commoners of the city who covered their expenses, excusing them all payment, both him and all his men.

After taking his leave of them all he left Bordeaux and headed for the kingdom of Navarre; he'd sent his Chapters there just as he had done to the Christian kingdoms of Castile, Aragon and Portugal and a number of other places where he thought he might be delivered of his undertaking. Through an officer of arms he had everywhere sent word of his Chapters and of his coming, making it clear that nowhere could or should he be detained further than the terms of his Chapters required.

Sir Jacques and his company pressed on till he entered the kingdom of Navarre, where he and his men enquired where the King of Aragon was to be found, and where the Prince[158] and Princess might be. He was told that the Prince and Princess were then residing in the city of Pamplona, but that the King of Navarre[159] wasn't there at present: he'd gone to spend a pleasant time in one of his cities on the border with Castile. Sir Jacques, thus informed, set off for Pamplona to find the Prince and Princess and to see if any knight or man of noble birth would answer his challenge by touching the device which, as I've said above, he wore on his right arm: a rich golden bracelet with a fine veil attached. All knights and squires with four lines of noble descent and without reproach would be entitled to touch it, in response to which Sir Jacques promised to fulfil and accomplish the terms set forth in his Chapters, which, as I've explained, he had sent an officer of arms ahead to proclaim. [f. 59v]

[158] Carlos, Prince of Viana (1421–61), the title given to the heir of the kingdom of Navarre.

[159] Referring to him confusingly both as 'the King of Aragon' and as 'the King of Navarre' may be explained by the fact that Juan, the King of Navarre at the time of Lalaing's visit in 1446, was to become King of Aragon (as Juan II) in 1458 – i.e. he was almost certainly King of Aragon at the time when this work was written. The King of Aragon in 1446 was Alfonso V (above, p. 80), but we are later told also that Juan, King of Navarre, was at this time regent of the kingdom of Aragon in his brother Alfonso's absence (below, p. 121). To complicate matters further, and to explain the important status of the Prince and Princess in this episode, Juan 'the King of Navarre' had first ruled only by right of his wife Queen Blanche I; on her death in 1441 he had seized the crown for himself, keeping it from their son Carlos (the Prince who is appearing here), to whom it had been bequeathed. There was much tension between father and son, which soon after the time of this episode was to turn to civil war.

35

How a knight of Navarre named Juan de Luxe asked leave and permission of the Prince to engage in combat with Sir Jacques de Lalaing, which request was refused

When the Prince and Princess heard of Sir Jacques's approach, they sent Jaime Díez,[160] principal squire of the Prince's stables, and a host of other nobles, knights and squires of the Prince's household, to welcome him with great honour and respect. And that very same day, on hearing of Sir Jacques's arrival, there came before the Prince a noble knight named Don Juan de Luxe,[161] who knelt at the Prince's feet and said:

'My redoubted lord, it will be in your gracious memory that I have previously craved leave to go and search distant realms such as England and France, bearing a device inviting combat with noble knights and squires, in the hope of growing in worth and reputation, and to win renown to enhance the house of my birth. As it happens, my lord, I've no need to suffer toil and hardship to achieve my goal: I can find such an adventure, if it please you, here in the kingdom of Navarre! I'm told that a noble knight, from a fine house and without reproach, has come here bearing a device which all noble knights and squires without reproach may touch. I consider myself to be so, my redoubted lord: I don't believe I've ever been guilty of a fault that warrants reproach. So I humbly pray your leave and permission, as a good lord should grant his loyal subject, to touch this gentle knight's device.'

Hearing his noble desire and brave request, the Prince of Navarre replied most courteously, saying:

'Don Juan de Luxe, you know my lord the King of Aragon and Navarre[162] has yet to be informed of this challenge to combat, or of the knight's arrival here; and you know – or should know – that the houses of Navarre and Burgundy have such strong ties, through both my sister and my spouse,[163] that I'm sure my lord the king will be quite opposed to combat between those of Burgundy and those of Aragon and Navarre. But I thank you, Don Juan de Luxe, for the honour and courage you show towards our house. And if it should please my father the king to have a baron or knight of his realms do

---

[160] '*Janmedis*'. Jaime Díez (de Aux y Armendáriz), lord of Cadreita, was a squire of the stables in the Prince of Navarre's household.

[161] '*Messire Jehan de Lusse*'. Juan de Luxe, lord of Domezain (near Bayonne), was head of the Princess of Navarre's household.

[162] Strictly speaking, this was not yet his correct title: see note 159.

[163] The Prince had married Agnes of Cleves in 1439; she was the sister of John, the 'young Duke of Cleves' who had taken Jacques de Lalaing to the Burgundian court. This phrase may be corrupt, as none of the Prince's sisters was tied by marriage to Burgundy.

combat with this Sir Jacques de Lalaing, I shall plead to him on your behalf:
you have my leave to be the first, before all others. But I'm sure he won't
allow it. Be content for the present and discuss it no more. But we wish you
and everyone to welcome Sir Jacques with honour, pleasure and good cheer;
we would have it so.'

Having heard the Prince of Navarre's response, and seeing he would have
no other, Don Juan de Luxe said no more: he had to accept it. [f. 61r]

<h2 style="text-align:center">36</h2>

*How the Prince and Princess of Navarre welcomed and fêted Sir
Jacques de Lalaing with great honour*

When Sir Jacques de Lalaing was about half a league from Pamplona, the
Prince's head squire and a host of knights and squires of his household
came before him and received him with all honour. They said the Prince and
Princess were delighted by his coming, and that he was most welcome in the
kingdom of Navarre. Sir Jacques, as adept and endowed with fine manners
as any man of his years, returned due thanks and shook their hands,[164] and
in spirited conversation they rode together into the city of Pamplona. They
dismounted before the Prince's palace, and a throng of knights and squires
escorted him inside. There they found the Prince and Princess who greeted Sir
Jacques and all his company with the utmost joy and courtesy. In his elegant
style he bowed to them as befitted their station, and delivered the greetings
of my[165] redoubted sovereign lord, my lord the Duke of Burgundy, as he had
been charged to do. He and his company were fêted and shown great honour
by the Prince and Princess.

After this fine reception, Sir Jacques was escorted to his lodgings by Don
Juan de Beaumont,[166] Don Pedro de Peralta, lord of Marcilla[167] and numerous
other noble men, who treated him with much joy and honour. Once he was
installed in the lodging provided they took their leave and departed and left
him with his companions; they spent the night most happily, delighted by the
honour and warm welcome they had received from the Prince and Princess.
He was lavishly served with dishes and entremets that night, for a number of
knights and squires of the Prince's household had stayed with him for supper

---

[164] Literally 'touched them by the hands'; it may be that, rather than a modern
handshake, the gesture was closer to a nudge of the fist as at the end of combat: see
note 132 above, p. 86.

[165] The use of the first person reflects the incorporation here of a herald's record.

[166] '*Jehan d'Ixsextre et de Beaumont*'. A line of the Beaumont family had established itself in Spain; Juan was Chancellor of Navarre.

[167] '*Pierre de Peraltre, seigneur de Mazilles*', Constable of Navarre.

at the Prince's bidding, to entertain and honour Sir Jacques. And when supper was over they engaged in conversation, exchanging questions of each other as they pleased. They were deep in talk for quite a while, till finally it was time to retire, when they took leave of one another and went their separate ways.

And so they spent the night till the following morning when all dressed and made ready. It wasn't long before the aforementioned lords arrived and told Sir Jacques they had come to escort him to the Prince and Princess, saying:

'Sir Jacques de Lalaing, my lord and lady and all their council are waiting for you to join them in the chapel to hear mass.'

'Sirs,' he replied, 'the honour my lord and lady show me I take not to be on my account but for the sake of my redoubted sovereign lord the Duke of Burgundy, to whom, God willing, I shall report the great honour they have paid me, for which I humbly thank them.'

And one of them replied: 'Sir Jacques de Lalaing, we know you by repute, and from what we have heard all honour is due to you.'

They all then left the house and mounted their horses and mules and rode to the palace and dismounted there; and you may be sure that as he passed through the streets along the way, the doors and windows were packed with men and women, ladies and damsels, townswomen and girls, all eager to catch a sight of Sir Jacques and his companions – and no wonder, for he was one of the most handsome young knights of the time, and richly apparelled, dressed in a splendid gown laden with orfrey.[168] He was tall and upright, well built in every limb, with a handsome, pleasant face, gentle, kind and courteous, but with the air of a courageous man indeed; and all he bore became him perfectly. Those who saw him riding by beheld him with delight – especially the ladies and damsels: you may be sure that some would gladly have exchanged him for their husbands if they could!

So through the city of Pamplona he rode till he arrived before the palace. There he dismounted and entered with his escort, and found the Prince and Princess accompanied by a host of knights and ladies. He bowed to them and they bade him and all his company most welcome.

'Sir Jacques,' said the Prince, 'you shall come and hear mass with us; after mass we shall speak to you.'

'As it please you, my lord,' he replied.

The Prince entered the chapel, and the Princess, holding Sir Jacques by the hand, entered after, and they heard mass together.

When mass had been said and sung they left the chapel and came to a rich chamber, splendidly hung with tapestry, where the Prince and Princess, the noble barons, lords and council all sat down; and Sir Jacques de Lalaing, at the Prince's command, was seated above all the rest. Once all were in their

---

[168] Elaborately detailed embroidery, often incorporating gold and silver thread.

seats the Chancellor of Navarre[169] rose, and at the Prince's bidding began to speak, saying:

'Sir Jacques de Lalaing, my lord the Prince and my lady the Princess bid me tell you that you are most welcome here.'

Sir Jacques rose and went down on one knee and thanked the Prince and Princess for their welcome. Thanks given, the Chancellor spoke, saying:

'Sir Jacques de Lalaing, it has come to the attention of my lord the Prince and all of us here that, by a herald of arms named Luxembourg, there have been broadcast in this kingdom, both at the Prince's court and elsewhere, the contents of a scroll on which are written the Chapters and Articles you wish to observe and accomplish if you can find a knight of four noble lines of descent and without reproach who will touch the device we see you wear on your right arm. This undertaking is inspired by great courage, and all princes are bound to admire you and pay you fitting honour. But for the present my lord the Prince bids me tell you that he does not deem it appropriate for men of the houses of Burgundy and Navarre to engage with each other in combat or challenge. Moreover, my lord the King of Navarre is unaware of your aim in coming, and he would certainly not permit it. The bonds of love and alliance between the houses are so strong that it is quite impossible to sunder them: if it please Our Lord they will last forever. Nonetheless, Sir Jacques, you may be sure that there are good and valiant knights in this kingdom who, for the enhancement of their honour and renown, would willingly have met your challenge to relieve you of your burden if my lord had given permission. The Prince has been strongly pressed to do so, especially by the lord of Luxe and a number of others; they would gladly have touched your device had they been allowed. Indeed my lord the Prince, my lady the Princess and all the ladies and damsels are taking it as having been done.[170] They therefore pray you be content.'

The Chancellor having spoken as instructed by the Prince of Navarre, Sir Jacques rose and thanked the Prince and Princess for the honour and courtesy they were showing him, and said:

'God forbid, my lord Prince, that I should ever be the cause or do anything to break or diminish the love and alliance between you and my redoubted sovereign lord: I'd rather have never been born! But you know that for as long as a man has vigour he should seek to enhance his honour and win renown, should strive with all his might to do and achieve anything on earth, both to advance and better himself and for the greater honour and acclaim of the house of which he is born.'

Such were the words addressed by Sir Jacques de Lalaing to the Prince of Navarre, in the presence of the Princess and all the barons, knights, ladies, damsels and other noble men. They delighted to hear him speak and admired

---

[169] Juan de Beaumont, introduced above.

[170] i.e. the will and intention were enough in their eyes, so honour is maintained.

and praised him for it, saying to each other that, if God let him live, he couldn't fail to achieve high and mighty honour: they'd never heard of a finer start to a career.

Then the Prince and Princess bade the barons and knights feast and entertain Sir Jacques and his company, with no expense spared, and their command was duly obeyed: Sir Jacques couldn't have been more grandly fêted. After dinner he was escorted to join the ladies, the Prince and Princess being present. Dancing and revelry began throughout the hall: trumpeters struck up a mighty din, and minstrels played gitterns,[171] harps and psalteries as well as they knew how: a most melodious sound it was. All were intent on joy and merriment. In short, not for a long time had a knight from a foreign land been shown such honour and been so highly fêted as Sir Jacques and his company were that day. He was delighted, as were his companions, for not a day went by during their stay in Pamplona but they were feasted so.

But it's commonly said that there's no feasting in the world, however grand, that shouldn't be set aside in the constant pursuit of a goal. And Sir Jacques, seeing there was nothing to be gained by staying there, since he found no one who dared to touch his device for fear of offending the Prince and contravening his command, was intent on continuing his quest: he would go to the King of Castile and elsewhere, to all those realms where he'd sent a herald with his Chapters proclaiming his challenge and announcing his approach. So he came before the Prince and Princess of Navarre and asked their permission to leave, thanking them for the great honour and kindness they'd shown him and his companions, and offering ever to be their servant and asking them so to view him, for there was no way he could repay their courtesy and honour; and he said that if it pleased God to return him to his sovereign lord the Duke of Burgundy, he would report to him his deep gratitude.

When the Prince and Princess heard that he wished and meant to leave, the Prince took him by the hand and said:

'Sir Jacques, we understand what you've undertaken and your eagerness to pursue it. We wouldn't wish to stand in the way of your going. We would rather have you stay than leave, but since it is your wish we are content, and pray that God will guide you on your path.'

Then the Prince took him by one hand and the Princess by the other. He kissed the Princess at his parting, as he did all the ladies and damsels; and then, having taken leave, he returned to his lodgings, escorted all the way by a host of knights and squires. And no sooner had those in charge of his purse agreed settlement with their host than the head of the Prince's household forbade the host and hostess to take anything, gold or silver, in payment for what Sir Jacques and his company had spent. Indeed, wherever he went in passing through the kingdom of Navarre all his expenses were defrayed, as were those of his companions.

---

[171] The gittern is a plucked, stringed instrument, often played with a quill plectrum.

As soon as he was ready he mounted, and found outside his lodgings a great throng of knights and squires who escorted him far along his way. Then they took leave of him, but gave him men to guide him till he'd left Navarre and entered the kingdom of Castile. There he dismissed the guides with a generous gift of wine with which they were delighted, and on their return they reported their gratitude to the Prince and Princess of Navarre. But we'll say no more about Navarre for now; we'll move on to Castile, as now you'll hear. [*f. 66v*]

37

How Sir Jacques de Lalaing came to the court of the King of Castile, and Sir Diego de Guzmán took up his challenge

As Sir Jacques de Lalaing left the kingdom of Navarre and entered Castile, he asked earnestly for news of where he might find the king. He was told by credible people that the king was then residing in the city of Soria, where he'd summoned the three estates of the realm. With him were a great number of dukes, marquises and counts and a host of knights and squires, and certain noble men informed him of Sir Jacques de Lalaing's approach. To meet him the king sent the Count de Guzmán, Grand Master of the Order of Calatrava,[172] along with Don Juan de Luna[173] and a great many other knights and squires, who all together greeted him with much honour and said that the king was delighted by his coming, being very eager to meet him, and he was most welcome in his kingdom.

'Sirs,' said Sir Jacques, 'I humbly thank the king and all of you for the honour you show me. God grant by His grace that I do something pleasing in his eyes!'

Then all, one after another, shook him by the hand,[174] and all his companions after. Then together they set off for Soria, where they saw Sir Jacques lodged in a house just outside the city which had been arranged and prepared for him, richly hung with tapestries and well supplied with the necessary, for two days previously he had sent ahead those in charge of his purse to make provision for them all, as their stay might well be long.

Now, it so happened that as Sir Jacques and his company and those sent to meet him were heading towards his lodgings at Soria, there came before him a knight named Sir Diego de Guzmán, brother of the count who was escorting him, and as he approached Sir Jacques he said:

---

[172] Luis González de Guzmán; the Order of Calatrava, founded in the 12th century, was Spain's oldest military order.
[173] This is probably Juan de Luna, Count of San Esteban de Gormaz, eldest son of the King of Castile's favourite, Álvaro de Luna, Duke of Trujillo.
[174] As before, literally 'touched his hand'.

'My good sir, dear brother and knight, I praise God my creator for your coming! By His grace He has chosen to have me find on my doorstep what I'd planned to seek in countless realms and provinces! I can't thank you and Our Lord enough! I'd been informed of your coming and your purpose by the herald you sent to proclaim your Chapters of Arms. It's clear to me that your challenge is inspired by the loftiest courage and honour; and so, to shorten your quest, I have managed to gain permission of my redoubted sovereign lord the King of Castile, and with your leave, and to please my beloved lady, I shall touch your device and undertake to fulfil and accomplish all the terms pronounced and proclaimed by your herald at the court of my sovereign lord. I shall be ready to answer your challenge to the best of my powers on the day appointed by my redoubted lord the King of Castile and León.' [*f. 68r*]

38

How Sir Jacques de Lalaing came before the King of Castile, and of the honour and favour shown him by the king and his barons

After Sir Diego de Guzmán had touched the device, Sir Jacques and his company were escorted to their lodgings where he was received with great honour by the King of Castile's men. They had been ordered to feast him grandly and then, next day, to take him and Don Juan de Luna to the city of Valladolid, where he was to stay till the king came and made further arrangements: he would do so very soon.

And you may be sure that once the feasting was done, Sir Jacques – along with Don Juan de Luna, appointed by the king to be his escort – left Soria and rode to Valladolid where they were given a most honourable reception. Sir Jacques and his company took lodging in the house arranged for him, where, while waiting for the king to come, he was grandly fêted by the knights, ladies and damsels.

Just a few days later the King of Castile[175] announced his arrival to the knights escorting Sir Jacques and ordered them to bring him to him. This they did: they led Sir Jacques to a broad, open field where they found the king running two bulls on which, as is the way in that country, he'd had a pack of huge mastiffs set to bait and destroy them. As Sir Jacques approached the king, ample space was given so that he and his men could come forward and pay their due respects. This Sir Jacques did with great aplomb, with his cultured elegance. He went down on one knee before the king and said:

'Most high, excellent, mighty prince, I know it will be in your royal memory that, with the leave and approval of my redoubted sovereign lord the Duke of Burgundy, I have undertaken with God's aid to carry a token of challenge to

---

[175] As noted previously, this is Juan II, r. 1406–54.

combat through most of the realms of Christendom. This I have made known by an officer of arms whom you allowed to proclaim my challenge in your noble majesty's presence.'

'Sir Jacques de Lalaing,' the king replied, 'we are well aware of this, and you are welcome here.'

Then he stepped up to the king, who took him by the hand and asked his news. Sir Jacques, as refined in manners as any knight of his years, replied to all the king's questions with impeccable courtesy and eloquence, and the king took great pleasure in hearing him speak. And his gaze was fixed upon him, too, for more than all others he looked a knight of quality indeed, which he was.

Riding and conversing with the king and in his company, Sir Jacques returned to the city of Valladolid. He accompanied the king to his palace and then took leave of him and rode back to his lodging with a number of knights and squires who'd been instructed by the king to escort him. There he dismounted, and they took their leave of Sir Jacques and returned to the king's court; but they were soon back to keep him company, and he gave them a splendid supper that night, regaling them with all that could then be found in Valladolid. After supper they engaged in conversation for a good while; then when the time came to retire, the knights and squires who'd supped with him took their leave and went their separate ways.

Next morning, as Sir Jacques was preparing to go and hear mass with the Dominicans (his lodgings being right close by),[176] the King of Castile's men arrived to accompany him. It was thus for several days during his stay in the city: they accompanied and visited him regularly, for the king had expressly bidden so; and so they duly did, guiding and escorting him wherever he wished to go.

It so happened in the days that followed that a number of important embassies arrived in Valladolid from France, Granada and Portugal; the king and his council were much occupied in dealing with them, and couldn't give their minds to fixing a day for the two knights to fulfil their challenge. So the king sent a message to Sir Jacques asking him to be patient: because of pressing business he couldn't give a date as early as he'd hoped. But he did name a date for him to be in Valladolid, when he promised he'd be there in person without fail; then they could engage in their feat of arms before him. Meanwhile, if he were so inclined, he could go and seek diversion in Castile or elsewhere, wherever he pleased. [f. 70r]

---

[176] This would be the church of the Dominican friary of San Pablo.

39

How the King of Castile told Sir Jacques de Lalaing to have patience,
that he could not do combat so soon; Sir Jacques resigned himself to
this, and to pass the time while awaiting the day he went to see the
King of Portugal

When Sir Jacques received the king's message from his knights,[177] he courteously replied that the date was quite acceptable since it was his royal pleasure. The delay was very irksome – he would much rather it had been less long – but there was nothing else for it: he would have to bear it and wait for another six months. Seeing time passing and not wishing to waste it, he told his companions that he'd decided, while waiting for the appointed day, to go and seek diversion in the kingdom of Portugal, to see the king and queen and the barons and knights of that land. They all applauded the plan, being eager as they were to explore strange lands, as all noble men have always done. So they made ready to take to the road, getting all in order. Sir Jacques sent the knights[178] who'd kept him company to inform the king of his journey; the king approved and sent him men to escort and guide him. Then Sir Jacques and his company set out.

Not far along the road from Valladolid was a city named Madrigal.[179] In residence there was the Princess of Castile, the King of Navarre's daughter,[180] and, hearing this, Sir Jacques headed there and paid his respects, humbly offering her his service. The Princess, with her ladies and damsels and the knights and squires of her household, received him most graciously, welcoming and fêting him with great respect and honour, being very pleased to see him. The Princess appeared indeed delighted by his coming, and so she was, and rightly so, for there was no more handsome, charming, courteous knight to be found in all Castile. The ladies gazed at him with wonder, dressed as he was in a rich crimson gown lined with sable which became him splendidly; his complexion was fresh and glowing, and being still only twenty-two[181] he had as yet no beard or moustache; his hair was fair and his eyes were clear and shining: so pleasing a sight he was that all the ladies were wishing their husbands or sweethearts had been like him! And truly, I, the author of this

---

[177] The MS suggests that he 'heard it from the clerics', but this is likely to be a scribal misreading of '*clers*' for '*chlrs*' (an often-used abbreviation of '*chevaliers*').

[178] See previous note: the same applies.

[179] Madrigal de las Altas Torres, south-west of Valladolid in the direction of Salamanca.

[180] Blanche (Blanca) of Navarre (1424–64), at this time married to the King of Castile's eldest son, though they were to be divorced (for non-consummation of their marriage) before he later reigned as Enrique IV.

[181] As noted previously, his age is inconsistently given: he was probably now 25.

work, had never seen a more handsome young knight in my time, or a more impressive figure of a man.

Now, to return to our story and continue: having been welcomed and fêted by the Princess and the knights, ladies and damsels of her company, Sir Jacques took leave of them and set off once more, heading for the kingdom of Portugal. He pressed on over mountains and through valleys, encountering many a city and castle, till he arrived in the kingdom and came to a city named Sabugal.[182] Here he met a squire by the name of Pedro Peixoto[183] who came before him accompanied by a number of noble men – some thirty horse or thereabouts. Approaching Sir Jacques he said:

'The king and those of his kingdom bid you welcome, sir, as is plain from the letter that he and his council have sent me.'

Hearing the squire's words and seeing the great honour shown him by the king in sending the squire to meet him, Sir Jacques gave him most courteous thanks; and he told the squire and his companions that he didn't attribute the honour to himself: he was sure it was for the sake of his sovereign lord the Duke of Burgundy.

'Sir Jacques,' the squire replied, 'the king and his barons wish to show honour and courtesy to all who come from the duke to Portugal; but truly, Sir Jacques de Lalaing, in light of your high renown and the fine reports of your deeds that have reached us and other Christian realms, all princes, knights and noble men are bound to honour you. And the king sends word through me bidding you most welcome in his realm of Portugal; he and all of his land are pleased to receive you, as is shown by the letter sent to me by him and his council, as I said.'

Then this squire and the gentlemen of his company came to Sir Jacques and he took them all by the hand, and they likewise greeted all who'd come with him. Then they rode on together and entered the city of Sabugal in the highest spirits. There Sir Jacques dismounted at the house prepared for him and his men, and shortly after they'd changed and donned their robes, supper was ready. He took his seat at table and the Portuguese squire with him; and what an array of delights was brought to Sir Jacques and his men: wines and meats aplenty, and sweetmeats and delicacies of many and varied kinds, lit by torches, wax tapers and candelabra; and trumpeters and minstrels played a host of melodious instruments in the style of their country, which Sir Jacques and his companions heard with much delight. In the land and city where they were, no better could have been provided for the Duke of Burgundy himself, or for his son the good Count of Charolais. But if I were to recount in full the dishes and entremets they were served I might overdo it, so I'll pass on!

[182] Just across the border going south-west from Salamanca; its impressive castle survives.

[183] '*Pierre Puissote*'. Peixoto was at that time castellan of Sabugal.

When supper was over and the tables were cleared they took Sir Jacques to relax in a garden where they conversed on various matters, and when it was time to retire the Portuguese gentlemen took their leave and went each to his own lodging.

Next morning, after hearing mass, Sir Jacques and his men made ready to depart, sending their mules and packhorses off with their chests and bags to head for the city of Évora,[184] where Sir Jacques had been told the King of Portugal was residing. Then he and his gentlemen mounted; but before they'd ridden from their lodging they found the Portuguese squire and his company at the gate, waiting to escort them. Into the fields they rode and set off after their baggage train on the road to Évora.

Before reaching there they came to a city called Estremoz,[185] where they met a great lord of the land named the Count of Engousance.[186] He received Sir Jacques and his company with much honour, and feasted him grandly, in perfect style, treating him and his men so graciously that Sir Jacques couldn't thank him enough. The count stayed a long while in the house where they were lodged; he didn't want to leave, such pleasure was he taking in listening to Sir Jacques converse, and seeing what a handsome, charming knight he was: he'd never been so pleased to meet a man. And thus the day passed and so did supper, where they were splendidly served with all that could be found. When it was time to retire the count took leave of Sir Jacques, offering him whatever service or honour he required. Sir Jacques thanked him for this most courteously, and wanted to escort him back to his house but the count wouldn't permit it.

So they went to rest till the following day, when they prepared to leave after dinner. This they did, riding on together till they stopped to rest at Evoramonte,[187] where they found a number of noble men sent by the King of Portugal to meet them. They welcomed Sir Jacques and his company with great honour and good cheer: if they'd been warmly fêted in the places they'd passed, they were even more so now!

Night went by and morning came. Before leaving, Sir Jacques had mass sung as was his custom; it was heard by him and his men with devotion. Then they mounted and set off for Évora, which was only four leagues from there.

As Sir Jacques drew near the city, there came before him a great host of lords, knights and squires, namely the lord of Miranda, Álvaro de Almada,

---

[184] East of Lisbon.

[185] About 30 miles north-east of Évora.

[186] Hard to identify with certainty (and the name is later rendered as 'Angossance'), but it may well be Afonso I, duke of Braganza: he was born near Estremoz and held lands there along with the castle of Evoramonte which is to be Jacques's next stopping-place.

[187] '*Montheure*': the castle of Evoramonte, a few miles north-east of Évora.

Rui Borges, João and Fernão da Silva and many more.[188] They welcomed him
with great honour, showing him and his men all respect, and escorted him to
the city where the king had arranged and prepared grand lodgings for him. He
and his company dismounted there, and were received by the host and hostess
and those appointed by the king to welcome him. You may be sure that they
wanted for nothing: the house was richly stocked with wine and food and all
that could be provided for a man's comfort and refreshment.

To keep him company that night there supped with him a host of noble
men of the king's household. They were served with a great array of dishes
and entremets of which I've no desire to give a long account; and when
supper was done and they rose from table, after giving thanks to Our Lord
they engaged in conversation till it was time to retire, when they took leave
of Sir Jacques and returned to their various lodgings. [f. 74r]

40

*How Sir Jacques de Lalaing was taken to pay his respects to the King
of Portugal, who received him with honour and favour, as did all the
princes of his court*

Next morning, once Sir Jacques was dressed and arrayed in his finest
robes, he and his men heard mass. Shortly after, at about ten o'clock, a
number of knights and squires from the king's household arrived and greeted
him, saying they'd been commissioned to escort him to the king. Sir Jacques
took them by the hands, courteously bidding them welcome, and said he was
ready to go wherever they wished if it was the king's pleasure. The mules
and horses were brought from the stables and he and his company mounted,
richly clad in silk and other splendid garments, and they rode from the house
and along the broad street that led to the royal palace. There they dismounted
and climbed the steps and entered the great hall, where they found Dom
Pedro and Dom Jaime of Portugal[189] accompanied by a host of knights and
squires, who received and welcomed Sir Jacques de Lalaing and his company.
Informed of who they were, Sir Jacques paid each of them due respect in
his accomplished way, having been well instructed since his childhood. With
respects duly paid, the two lords took Sir Jacques, one on either side of him,
and escorted him to the king's chamber. The king[190] was accompanied by

---

[188] These are probably the names to be understood from the MS's renderings: '*le
signeur de Mirande, Alvro d'Abmarde, Ru Borges, Jehan et Frantelle de Silves*'.

[189] Pedro and Jaime, the teenage sons of Pedro, Duke of Coimbra, who was the
son of King John (João) I of Portugal and regent at this time (1439–48), being the
young King Afonso's uncle.

[190] Afonso V (r. 1438–81), at this time in his early teens.

Dom Pedro of Portugal, Duke of Coimbra, the Count of Angossance,[191] and Dom Fernando, the king's brother.[192] Sir Jacques bowed to the king and to the princes with him, and presented the letter from his sovereign lord Duke Philip of Burgundy and Brabant, saying:

'Most high, excellent, mighty prince, I am sure you will remember that I have leave and permission of my redoubted sovereign lord, your good uncle the Duke of Burgundy,[193] to bear through most of the realms of Christendom a token declaring a challenge to arms: your royal majesty has been informed of this challenge, and I have come to accomplish with God's help what is set out in those Chapters.'

Once Sir Jacques had said all he wished to say, the king replied most kindly, saying: 'Sir Jacques de Lalaing, welcome to my kingdom of Portugal; it is small, but out of honour and respect for our dear and much-loved uncle and aunt of Burgundy we wish to do whatever service and favour we can for you. And with regard to your request, you know the answer is a delicate matter, but for the moment go and rest and be patient awhile.'

After the king's reply Sir Jacques bowed deeply to him once more as he took his leave, and in turning away he likewise bowed humbly to the Infante Dom Fernando the king's brother, and to the Infante Dom Pedro, Duke of Coimbra, and to several princes and lords of the blood royal, who all showed him great honour. Then he and his men returned to his lodging, accompanied as stated above. [f. 75v]

41

How Sir Jacques de Lalaing came once more before the king, and of the reply that he was given

Next day after dinner, around the hour of vespers, a number of knights and squires sent by the king came to find Sir Jacques in his lodgings. They escorted him to the palace, where he found the king accompanied by princes, knights and squires in great numbers, together with his council. He bowed to the king and to them all in his accomplished manner, and after all respects had been paid, silence fell in the palace. And then, in the presence of the king, Sir Jacques was told by one of the most eminent of the council:

'Sir Jacques de Lalaing, you are most welcome. The king bids me tell you that he was informed of your coming some time ago by a herald, who presented to him certain Chapters of Arms stating that, by the leave and

191 The Count of 'Engousance' (probably Braganza) who appeared above, p. 105.

192 A year younger than Afonso, having been born in 1433.

193 Duke Philip was Afonso's uncle through marriage, having taken the king's aunt, Isabella of Portugal, as his third wife in 1430.

permission of my lord the Duke of Burgundy, you are bearing a token of challenge to combat through most of the realms of Christendom. You have not forgotten the kingdom of Portugal! But the truth is, as you know, that the King of Portugal and the Duke of Burgundy are bound in such firm and friendly alliance that the bond and affection can never be undone. For that reason the king has instructed me to tell you that he has no wish to permit any of his household or kingdom to engage in combat with any from the house of Burgundy. But if there were anything that the king and the princes of his blood, or his knights and squires, could do to please the house of Burgundy, they would wish to do it to the full.'

Other words were addressed to Sir Jacques by the princes, barons and knights, in response to which he made such apt and measured reply that they could not have marvelled more at the worth and sagacity of that young knight. They said to each other that the father and mother who had given birth to him should count themselves blessed indeed. So highly did they praise him, such was their esteem, that they said that never in their time had they seen a young knight more clearly destined to achieve the heights of prowess and renown, which should be the goal of all noble hearts.

After Sir Jacques had been there a fair while, wines and cordials were served. Shortly afterwards he took his leave of the king, and was escorted by a host of knights and squires to the chamber of the queen, who received him very graciously. After he had bowed to her, he was likewise grandly welcomed and warmly received by the princesses, ladies and damsels of her company. That day, when he entered the Queen of Portugal's chamber, all her ladies – who included princesses – were most richly dressed and adorned in the style of that country and as befitted each her station. I assure you Sir Jacques was viewed with great pleasure; and truly, he of all knights was worthy of welcome in such high places, given his handsomeness, humility and wisdom. I, the author of this book, can tell you in all honesty that God and Nature had overlooked nothing in his making, and without disparaging or diminishing any other, I had never known in all my days the equal of that young knight, the subject of this story. To return to which, and to continue: after paying his respects and salutations to the queen and princesses and ladies in great numbers, Sir Jacques took his leave of them and was escorted to his lodgings by a host of knights and squires, who then took leave of him and returned to the palace.

Sir Jacques and his men stayed there for some two days before they returned to court, but every day they were visited, and the king's household constantly sent him wine and food and all they thought he and his company might need. [f. 77r]

42

How Sir Jacques de Lalaing and his men were feasted at the palace
by the King of Portugal, in the presence of many princes of his
blood and lineage

Two days after Sir Jacques's appearance at court, the King of Portugal decided to hold a stately feast in honour of Sir Jacques de Lalaing, and ordered the heads of his household to arrange a grand, ceremonious dinner. The Infante Dom Pedro, Duke of Coimbra, presented the water to the king. Having washed his hands, the king sat down at the centre of the table; seated at his right was the Duke of Coimbra, and at the king's left hand was Sir Jacques de Lalaing. The King of Portugal was served that day in splendour, for as each dish was brought to the table it was preceded, with a glorious din, by trumpeters, minstrels, kings of arms, heralds and pursuivants, all arrayed in the coats of arms of the king and of the princes present, of the blood royal and others, too, a most handsome sight to behold. And all of the king's household, of every degree, went to the utmost lengths to fête Sir Jacques and his company. But all the dishes and entremets served to the king I'll not describe at length.

When dinner was over the king rose from table and thanks were given to Our Lord. Then the king took Sir Jacques by the hand and led him to one of the windows of the hall. He spoke to him on a range of matters, and Sir Jacques's replies were so eloquent that the king was most impressed and pleased, and praised him highly in his heart.

When all the conversation was done, around the hour of vespers, everyone withdrew, the king joining the ladies; and Sir Jacques came and paid his respects to the king and queen in his polished fashion. Then the dancing began: the king danced first, leading the queen, and when they had finished their dance he took her by the hand and called Sir Jacques de Lalaing and said:

'Sir Jacques, you must lead the queen in the next.'

Sir Jacques thanked the king, as he did the queen, for the honour they were paying him. Then dancing began throughout the hall, with minstrels playing all kinds of dulcet instruments, a great joy to see and hear.

Sir Jacques was highly fêted by the king, the queen, the princesses, ladies and damsels who were present in the palace that day. And when all the dancing and revelry were done, wines and cordials were served in the customary fashion. Then Sir Jacques took leave of the king and queen and ladies, and he and the other princes, barons and knights all retired to their lodgings. [*f. 78r*]

43

More on this matter

As you've heard, Sir Jacques and his men couldn't have wished to be treated more grandly by the King and Queen of Portugal. When the king and queen decided to go hunting and sporting in the fields they sent word to Sir Jacques to join them with his men, as he'd done several times during his stay, which lasted some thirteen or fourteen days. And all of this was done to fête and honour him: the king, the queen, princesses, ladies and damsels did all in their power to do so, as much out of respect for the Duke of Burgundy as for his own sake. Sir Jacques didn't know how to thank them enough for what they'd done for him and strove to do daily.

But he realised he couldn't stay longer in Portugal if he were to meet the date set by the King of Castile for his return to accomplish his feat of arms. So he came before the King and Queen of Portugal one day and thanked them most humbly for the honour and welcome he'd received from them and the princes, princesses, barons, knights, ladies and damsels and all the nobles of the realm, and for the cordiality he'd been shown while passing through the kingdom, which he attributed not to himself but took to be for the sake of his sovereign lord the Duke of Burgundy, to whom, on his return by the grace of Our Lord, he would express his deep gratitude. Then the king replied, saying:

'Be assured, Sir Jacques, that for love of our dear uncle the Duke of Burgundy and our aunt his wife the duchess, we and our people wish to do all in our power to please, serve and honour any who come here in their name; and after the duke and duchess themselves, but ahead of all knights we have ever seen here in our kingdom, we wish to do all possible to please you, and only wish we could have done more: we see you so full of noble qualities that you are worthy of every favour. But you are a truly gentle knight and will bear with all that you have encountered here.' [*f. 79r*]

44

How, after all the celebrations, Sir Jacques de Lalaing took leave of the king and all the princes and made his way to Castile, where the King of Castile received him with great honour in his city of Valladolid

When Sir Jacques heard the king speak so warmly, he went down on one knee and thanked him for the honour he had shown him, and offered him his person, wealth and service – and likewise those of his lineage – should he ever request them: they would obey and fulfil his every good command. The king took him by the hand and bade him stand, saying:

'Rise, Sir Jacques; no one can pay you too much honour or reward. I pray that God will bring you all fulfilment.'

And so Sir Jacques took leave of the King and Queen of Portugal and of the princes, princesses, barons, knights and squires and ladies and damsels of the court. Many gifts were offered him – jennets, fine coursers,[194] mules – but the only gift he accepted, presented by the king and queen and the Infante Dom Pedro, was a splendid golden chain of the Order of Portugal,[195] garnished with diamonds, rubies and pearls. For this he thanked the king and queen and princes deeply.

After leave had been taken and the wine and cordials brought, he and his company departed and returned to their lodgings, accompanied as ever by men of the royal household, who settled handsomely with Sir Jacques's host and hostess: all expenses incurred by him and his company, there and elsewhere in the course of their stay, were paid in full. The king also provided men to guide and escort him right through the kingdom.

That night Sir Jacques's companions made ready, preparing and packing for departure early next day. And leave they did: in the morning, once Sir Jacques had heard mass, he and his gentlemen left the city of Évora and took to the road with the men commissioned by the king, who guided and escorted them till they entered Castile. There they took leave of Sir Jacques, who thanked them deeply and earnestly prayed them to commend him to the king and queen, which they promised to do.

Then they left them, and Sir Jacques and his company rode on through Castile until – passing over the stages of their journey and their stops along the way, where they encountered nothing worthy of record – he came to the city of Valladolid, where the day had been set for him to meet Sir Diego de Guzmán in combat and accomplish the terms of his Chapters of Arms.

Once Sir Jacques had arrived at his lodging, the King of Castile sent a number of knights and squires, among them a baron named Juan de Luna,[196] who came before him and said they were to escort him to the king. He replied that he was at the king's command, and he and his men, all ready, mounted and rode together to the royal palace with their escort.

On arrival he bowed to the king, who gave him a grand and joyous reception, saying: 'Sir Jacques de Lalaing, you are most welcome! I am sure you know it has long been the custom that when a knight arrives in a kingdom from foreign parts he is rightly given worthy men to guide and advise him; and though we know you to be good and wise and thoroughly adept and skilled

---

194 The jennet was a much-admired Spanish horse-breed, light but strong; 'courser' implies a fine horse, bred for speed, much prized for hunting and often used in combat.

195 Presumably the Order of Aviz, the Portuguese chivalric order founded in the 12th century.

196 *Jehan de Lune*, who appeared above, pp. 100–1.

in arms, I am giving you as companion Juan de Luna here present, to serve
you as occasion demands in every way he can: such is our will and pleasure.'

Sir Jacques went down on one knee and thanked the king. Then wines and
cordials were brought before he straightway took his leave and was escorted
to his lodgings.

There he stayed for three weeks before he knew the day appointed for the
combat. But finally the king sent knights to inform him of the date and to bid
him prepare. When Sir Jacques heard them name the day he answered, saying:

'I assure you, sirs, I have long been ready and eager to fulfil my purpose
in coming here!' A number of kings of arms and heralds were present, and he
said to them: 'Sirs, you know and have seen my Chapters of Arms, which state
that I should not be kept waiting for more than six weeks. That said, I wish to
abide by the king's will and pleasure, and will be ready on the day assigned.'

The kings of arms and heralds, hearing Sir Jacques's reply, took leave of
him and returned to the king to report his response. The king was delighted,
and declared in the presence of his barons that if Sir Jacques were to live
long enough, he looked sure to win high honour and to enhance the standing
of his friends and kin. [*f. 81v*]

45

How Sir Jacques de Lalaing entered the lists to do combat in accordance with his Chapters of Arms

The kings of arms and heralds having made their report to the king, orders
were given to the constables and marshals to set up and arrange the lists.
This they did in the Square of the Dominicans;[197] there the lists were set – as
was an array of stands, for a large number of knights and great lords, not
only from Castile but from Portugal, Navarre and Aragon, and ambassadors
from France, too, were there that day in response to the news that had spread
abroad: everyone was eager to see the event, so orders had been given for
several stands to be built so that all could watch in comfort. Among the others
there were four main stands right next to the lists, in two pairs adjoined to
each other: the king's stand and the queen's stand were on the east side and
the judges' stands on the west; Diego de Guzmán's pavilion was pitched to
the south and Sir Jacques de Lalaing's at the opposite end.

And so the day came when the two champions were to do combat: it was
the third day of February. At about nine in the morning sixteen men came into
the field in full armour; they took up positions on foot between the two lists
(they were double barriers, you will understand), placing themselves at the

---

[197] '*la place des Frères Prédicateurs*'; this is now the Plaza de San Pablo, the large
square on which stood the Dominican friary mentioned above, p. 102.

four corners to guard the field against any incursion; they were armed with axes, guisarmes[198] and other weapons. Shortly after came the queen in fine array; she mounted her stand – which was not so much a stand as a handsome house, splendidly roofed and hung with richest tapestry. This 'house' and the next were adjoined, so that the steps up to the king's stand were from Sir Jacques's end but the steps up to the queen's were from Guzmán's. The king arrived straight after, accompanied by Álvaro de Luna,[199] Grand Master of Santiago,[200] by the bishop of Palencia,[201] the Count of Benavente[202] and a host of other knights and squires, and he climbed up to his stand.

Then, around ten o'clock, Sir Jacques de Lalaing received the king's leave and permission to come and arm in his pavilion. He left his lodgings on foot, wearing leg armour and dressed in a full-length robe of scarlet[203] lined with sable and laden with orfrey. Before him rode the gentlemen he'd brought with him, in rich garb and array, and he was flanked by two eminent knights, Don Juan de Luna (who advised him all day long) and another knight of the royal household. He was accompanied too by several gentlemen from the embassy sent from France to the King of Castile, and by some of those of his own household, on foot, some holding his horse by the reins and others as a surrounding escort. Behind him, led by his armourer, was a most handsome destrier loaded with a pair of panniers containing all his armour; the panniers were covered with a gorgeous cloth of gold. In this fashion he proceeded to the lists, and entered his pavilion where he armed in his own good time. Once he was armed he came and bowed to the king and queen and all the others that he saw there in the stands. He came first before the king's stand and went down on one knee, saying:

'Most high, excellent, mighty king, may it please your majesty to know that I am ready and equipped to fulfil and accomplish the terms of my Chapters of Arms, with the aid of God and my lord Saint George, and I pray, most high, excellent, mighty prince, that you may show me all true justice, as I have perfect trust you will.'

And in the presence of all the king replied: 'Sir Jacques de Lalaing, you are most welcome, and I shall willingly do as you ask.'

On hearing this response Sir Jacques withdrew and returned to his pavilion – of white silk it was, and splendidly adorned with his coat of arms. There

---

[198] As before, 'axes' refers to pollaxes (see note 116 above, p. 82). The guisarme is similarly a pole weapon, but is distinguished by incorporating a hook.

[199] Álvaro de Luna, Duke of Trujillo: see note 173 above, p. 100.

[200] '*Saint Jacques*': the Order of Santiago, founded in 1170; Álvaro de Luna was Grand Master 1445–53.

[201] The MS reads 'Valence' but this is surely not Valencia, which was outside Castile; Palencia, however, is a city immediately north-east of Valladolid.

[202] North-west of Valladolid.

[203] A red-dyed, luxury woollen cloth.

his arming was completed and he waited for his opposing champion, ready to fulfil the terms of his Chapters. Now that he was armed, the gentlemen of the French embassy who had accompanied him left and went to take their seats in the stands allotted them. [*f. 83r*]

46

How Sir Diego de Guzmán entered the lists to do combat with Sir Jacques de Lalaing

With all this duly done, between eighty and a hundred men appeared, fully armed and lances in hand; with the others who'd arrived before them[204] they were positioned to guard the field against any encroachment or interference. Very soon after came the guards who were to restrain the champions when the moment came:[205] ten wise, judicious gentlemen they were, of great experience.

But Sir Jacques stayed in his pavilion, waiting for his adversary, for a long while: it was fully three hours after noon before Diego de Guzmán made his due appearance in the field. He was accompanied by a host of knights and squires and by his brother Sir Gonzalo[206] de Guzmán at his right hand and Don Felip Boyl[207] at his left. Behind him came four officers of arms – two heralds and two pursuivants – mounted on four coursers caparisoned to the ground, these trappings bearing the coats of arms of Guzmán's four lines of descent. The officers of arms were similarly clad, each sporting the coat of arms borne by the four horses. In this array, and fully armed, Guzmán entered the field. As soon as he'd dismounted at his pavilion he came to make his bow to the king; after paying his respects to the king and queen he returned to his pavilion.

Then the constable Don Juan de Luna, son of Álvaro de Luna, and the marshal Pedro de Herrera,[208] appointed judges of the combat,[209] informed the champions that neither was to leave his pavilion till the trumpets had sounded three times; after they'd sounded a third time, and not before, they were both to leave their pavilions. This was proclaimed, with trumpet fanfares, at the

---

[204] i.e. the sixteen mentioned above.

[205] i.e. at the end of the combat, or if either party were in difficulty.

[206] '*Gayssal*': this is the Count of Guzmán referred to above, p. 100.

[207] '*Philippe de Vul*': the MSS give a number of variant readings of a name rendered in Lefèvre's letter as '*Phelippe Bril*'. This may well be the Aragonese knight Felip Boyl, lord of Massamagrell (just north of Valencia), recorded as fighting a duel in England in 1445 at the court of Henry VI.

[208] '*Pedro de Herie*'. Pedro García Herrera was Marshal of Castile.

[209] i.e. they would supervise and 'referee', while the king, the official 'arbiter' as declared in the Chapters of Arms (above, p. 93), would provide final judgement.

four corners of the field. After the required announcement of regulations, the champions' axes and swords were brought before the judge. It was found that Diego's axe had an illicit device and was not as prescribed in the Chapters, so he was given another, despite the fierce protestations of Don Felip Boyl. Once the axes and swords had been inspected, the announcements and regulations were proclaimed three times in the king's name at the four corners of the lists. Then the trumpets sounded as arranged; but Sir Diego forgot the judges' ruling, and as soon as the first fanfare ended he burst wildly from his pavilion. His advisers quickly grabbed him and led him back, but he did the same at the second blast, and the King of Castile was most displeased and called angrily to him from the stand, loud enough for all to hear. [*f. 84v*]

47

How Sir Jacques de Lalaing and Sir Diego de Guzmán fought on foot before the King of Castile, and Sir Jacques left the combat with very great honour

When Sir Jacques de Lalaing heard the third trumpet blast, with great composure and assurance he came to his pavilion door. Then, making the sign of the cross, he stepped forth, switching his axe from left hand to right, and marched forward some four paces; then he bowed to the king and queen. And Diego de Guzmán marched fiercely to meet him, visor lowered. Sir Jacques, his visor still raised, saw his adversary coming, and the two of them engaged, fighting with their axes, exchanging such terrible, awesome blows, thick and fast, that from their fine steel armour leapt flaming sparks. So well did they fight and so cruel were their blows that the king and all those watching said they'd never seen a combat to compare. Then Sir Jacques de Lalaing, who could see how fired his opponent was, turned his axe on end and with the pointed heel struck three times in quick succession through Diego's visor, inflicting three wounds in his face. And all the while Sir Jacques's own visor was still raised. With the first blow he struck him on the left eyebrow, with the second on the right side of his forehead and with the third he struck him above his right eye.[210] The battle didn't last much longer, as Sir Jacques now dashed the axe from Diego's grip. Finding himself disarmed, Diego rushed at Sir Jacques, arms outstretched, aiming to seize him and haul him bodily from the lists as two months before he'd boasted he would do; but Sir Jacques, seeing what he planned, thrust out his left hand to fend him off and push him back. In doing so he threw his axe down in the sand and took

---

210 The MS reads 'ear', but this seems unlikely given that the wounds are inflicted through the visor's eye-slit, and Golden-Fleece's letter to Jacques's father, from which this passage is directly copied, gives 'eye'.

hold of his sword-hilt, ready to draw. Then the King of Castile, seeing that one had had the better of the contest (well though they both had fought), threw down his baton to signal that the challenge was complete. Then the field-guards who'd been assigned to the task parted the two champions and led each to his pavilion.

A short while after, Sir Jacques de Lalaing came and presented himself before the king, going down on one knee and saying:

'Most high, excellent, mighty prince, I know it will be in your noble memory that I said in my Chapters that if I left the lists fit and well after the combat on foot, and if my opponent was willing, then within three days I would engage with him on horseback till four lances were broken, out of love for my lady.[211] You see me, sire, ready to do so by your noble leave.'

The King of Castile replied, saying: 'Sir Jacques de Lalaing, we consider the challenge accomplished and done, both on foot and mounted.' He added that it was not his wish to see any further combat – between the two of them, that is, but if together they were to take on two others, he was happy for them to do as they wished. And then he said: 'Sir Jacques, you have fought very well.'

Then the king bade the Grand Master of Santiago[212] go down from the stand and send the two champions before him. And so he did: he left the stand and summoned Diego de Guzmán and Sir Jacques and took them by the hands and bade them touch together, saying as follows:

'It is the king's wish that, no matter what has happened between you here, neither should feel rancour or ill will towards the other; the king wishes you to forgive one another and be henceforth friends, like brothers. He expressly commands that it be so, and hopes the time may come when the two of you together, if it please God, may test yourselves in combat against two others.'

Then the two champions, hearing the king's wish and command, pardoned one another and touched hands and embraced in love and brotherhood. Then they left the king's presence and mounted and rode from the lists together, taking each other by the hand and remaining so till they parted and went to their separate lodgings. [*f. 86r*]

48

How the two knights, having left the lists and returned to their lodgings and disarmed, dined together, and shortly after exchanged most honourable gifts

When the two champions had parted and ridden from the lists, the king and queen and everyone left the stands and all returned to their lodgings. Sir Jacques meanwhile dismounted at his, accompanied by his men and by

---

[211] i.e. probably the Virgin Mary, as noted above, p. 92.
[212] Álvaro de Luna: see note 200 above, p. 113.

a host of other knights and squires from the royal household and the French embassy; as he went inside he thanked them profusely for the honour they had shown him.

Then, once Sir Jacques was disarmed and refreshed, the Constable of Castile[213] arranged a supper to which he invited the two champions and a host of other barons and knights who joined them there. Of the dishes and entremets they were served I've no desire to tell, for nothing was spared that silver or gold could buy that day: the supper lasted long! When it was over they rose from table, and after grace had been said they all engaged in conversation. Then wine and cordials were served before they took their leave of the Constable.

But as Sir Jacques was going, Diego de Guzmán glibly avoided taking leave of him. Sir Jacques returned to his lodging and stayed there for two or three days, not leaving, because he'd been told Diego was displeased with him but he didn't know why. But the following Monday Diego sent him a message requesting that he spend four lances in combat with him as laid down in his Chapters. Sir Jacques replied that he was ready and willing to do so but was observing the king's command. The king was informed of this request made by Diego of Sir Jacques, and sent word that he was to speak of it no more and should accept the decision he'd made on the day they'd fought on foot: that was the end of the matter. What's more, Guzmán was taken aside and told that the king did not appreciate what he'd done and how he'd behaved towards Sir Jacques. So to assuage the king's wrath, six days or so later Diego, accompanied by his brother the Count of Guzmán and a number of other knights and squires, came before Sir Jacques in most amicable fashion, to the extent that Diego said to him:

'Good sir, brother and friend, whatever you may have been told, my brother and I and all our friends and kin are entirely at your command, at the service and pleasure of you and yours. For I know you to be such a noble knight, of such high renown, that all knights and squires are bound to honour you, and in doing so can earn only praise and honour.'

Hearing him speak so courteously, Sir Jacques thanked Diego humbly, saying: 'Sir, brother and friend, for the great honour and satisfaction you have granted the house from which I come, by discharging me of my undertaking, I thank you. Be assured that we of the house of Lalaing, our kinsmen and our friends, and I myself above all, will be bound and obliged to you and yours, now and as long as I live.'

Then embraces were exchanged between them all, and many friendly words, and so charmed were they by the conversation and by Sir Jacques's great humility that they couldn't stop talking about it: he couldn't have impressed

---

[213] There may be confusion in the record: Juan de Luna is referred to as constable above, p. 114, but the Constable of Castile at this time was in fact his father Álvaro de Luna.

them more. Then wine and cordials were served, and they all drank together. And shortly afterwards Diego de Guzmán sent for a handsome courser, caparisoned in crimson satin, and presented it as a gift to Sir Jacques who received it very happily and thanked Diego. Then they took leave of each other, but next morning Sir Jacques de Lalaing, so generous and courtly, in recognition of the courtesy shown him by Diego, had a very fine destrier made ready, caparisoned in rich blue velvet laden with orfrey, and with a saddle covered in violet velvet. It was presented to Guzmán by one of Sir Jacques's squires and a herald named Luxembourg; Diego accepted it with delight and sent thanks to his brother and companion: he was overjoyed by the gift. [f. 88r]

49

How Sir Jacques de Lalaing came to court and took leave of the king,
queen, barons and knights of the kingdom of Castile

Next day after dinner, around the hour of vespers, Sir Jacques de Lalaing, accompanied by a host of knights and squires from both the royal household and his own, went to the palace where he was received most honourably by the princes, knights and squires of the court, and met with great cheer. After wine and cordials had been served he was escorted to the chamber of the queen, in whose company that day were many notable ladies and damsels who greeted him very graciously. To fête and honour him there was dancing and entertainment, in the course of which he danced with the queen; and so finely did he conduct himself that he was praised and admired on all sides for his handsome looks, his wit and for his courteous speech and manners; all, men and women alike, did their utmost to honour and please him.

When the dancing and the merriment were done, wine and cordials were served. Then Sir Jacques took his leave of the queen and of all the ladies, damsels, knights and squires and returned to his lodging, grandly accompanied by men of the king's household and the gentlemen of his own company.

Some six days later, realising there was little point in staying longer and that he'd accomplished what he'd come for, Sir Jacques went to the king to take his leave. As he came before him he went down on his knees and thanked him most humbly for the honour and justice he had received from him and the people of his kingdom, saying:

'Sire, I am bound all my life to be the good, humble, loyal servant of your majesty and of all the people of your realm, for I have been courteously treated everywhere.'

'Sir Jacques,' the king replied, 'you have been most welcome here. And if there is anything you need and would like from us or our people, then, for the valour and worth we have found in you, it will be granted.'

Sir Jacques thanked the king most humbly and then took leave; and he went to take leave likewise of the queen and all the ladies and damsels before returning to his lodgings. He'd barely arrived before the King of Castile sent him a robe of crimson and cloth of gold lined with finest sable; he returned many thanks to the king.

Having taken leave of the king, queen, ladies and damsels, and of the Constable and the other princes, knights and squires, Sir Jacques had everything prepared and arranged that night, with chests packed and mules laden for him and his men, and guides and others found to provide an escort.

Next day he left Valladolid. But he didn't want to leave Castile till he'd taken leave of the Prince[214] who was four leagues away in a town called Medina del Campo.[215] There he paid his respects to the Prince and all his company, thanking him most humbly for the favours and high honours paid him by his father the king and the people of his kingdom, and respectfully offering him his service. The Prince and the attendant barons received him with much honour, and the Prince had a knight well versed in French reply to him:

'Sir Jacques de Lalaing, you are most welcome, and we must thank you for the honour you have shown the king and those of us present, and the whole kingdom. You have been welcomed only modestly; kindly pardon us on this occasion, and my lord the Prince bids me say that if there is anything you need or he can do for you, he will provide it very gladly.'

Sir Jacques thanked him most humbly and took leave. He returned to his lodging, where many gifts were sent to him by the Prince – wines and meats and other presents.

Next morning he departed, heading for Madrigal[216] where he knew he'd find the Princess of Castile – the Prince's wife, the daughter of the King of Navarre.[217] He pressed on till he reached the city, and dismounted before the Princess's residence. She was informed at once of his arrival. He went up to the hall, and to meet him came a host of knights and nobles who greeted him and bade him very welcome to the Princess's house. They escorted him to a splendidly decked and furnished chamber where the Princess was seated. Sir Jacques stepped forward in all humility, well versed in manners as he was, and bowed to her and offered her his service, and gave her courteous thanks for the great honour and fine reception shown him by the King of Castile and by the Prince and other noble barons and knights: they were well worthy

---

[214] Enrique (1425–74), later to reign as Enrique IV.

[215] South-west of Valladolid.

[216] Madrigal de las Altas Torres, as above, p. 103. It is further still south-west of Valladolid.

[217] Blanca, who appeared above, *ibid.*

of recognition and repayment, and he had every intention of expressing his thanks to his redoubted sovereign lord the Duke of Burgundy.

With all thanks duly given, Sir Jacques took leave of the Princess and made his way to his lodgings, to which she saw him escorted with great honour and where he was joyously received. And splendid gifts were brought to him – wines and meats and other delicacies, all the finest things available; and a knight said to him:

'My lady the Princess sends her respects, and prays you be content with the little cheer we offer you: we were not informed of your coming. But she is fully mindful of her obligation to the house of Burgundy in view of its ties with Navarre, the kingdom from which she comes.'[218]

Then they took leave of Sir Jacques, who earnestly entreated them to commend him to the Princess's good grace: he considered himself her humble servant evermore. And with that they left. [f. 90v]

50

How Sir Jacques de Lalaing, having taken leave of the King and Queen and Prince and Princess of Castile, departed and came to the kingdom of Navarre, where he was most honourably received and entertained by the King and his son the Prince and the Princess

Next morning, having arranged the previous evening that everything be made ready for departure, Sir Jacques set out, heading for the kingdom of Navarre. He rode on till he came to a city named Caval[219] where he found the archbishop of that place, who had sent a party of noble men to meet him – some twenty-four horse or thereabouts – along with other officers of Castile. All of them together escorted Sir Jacques to his lodging. Then that evening the archbishop sent a number of other nobles to Sir Jacques, saying:

'You are most welcome, sir. Our master sends his respects, cordially praying that tomorrow you will accept his hospitality at dinner: he will consider it an honour and a pleasure.'

Sir Jacques hesitated – he would gladly have excused himself; but after attempting a number of apologies he agreed to go.

And so he passed the night; and next morning, after he and his gentlemen had heard mass, he made his way to the archbishop with the men of his household and those who'd been sent to escort him. He found the archbishop in a lovely, most delightful garden, and there he bowed to him. The archbishop, seeing him approach, strode forward and bowed to him in return, and bade

[218] As noted above, p. 95, in 1439 Agnes of Cleves, niece of Duke Philip of Burgundy, had married Prince Carlos, the King of Navarre's eldest son.

[219] This is probably Ávila, south-east of Madrigal, continuing the southward loop from Valladolid before heading northward again to Navarre.

all his company welcome; Sir Jacques greeted the archbishop's men likewise. Then he was led to the hall, where the tables were set, and after the washing of hands they took their seats and were served the finest and most delicious food that the town then had to offer. When dinner was done and they rose from table, the archbishop and Sir Jacques took each other by the hand and went to lean at one of the windows of the hall where they conversed together at length. Their men engaged in conversation likewise. And then, when the talking was done, the archbishop offered Sir Jacques an array of mules and horses, but he would accept none. Then wine and cordials were served and they drank as much as they pleased, after which Sir Jacques took leave of the archbishop, offering him all possible service. He returned then to his lodging where he spent the night, resting till the following morning when he departed after hearing mass.

He journeyed on past towns and castles till he reached the kingdom of Navarre and came to a city called Tudela, where he stayed for just one night. He left after hearing mass and stopped next at Marcilla,[220] at the house of Don Pedro de Peralta,[221] where he and his men were received with great honour.

Next morning after hearing mass and dining with much good cheer, Sir Jacques took leave of this lord and set out once more, pressing on till he came to Olite in Navarre, and found that just one league away was a city named Tafalla, where the Prince and Princess of Navarre were then residing.

And you may be sure of this: that if Sir Jacques de Lalaing had been finely entertained when he'd first passed through Navarre, he was even more so on his return. For the five days that they stayed there, Sir Jacques and his company were fêted in every possible way by the Prince and Princess and their entourage: they could have wished for nothing more.

Then, at the end of those five days, he took his leave of the Prince and Princess and the knights and squires and ladies and damsels and departed, setting out to meet the King of Navarre,[222] who was then in residence in the city of Zaragoza in Aragon, accompanied by a host of Navarrese nobles including in particular the eminent squire of the stables Jaime Díez.[223] When Sir Jacques arrived in Zaragoza, the king – who was at that time regent and governor-general of the kingdom of Aragon on behalf and in the name of his brother King Alfonso[224] – had ridden from Zaragoza Castle, which had entrances to both field and town, and gone hunting. As Sir Jacques rode into the town he

---

[220] About 20 miles north of Tudela.

[221] '*Pierre de Peraltre*'. Peralta, who appeared above (p. 96), had married Anne of Brabant, illegitimate daughter of Anthony of Burgundy (Duke Philip's bastard son). His father had built Marcilla Castle, which is presumably where Jacques de Lalaing has stopped.

[222] See note 159 above, p. 94.

[223] '*Jemmedis*', who appeared earlier as '*Janmedis*' (above, p. 95).

[224] Alfonso V 'the Magnanimous', r. 1416–58. See previous notes above, pp. 80,

was told the king was out at sport, so he promptly sent his baggage train to find lodgings in the city while he and his gentlemen hurried out to the fields to find the King of Navarre. The king, informed of Sir Jacques's arrival, was looking towards the town, and seeing him approach he drew rein and stopped, along with the knights and squires then with him. Sir Jacques saw the king and dismounted and bowed as he knew was due, and the king most courteously and humbly said to him:

'Sir Jacques, you are most welcome! We know what business has brought you to the kingdom of Aragon.'

'Sire,' he replied, 'I know you have been informed of the reason for my coming to your royal majesty. And knowing, too, that you are sovereign regent of Aragon, I pray and request you by your kind grace that, if any knight or squire, noble in name and arms, will touch the token of challenge that I bear on my right arm, you will grant leave and permission to perform and fulfil the terms of my Chapters of Arms presented to you by a herald named Luxembourg.'

At the king's command the reply was given: that Sir Jacques was very welcome, and that he would have a response to his request with which he should be content. With that Sir Jacques took leave of the king, and was escorted to his lodging, a house of great magnificence called the 'Bouticle de Fonde'[225] where princes and magnates were always lodged, and where that night he was grandly entertained by the king's men.

Next morning after mass had been heard, a number of knights and squires of the royal household came to Sir Jacques and escorted him to pay his respects to the king, who received him most graciously and said:

'Sir Jacques de Lalaing, you are very welcome here. We are mindful of the request you made of us yesterday in the fields, and are well aware of the Chapters you sent us, presented by a herald of arms. But Sir Jacques, we would ask you to bear in mind the alliance between our beloved son of Navarre and our much loved daughter his wife, the niece of our dear friend the Duke of Burgundy, as well as other alliances forged by our ancestors. In light of this it would be neither right nor reasonable to allow combat between knights or squires of our kingdom of Navarre – or of the kingdom of Aragon, the government of which it has pleased my dear brother to entrust to me – and those of the house of our much-loved Duke of Burgundy. On no account would we permit it. So we pray you be content to bear your token of challenge no longer – unless it be touched by a knight or squire outside our realms of Navarre and Aragon; in which case, if any men of our kingdoms be required to serve or help you we would have them do so wholeheartedly, but that is all.'

---

94. It was from his court that the knight Boniface had come issuing challenges to combat (above, pp. 75, 80).

[225] In old Zaragoza there was a street known as the Botigas Fondas (literally 'deep shops' in Catalan), presumably the site of this grand house.

Sir Jacques, hearing the king's decision, thanked him humbly. Then they conversed about other subjects, and he was entertained by the king that day with very great honour.

During the time he was there, which was Holy Week, he was visited and fêted at the king's command and instruction, and when he departed the king defrayed all the costs and expenses he had incurred.

On the Monday after Easter[226] Sir Jacques took leave of the king and of the princes, knights and squires of his household and set out, passing through the kingdom of Aragon by way of Lérida [227] and into the county of Barcelona. He journeyed on till he came to the abbey of Our Lady of Montserrat.[228] He and his men were welcomed and feasted by the abbot and the monks, and he slept that night, but that night only, there at Montserrat.

Next morning he heard mass and made his offerings to the Virgin Mary, and then set off and made his way to Barcelona, where he found the Queen of Aragon, King Alfonso's wife, at that time regent of the county of Barcelona and Roussillon.[229] When the queen was told of Sir Jacques de Lalaing's arrival, she sent a company of knights and squires to meet him. They welcomed him with great honour and many fine, respectful words and escorted him to his lodging; and as they left the house they said:

'Sir Jacques, have patience for today. Tomorrow the queen will send for you, to receive you and hear what you wish to say – though she has been informed of the reason for your coming by a herald, who presented certain Chapters of Arms which have made a number of knights and squires very eager to see you here.'

With that they took their leave and returned to the queen. [f. 94r]

51

How after leaving Navarre Sir Jacques de Lalaing made his way to the Queen of Aragon, then at Barcelona, hoping to find knights or squires willing to accept his challenge, but the queen would not allow anyone from her kingdom to answer his request, because of the alliance between her husband the King of Aragon and the Duke of Burgundy

Next morning, a host of knights and squires came to Sir Jacques's lodging and told him that the Queen of Aragon had sent them to fetch him. Sir Jacques courteously bade them welcome and said he was ready to obey the

---

[226] 25 March 1448.

[227] Lleida, east of Zaragoza.

[228] North-west of Barcelona; the Benedictine abbey is famous for the statue of the Black Virgin.

[229] This is Maria of Castile, who was regent of the kingdom as well as of the county for long periods during her husband's absences, preoccupied as he was with campaigns to reconquer the kingdom of Naples (see note 108 above, p. 80).

queen's good commands. They mounted all together and made their way to the queen. Sir Jacques went down on one knee and paid most humble respects, and the queen, seeing him kneel, received him very graciously and bade him rise. Then she had an elderly knight tell him:

'Sir Jacques de Lalaing, you are most welcome in these lands. The queen has been informed of your purpose in coming here: it was made plain by an officer of arms who brought and proclaimed certain Chapters of Arms bearing your signature and seal; in light of which, Sir Jacques, the queen bids me tell you that she is not happy to have any man of any degree accept your challenge to do combat in whatever manner. This is not meant as a reproach to you – she has nothing but respect for your great nobility. It is because she wishes to uphold to the utmost the great friendship and alliance existing between her and her dearly loved cousin of Burgundy, and such is the wish of her lord and husband the King of Aragon.'

No more was said on the matter; they spoke of other business. And when the conversation was done Sir Jacques took leave of the queen and returned to his lodging, escorted by a host of knights and squires.

The night passed. Next day he and his men heard mass; and then, between six and seven in the morning, the queen sent two noble knights to Sir Jacques, accompanied by a number of squires, who requested him on the queen's behalf to desist from wearing his token of challenge in case some knight from foreign parts should touch it, which she would never permit. Nor would she allow a place for them to conduct their deed of arms. Nor was it appropriate to refer to ladies in such matters. And above all she was so commanded by her husband the king and had been so notified by her brother-in-law the King of Navarre. Sir Jacques de Lalaing's reply to this was that he had sent an officer of arms, a notable and well-respected man, through a good many realms and provinces of Christendom, from whom he had had reliable reports which made no mention that the queen or any princes, knights or squires disapproved of his wearing the token. And in all honesty it might appear to some that he had removed it for another reason, of which he was innocent; and so he entreated the queen, for the sake of his honour and as an act of kindness, to withdraw her command lest some knight or squire or anyone else thought he had removed it out of cowardice or the like, which would do great harm to his honour. And if some knight or squire who met the requirements laid down in his Chapters were willing to touch his device, he would be happy for him to appoint whichever arbiter he deemed fit, be it the King of France or Spain[230] or England or any other Christian prince, and wherever he pleased he was ready to accomplish his deed of arms with the aid of God, as laid down in his Chapters. [f. 95v]

---

[230] i.e. Castile.

52

How Sir Jacques, having taken leave of the Queen of Aragon, headed for the Dauphiné and was warmly welcomed by the King of France's treasurer; from there he went to the Dauphin who received him with great honour

After hearing Sir Jacques's reply, the queen's knights left and returned to her and gave their report, relaying exactly what he had said. Then the queen assembled her council; they decided to send another embassy of knights and squires to Sir Jacques, and this was done. When they arrived they greeted him most courteously on the queen's behalf and said:

'Sir Jacques, the queen thanks you for the honour you pay us in these lands by bearing such a worthy challenge to arms. She recognises that it is prompted by noble courage, and there are a good many knights and squires who have been hoping you would come here, being eager to take up your challenge. But the queen has issued a general ban, and forbidden some individually; and so we as her ambassadors ask again that you be content to comply, and accede to her request that you remove your token and wear it no more in the counties of Barcelona and Roussillon.'

Having heard the knights out, and taken fully on board the queen's request, Sir Jacques replied most courteously, saying: 'Sirs, I have always been and am and will strive throughout my life to be the servant of ladies: I consider myself so bound. Which is why I pray you consider my case, and ask that the queen graciously withdraw her command. That said, I am ready to obey as is right and proper. So if any knight or squire will do me the honour of fulfilling the terms of my Chapters, I ask that he let me know his intentions, and he will have news of me in the Dauphiné – the land of my lord the Dauphin, eldest son of the most Christian king of France. Meanwhile, honoured sirs, I pray you do me the favour of commending me to the queen's good grace, and tell her that, since her wish is such, I shall indeed obey her will and command.'

Sir Jacques's reply thus given, the embassy took leave and went to report to the Queen of Aragon.

The night passed. Next morning Sir Jacques and his men came to take leave of the queen, ladies, damsels, knights and squires, and humbly thanked her for the honour, courtesy and kindness he had been shown at her command, both by her court and by the people of the city of Barcelona. To this the queen replied:

'Sir Jacques, you have not been shown all the favour I would have wished. I pray you bear with us patiently; if you have any further business here we will gladly see it done.'

With that Sir Jacques departed. His men were ready, and they mounted and rode from Barcelona, accompanied by a body of knights and squires of the queen's household who escorted him for a time before they took their leave and turned back.

Sir Jacques, still wearing his token of challenge, rode with his company through the county of Roussillon till he came to Perpignan, and then to Narbonne, and kept going day by day till he reached Montpellier. Some three leagues from there he met a man by the name of Jacques Coeur, at that time the treasurer[231] of France, who was on his way to see one of his sons installed as bishop of Maguelone.[232] As they met, this treasurer showed great respect and honour to Sir Jacques de Lalaing, saying:

'Sir Jacques, all my wealth counts for nothing unless you help me! I've been longing for you to come this way!'[233]

'My lord treasurer,' Sir Jacques replied, 'tell me what you want from me – I am yours to command. If it's something I can do with my honour safe, I will do it very gladly.'

The treasurer was delighted by Sir Jacques's response, and immediately asked him to come and spend a day or two at Montpellier, a request which Sir Jacques readily granted. He stayed there from the Friday evening till the following Monday after mass, and on the Sunday the treasurer entertained him with a splendid dinner. After dinner they discussed a number of matters; and in the course of this the treasurer took him by the hand and led him aside with three or four gentlemen of his household. He took him to a counting house containing a vast quantity of gold and jewels and other riches. He looked at Sir Jacques and, smiling, said:

'I'm well aware, Sir Jacques, that you've been away from your country for a long while now at great expense and cost, so I pray you do me the honour of taking whatever you need; for truly, I would as gladly give it to you as to any knight alive, out of honour and respect both for my redoubted lord the Duke of Burgundy and for your worthy self.'

Sir Jacques, seeing the great honour and favour proffered by the treasurer of France, replied thus: 'My lord treasurer, I thank you with all my heart for your generous and gracious offer. For the kindness you have shown, I and all my kin are forever in your debt, and if there were anything I could do to please you I would do it gladly. I shall thank my redoubted sovereign lord

---

[231] '*argentier*': with his immense personal fortune, the merchant Jacques Coeur (c.1395–1456) was a major financier, funding royal campaigns and being made master of the mint and steward of royal expenditure.

[232] On the coast just south of Montpellier.

[233] This apparently extravagant greeting might be explained by Coeur, as a royal councillor, being hungry for information from Jacques de Lalaing about affairs in Spain and Burgundy.

the duke for the favour you have done me in his honour; but when I first set out with his leave and approval he provided me with all I needed, so I pray you pardon me out of respectful thanks to him.'

Then the treasurer replied, saying: 'Sir Jacques, if you've left any valuables as surety, as sometimes happens in the course of men's affairs (especially in your worthy line, where so much honour's involved), there's hardly a kingdom or a province where I don't have agencies: I'll very gladly write to them and have your valuables redeemed and sent wherever you wish.'

Sir Jacques gave him many thanks.

I've no wish to recount at length the entertainment and favours the treasurer provided and arranged, with dancing and revels attended by many a lady and damsel and the foremost women and maidens of the town; but he did so most magnanimously, as if Sir Jacques had been a son or brother, and was just as generous to Sir Jacques's men out of love for him.

After supper that Sunday, and after wine and cordials, Sir Jacques took leave of the treasurer, who pressed him to stay next day till after dinner, but Sir Jacques entreated him to be content. So they embraced, and he escorted him back to his lodging where they took leave of each other once more.

Night passed, and next morning after hearing mass Sir Jacques left Montpellier and rode by way of Béziers and Nîmes and arrived at Avignon.[234] There he made his offerings to Saint Peter of Luxembourg[235] and was grandly fêted by the Cardinal of Foix,[236] papal legate in Avignon.

After taking leave of the cardinal he left Avignon, and rode on with his men till they reached the Dauphiné. He went to meet my lord the Dauphin, who was then residing in a private retreat[237] near Valence. There he paid his respects, and the Dauphin received him with honour and entertained him liberally, after which Sir Jacques took leave of the Dauphin and departed. [*f. 99r*]

[234] This seems an unlikely route: unless he went west before going east, he would have passed through Nîmes but not Béziers.

[235] Pierre de Luxembourg had died there in 1387, aged only seventeen, but had even earlier been appointed Bishop of Metz by the Avignon-based 'Antipope' Clement VII. Driven from Metz he had moved to Avignon where he brought about his own death through extreme self-imposed penances. This was evidently deemed impressive: miracles were attributed to him, and in 1432 he was named patron saint of Avignon.

[236] Peter of Foix the Elder (1386–1464), later appointed Archbishop of Arles.

[237] '*maison de plaisance*'. The Dauphin, the future Louis XI, appeared above, pp. 58–9, 64.

53

How Sir Jacques, having taken leave of the Dauphin, left and came to
Burgundy, where he was grandly fêted by many knights and squires
of that country, and then departed and came to Flanders where the
Duke of Burgundy received him with great favour; and also of
his return to Lalaing

After leaving my lord the Dauphin, Sir Jacques de Lalaing made his way to
Lyon on the Rhône, and from there pressed on till he came to Burgundy,
where he was splendidly fêted by the knights and squires, ladies and damsels
and people and officers of that country: it's more the custom to do so there
than anywhere one might go.

Having stayed a short while in Burgundy, he rode on across Champagne
and headed for Flanders, knowing as he did that his lord the duke was at
Bruges. And there he came and bowed before him and thanked him for all
the favours accorded him – for the sake of the duke and in his honour – in the
kingdoms and provinces to which he'd been. He was received most warmly
by his sovereign lord the duke, by the Count of Charolais his son, and by the
counts and barons and knights and all the officers of his court. And so it was,
such being Lalaing's favour in the sight of Our Lord, that he returned with
honour and praise – and having suffered no harm or loss to himself or to any
of his men – to his redoubted sovereign lord Duke Philip of Burgundy. The
duke welcomed him most cordially and with great cheer, asking him about
all he'd seen and found in the course of his journey. Sir Jacques replied so
eloquently that the duke listened with delight and pleasure, as did all the
barons and lords of the court, especially his two uncles the lord of Créquy
and Sir Simon de Lalaing, who loved him very dearly for the fine promise
they saw in their nephew, giving as he did every sign that he would achieve
great heights of honour and enhance the standing of all his friends and kin.

After spending several days in the house of his sovereign lord the duke, Sir
Jacques took leave of him to go and visit his father and mother, the lord and
lady of Lalaing; they'd already been informed of their beloved son's return
and were longing with all their hearts to see him. He was eager likewise to see
them, and he took leave of the duke and rode hard, he and his men pressing
on till he arrived at the castle of Lalaing, to the great delight and happiness
of the lord of Lalaing and the lady his wife. And many other knights and
squires, ladies and damsels, when they heard of his arrival, gave him a joyous
welcome, and rightly so. The lord and lady, seeing their much-loved son return
with his men without any mishap, gave Our Lord devoted thanks and praise.
The lady of Lalaing kissed her son over and over, for she loved him more
than any of her other sons; of all her children he was the dearest, along with
a daughter, a fair damsel indeed, who was later married to the lord of Bossu,

a great baron of Hainaut.[238] Sir Jacques was the eldest of them all; the second son was later appointed provost of the church of Saint Lambert at Liège,[239] a fine and venerable man; the third was Sir Philippe de Lalaing, of whom we shall speak later; and the fourth son, named Anthoine, was knighted at Reims at King Louis's coronation.[240] On that day when Sir Jacques returned, all four sons found themselves together: it was a great joy to the lord and lady. And to celebrate his arrival a splendid feast was held, attended by a great host of knights, squires, ladies and damsels, most of them being their relations, friends and neighbours. And they had good cause to celebrate, not only for Sir Jacques's return but for the great honour and enhanced esteem he'd brought to all his friends and kin – and they could see he promised even more! The lord of Lalaing listened insatiably as his son recounted what had happened on his journey. As for the lady of Lalaing, she was every bit as happy: so delighted she was to listen and talk to her son that her heart was soaring with joy; and when alone around the house she would repeatedly give thanks to Our Lord, devoutly praying that He would guard and preserve her beloved son from trouble and harm.

And so, as you've heard, there was great celebration at the castle of Lalaing for the return of the gentle knight. When all the feasting was done, all went their separate ways, taking leave of the lord and lady and of Sir Jacques, who thanked them for the honour they had shown him. [*f. 101r*]

54

How Sir Jacques sent his Chapters of Arms to the King of Scotland, having first sought leave of his sovereign lord the Duke of Burgundy

Sir Jacques's thoughts were ever set on ways to scale still further the heights of prowess and renown, striving with all his heart to enhance the honour of the house of his birth, and he knew that Idleness was the mother of vice and the wicked stepmother of virtue. To avoid and escape Her he decided, having spent several days at the house of his father the lord of Lalaing, to send a letter to the kingdom of Scotland, to master James Douglas.[241] This letter, I understand, contained the Chapters he'd been sending everywhere, detailing his challenge to arms; but whatever his words or tokens of challenge, they would be issued only with the leave and approval of his sovereign lord the Duke of Burgundy, to whom he now went to inform him of his intentions.

---

[238] Isabel, who (as mentioned above, p. 42) married Pierre I de Hénin, lord of Bossu, a knight of the Golden Fleece.

[239] As mentioned above, p. 41.

[240] i.e. the coronation of Louis XI in 1461.

[241] *'du Glas'*. James Douglas (1426–91), some five years younger than Lalaing, was to become 9th Earl of Douglas in 1452 following his brother's murder.

When Duke Philip heard the young knight's wishes and saw the letter he'd dictated to be sent to Scotland, he was overjoyed and said: 'Sir Jacques, may God by His grace grant you all fulfilment. I see you desire and crave the honour and glory of true nobility and high renown. Be assured I shall support you in all you undertake; go boldly and carry out your mission.'

Sir Jacques thanked the duke most humbly, and showed him the letter he meant to send to Scotland, the tenor of which was as follows. [f. 101v]

55

How, with the duke's permission, Sir Jacques sent the herald Charolais with a letter to master James Douglas in Scotland

'Know, most honoured sir, that I am presently sending Charolais Herald to the kingdom of Scotland with certain Chapters of Arms. Because of the great virtues, honour and valour I know to be in your noble person, I crave your acquaintance, if it please you, more than that of any other, in light of the desire and ambition I know you have for the illustrious profession of Arms. And since moreover I would consider myself most fortunate if I could in some way serve your fair lady, and in doing so learn from you something to my benefit, I have expressly instructed Charolais Herald to address himself first to you and to show you first my aforesaid Chapters.

'At the same time, most honoured sir, not knowing the current state of your affairs and whether you are presently able or inclined to concern yourself with so small a matter, I shall not press my request too hard; but I would pray you do me the favour of directing Charolais to some knight or squire who meets the conditions laid down in my Chapters. I would also ask that you help persuade the noble and excellent prince the King of Scotland[242] to give his gracious leave for my token of challenge to be touched as required, so that the deed of arms prescribed in my Chapters may be accomplished in the presence of his royal majesty. In the event that the one who will do me the honour of fulfilling my challenge prefers not to do so before his majesty, I offer to perform my deed of arms before the illustrious and mighty prince the Earl of Douglas.[243]

'This comes with my prayer to you and all others that no malice or unpleasantness be inferred, for by my soul, my mind is set only on honour and virtue and on following the path of nobility. You will do me a perfect favour and give me singular pleasure, and I shall consider myself forever beholden to you, if it will please you to write back via Charolais informing me who will do me the honour of answering my challenge, and who will be arbiter, and the place and day appointed, so that I may prepare and arrange accordingly.

[242] James II (r. 1437–67).

[243] i.e. James Douglas's elder brother William, 8th Earl of Douglas (1425–52). He had succeeded his father as earl in 1443.

For my part I shall be there without fail – with the aid of God, who I pray will grant you joy of your fair lady and the fulfilment of your every happy and gracious desire.

'To assure you, my most honoured lord, that this is all sincerely meant, I have signed this letter by my own hand on this ___ day of July in the year of Our Lord 1448.'

This letter duly dictated and written, Sir Jacques showed it to his lord the Duke of Burgundy in the presence of his two uncles, the lord of Créquy and Sir Simon de Lalaing, lord of Montignies, and several other knights and squires, all of whom gave it their approval. So it was entrusted to Charolais Herald who, instructed in his mission by Sir Jacques, set off with the duke's consent and made his way to Dunkirk where he boarded ship and, thanks to a fair wind, landed in Scotland in a mere few days. Once ashore he sought the whereabouts of master James Douglas, and was told by some who were well informed that he was residing in a small city with a castle named Elgin, and there he found the Earl of Douglas and his brother master James. He greeted the earl and gave master James the letter containing the Chapters from Sir Jacques de Lalaing. [*f. 103r*]

56

Master James Douglas's reply to Charolais, and the letter he addressed to Sir Jacques de Lalaing; and how Sir Jacques came to Scotland, and six fought in the lists before the Scottish king

When Charolais Herald presented master James with the letter he was mightily intrigued, eager to know what it contained. He broke the wax and opened it and read it from start to finish, including the Chapters previously proclaimed in other realms and provinces. Having read it Sir James showed it to the Earl of Douglas and a number of other barons and knights there present.

The letter duly perused, Charolais was bidden most welcome and told to have patience, for he would soon have a response to its contents. Then master James went to see the king, who gave him permission to answer and accept a date to do combat in accordance with the terms laid down in the Chapters. So a letter of reply was dictated and written, the content of which was as follows:

'Honoured sir, with fulsome greetings may it please you to know that I have received your fine and most agreeable letter and fully appreciate the honour you have shown and offered me. As for your desire to meet and engage in arms with me and some of my companions, as declared in your Chapters, I thank you very dearly. In terms of your willingness to come here to the kingdom of Scotland, to perform this deed of arms either before my sovereign lord or – if he were for any reason unable or unwilling to

attend – before my brother and redoubted lord the Earl of Douglas, kindly
be assured of this, in response to your letter and the Chapters therein:

'Regarding your coming here, you will be given a most cordial welcome,
and with God's help will be served by me or my kinsmen or others according
to your wishes and the terms of your Chapters; and you will have either my
sovereign lord or my brother as arbiter as you desire, and one or other will
appoint an appropriate date and place for combat. The date will be around
the end of January, and within a reasonable time of your arrival, which
you say in your letter will be about then, so that you are not made to wait
more than a fortnight. Furthermore, when the combat you have undertaken
is accomplished and fulfilled according to God's will, I think you will be
asked – as is the custom in this kingdom of Scotland, so that we may have
more instruction from you in the noble practice of Arms – to engage with
another gentleman who answers the requirements of your Chapters. Thus
you may return to your country with still greater honour and praise. And
may God grant you and all valiant and noble men a good and long life.

'In witness of all the above, I have had this letter written at Elgin and
placed my seal upon it on the twenty-fourth day of September in the year
of grace 1448.'

    This letter written and sealed as you've heard, it was delivered to Charolais
Herald who, having taken leave, promptly departed and boarded a merchant
ship bound for Sluis. The duke was then in residence there, along with Sir
Jacques and his two uncles, the lords of Créquy and Montignies. When
Charolais entered the duke's court, there were a great many knights and squires
eager to hear his news. Charolais went up to the duke's chamber, where he
found the duke had just dined; he bowed to him most humbly and then gave
Sir Jacques the letter, which he opened, and it was read before the duke and
everyone present. They all began discussing it, and after this reading and
due deliberation it was decided, with the Duke of Burgundy's approval and
consent, that Sir Jacques de Lalaing would travel to Scotland to accomplish
his deed of arms, as he yearned more than anything to do.
    He prepared and equipped himself splendidly, quite perfectly, and once
he was fully ready to depart he returned to Sluis in Flanders, took leave of
the duke and put to sea. His ship was suitably fitted and stocked with wine
and all manner of provisions, and he was grandly accompanied by knights
and squires, among them his uncle Sir Simon de Lalaing, lord of Montignies,
and a squire, noble in name and arms, a native of the land of Brittany named
Hervé de Mériadec,[244] eminent squire of the stables at the Duke of Burgundy's

---

[244] Mériadec is in southern Brittany, between Auray and Vannes. Hervé appeared
briefly above, p. 78.

court. They were not planning to engage in arms, but did not neglect to take armour and weapons in case adventures befell them on the way, and they were splendidly dressed and apparelled, too, and had packed a good deal of silver plate and other valuables.

All prepared and boarded, Sir Jacques and his company put out from Sluis some time in December, and sailed without troubling incident till they reached Scotland and the city of Edinburgh. The men of master James Douglas's council were there at that time, and as Sir Jacques and his company arrived he was met by a party of Scots who welcomed him on master James's behalf. But in the exchange of words that followed they wanted to know why he'd challenged master James to combat, and it was clear from their manner of asking that they were far from happy. But they were told it wasn't prompted by hatred, envy or any ill will; it was rather to do him the greatest honour that Sir Jacques ever could, for the illustrious house of which master James was born, and his high renown and valour, made Sir Jacques more eager to meet him than any lord in Scotland. At this James Douglas's men were satisfied.

When master James and Sir Jacques then discussed the matter in full, they agreed to bring to the combat two companions each – men noble in name and arms – and this they did. On his side Sir Jacques took his uncle Sir Simon de Lalaing, lord of Montignies, and Hervé de Mériadec, while master James, to accompany him and fight alongside him, took two noble, mighty lords, one named the lord of Halkhead[245] and the other also named James Douglas,[246] both renowned everywhere as valiant knights of great physical strength. The matter thus concluded, the King of Scotland agreed to be their arbiter and appointed a time and place: lists were duly built and erected at Stirling.

With all arranged and the date fixed,[247] both parties prepared and made ready to be in the lists, all six together, on the appointed day of combat. They were most honourably received by the King of Scotland who, after they'd been duly fêted, provided two eminent knights to escort and advise Sir Jacques, his uncle Sir Simon and Hervé de Mériadec, as is customary.

The day arrived, and the king came and took his place on high in his stand. Sir Jacques de Lalaing, his uncle Sir Simon and Hervé de Mériadec entered the lists unarmed; Sir Jacques and Sir Simon were dressed in robes of black velvet, long and lined with sable, while Hervé was clad in a short robe of black satin, sable-trimmed. Behind them their armour was carried in two chests draped with the arms of Sir Jacques de Lalaing, superbly

---

[245] '*Haguet*'; this is John Ross, 1st Lord Ross of Halkhead (Hawkhead, near Paisley in Renfrewshire), 1429–1501.

[246] James Douglas of Ralston, from the Douglas family of Lochleven (Kinross, Perthshire).

[247] 25 February 1449.

embroidered; and they were grandly accompanied by the noble men who had
sailed there with them, as well as those appointed by the King of Scotland
to be their escort. All three came and dismounted before their pavilion and
entered, and then went to make their bows to the King of Scotland. Then
they returned to their pavilion and found their armour ready and in order,
and they were armed at leisure. And leisure they had aplenty, for their
opponents waited more than three hours before they came. When the hour
arrived, master James Douglas, the lord of Halkhead and the other James
Douglas came to the entrance of the lists, grandly accompanied by the Earl
of Douglas and other great lords, knights and others numbering, it was said,
a good four or five thousand men. Fully armed and clad in their coats of
arms, the three champions dismounted at their pavilions; then, as they came
and bowed to the King of Scotland, all three of them asked to be given the
order of chivalry, and this the king freely granted, coming down from the
stand and knighting all three. Then they left and entered their pavilion, while
the king returned to his stand.

Watching from their pavilion, Sir Jacques de Lalaing, his uncle Sir Simon
and Mériadec saw the three knights returning from the king's presence and
identified them by their coats of arms; they decided that Sir Jacques would
fight Sir James Douglas, Mériadec the lord of Halkhead (deemed to be the most
powerfully built) and Sir Simon would confront the other James Douglas. In
terms of weapons, they were to do combat with lance, axe, sword and dagger,
either *à outrance*[248] or till the king bade them stop. But at the Scots' request
the throwing of lances was forbidden, for they were very confident in fighting
with them; so uncle, nephew and Mériadec decided neither to throw them at
the enemy nor fight with lances at all: when the time came to engage they
would cast their lances behind them and do battle with their axes.[249] Now,
according to their terms of combat, each man was allowed to aid a companion,
so Sir Jacques de Lalaing said to Mériadec:

'I think you'll be the first to see off his opponent, in which case I pray
you, I insist, no matter what you see befall me, don't help me or intervene in
any way: leave me to deal with whatever fortune, good or ill, God chooses
to bestow on me.'

All three agreed to abide by this. [*f. 107v*]

---

[248] 'to the limit' – i.e. under conditions of war, in which death or serious injury was
very possible; unlike previous challenges (with Boniface, for example, and in Castile)
in which combat has continued until conditions have been fulfilled, the implication
now is that it will stop only when one party yields or the arbiter (the king) intervenes.

[249] As noted previously (above, p. 82), these are pollaxes.

57

*How Sir Jacques de Lalaing, his uncle Sir Simon and Hervé de
Mériadec fought three Scottish knights in the lists before the Scottish
king and emerged with very great honour*

When the six champions were armed and ready to leave their pavilions, they awaited the announcements, prohibitions and regulations customary at combats in the lists. These were promptly proclaimed at the four corners in the King of Scotland's name, along with three trumpet fanfares, and as these ended out of their pavilion came the two Lalaings and Mériadec, fully armed with all their weapons and wearing their coats of arms, Sir Jacques between his uncle Sir Simon and Mériadec. Then the Scots emerged from their pavilion, armed and weaponed and each clad in his coat of arms, with Sir James between his two companions. In great strides they marched fiercely towards each other, and a fine and splendid sight it was. As they drew close, Mériadec, seeing the lord of Halkhead was on Sir Simon's side, wanted to cross in front of Sir Jacques to fight Halkhead, but Sir Simon called out:

'Stay as we are!'

And together they came to join battle. The Lalaings and Mériadec cast their lances behind them as planned, and gripped their axes and started dealing mighty blows upon the Scots, who defended with their lances. Sir Jacques was fighting Sir James Douglas, whose lance didn't stay in his hand for long, so he took up his axe but didn't fight long with that, either, Sir Jacques dashing it from his grip as he had the lance. Then Sir James, enraged and dismayed to find himself deprived of both lance and axe, whipped out his dagger and aimed to strike Sir Jacques in the face – for he was fighting without a visor, his face uncovered. But Sir Jacques, seeing him coming, thrust his left hand forward and forced him back. Undaunted, Sir James strove again with all his might to strike him in the face; then Sir Jacques threw down his axe and with his left hand seized hold of Sir James between bevor and visor,[250] in so tight a grip that he couldn't get at him, and with his right hand he drew his sword, a slender tuck,[251] and gripped it near the point so he could use it like a dagger, having lost his own though he didn't know how – some say the man who was meant to provide it failed to do so. As he prepared, as I say, to use his tuck as a dagger, he aimed the blow at Sir James over the top of the hand that was gripping the bevor, and in doing so the tuck slipped from his grasp and

[250] i.e. by the gap between the armour plate protecting the neck (the bevor) and the visor above. This is my understanding of the phrase '*prit ... par le wid* [or *vuide*] *de la pièce*'.
[251] '*estoc*', a sword designed for fighting against plate armour, being long and straight with no cutting edge but sharply pointed.

he was left without a weapon. Finding himself unarmed, he quickly, sharply, seized Sir James with both hands between bevor and visor, and by main force dragged him back to the foot of the royal stand. Twice he lifted him bodily, aiming to haul him to the ground. He had him gasping for breath, for sure – and with good reason, for Sir James was fighting in a bascinet with the visor closed, while Lalaing, without a visor, was breathing freely. Sir James was doing anything but, as became clear when the king threw down his baton and they opened Sir James's visor!

But we'll leave the battle between these two and turn to the others, and tell how Sir Simon fared against Halkhead. As explained above, the lord of Halkhead entered the fray and began the fight with his lance, in which he had great confidence; but it wasn't with him for long: Sir Simon, a skilful, strong, courageous knight, experienced in combat, soon deprived him of the lance. They came at each other then with axes and exchanged tremendous blows, for they were both of tall and mighty build: outstanding knights they looked indeed, and so they proved themselves that day. Halkhead's strength was very great, as he showed with the terrible blows he dealt Sir Simon de Lalaing; but Sir Simon ably parried them with his axe and returned some awesome blows when he saw the chance, for he had exceptional self-control and skill, and knew exactly how to wear an opponent down. They fought for a long while and with great valour, but it wasn't to last much longer: in his passionate haste and eagerness to strike and vanquish Sir Simon, the lord of Halkhead began to tire and run out of strength and breath. Sir Simon, wily, cool and disciplined, seeing it was time to show his hand, struck out fiercely with point and edge, thrusting him back with his pollaxe; he had his opponent so hard-pressed that with his axe he drove him staggering back down the lists. It was clear to all that if the battle continued the lord of Halkhead would be the worse for it, and so he would have been, had the king not intervened.

Now we must speak of the brave and noble Breton squire Hervé de Mériadec, who that day confronted and did battle with Sir James Douglas, close kinsman of the Earl of Douglas;[252] a most noble knight he was, well built and very skilled. Together they came and engaged. The Scottish knight lowered his lance and aimed to strike Mériadec with a thrust to the face, but he missed and caught him on the left sleeve of his coat of arms; in attempting to follow through, the lance glanced off the forearm, and Mériadec strode right in and landed an axe-blow on the cheek of his bascinet that laid him flat out, face down, stunned. Seeing his opponent on the ground, and knowing that the Chapters allowed each man to go to his companions' aid, Mériadec looked to see if they needed help. But then he saw Douglas, sharp and fit, already kneeling and nearly back up; so he turned to face him once again, and clutching his axe in both hands he used the shaft to beat him back to the ground, head down, with a blow that gravely hurt his back and laid him out.

---

[252] And therefore, of course, closely related also to the other Sir James.

There's no doubt that if he'd wanted to destroy him it was in his power and he could have done so freely, for the combat was *à outrance*; but on neither occasion that he saw him down would he touch him, which was nobly done and should be counted to his very great honour. Again Mériadec turned to his companions and marched to their assistance – but they didn't need him; and again Douglas was back on his feet with axe in hand, and Mériadec returned to face him. They fought now for a good while, but along with the others they were parted by the guards when the king threw down his baton. But you may be sure that the noble squire Mériadec was one of the finest and strongest fighters you could find, and the rest of their contest, after Sir James had recovered from his fall, was to the very great honour of Mériadec, who rained mighty blows upon him and drove him hither and thither at will.

These deeds of arms proclaimed, performed and now accomplished, with master James Douglas and Sir Jacques de Lalaing locked together as described above, and Sir Simon and the lord of Halkhead likewise fighting bravely with their axes, the King of Scotland, aloft in his stand, delayed no longer and threw down his baton. The guards appointed to the task took hold of the champions as instructed and led them before the king, who told them they had all fought well and valiantly, and that he deemed the deed of arms complete and wished them to be good friends henceforth.

And so, as you've heard, the combat was accomplished before the King of Scotland, and they returned to their separate lodgings. In the days that followed the king feasted them lavishly and gave them splendid gifts for which they thanked him. And after the festivities Sir Jacques de Lalaing, his uncle Sir Simon and Mériadec and those who'd come to Scotland with them took leave of the king and departed. [*f. 111r*]

58

How Sir Jacques de Lalaing, his uncle Sir Simon and Hervé de Mériadec took leave of the King of Scotland and came to England, to King Henry in London

Once the baggage was packed and arranged and they'd taken leave of the King of Scotland, they put to sea and headed for London in England, though Hervé de Mériadec took to the road instead, and made his way across country through the kingdom of Scotland and right through England till he reached London. There Sir Jacques de Lalaing and his uncle the lord of Montignies arrived, and they found themselves together once more.

A good while beforehand Sir Jacques had sent Charolais Herald to King Henry of England,[253] both to secure safe-conduct for himself and his company and to seek permission to bear his token of challenge at the king's court and

253 Henry VI (1421–71, r. 1422–61, 1470–71).

throughout his realm. With him Charolais had taken the Chapters of Arms, the same as had applied to the combat fought by Sir Jacques against Diego de Guzmán before the King of Castile. But Sir Jacques and his uncle Sir Simon and Hervé de Mériadec were in England, in London, for quite a long time, and were given little in the way of welcome, and King Henry would not permit any man in his kingdom to engage in arms with Sir Jacques and his companions.

In view of their poor reception they left London and put to sea at the port of Gravesend; they had a fair wind and soon landed at Sluis in Flanders, where they stayed and rested awhile. Then they set out and arrived in the city of Brussels where Duke Philip of Burgundy was at that time, and he received them joyfully and with good cheer, and rightly so: they fully deserved it. They were a long time in conversation with the duke, recounting their adventures, just as you've heard. The duke listened to it all with delight, and gave them a joyous, warm reception, as did all the princes, barons, knights and squires of his court; they were likewise received by the duchess with great happiness and joy, and by all the ladies and damsels of her company.

And then a few days later, after all the festivities, news arrived at the duke's court that a gentleman was coming from England – a native of the realm by the name of Thomas[254] – with the aim of engaging in arms with Sir Jacques de Lalaing. [*f. 112r*]

59

How, after Sir Jacques de Lalaing, his uncle Sir Simon and Hervé de Mériadec had left England and returned to the Duke of Burgundy's court, news arrived that an English gentleman had crossed the sea intending to engage in arms with Sir Jacques

The duke and the barons of his court, and Sir Jacques above all, were delighted by the news. And this English squire had written that his wish was to do combat before the duke in accordance with Sir Jacques's Chapters: that is, that each would wear armour customary in the lists and would fight with axe and sword till one of them was brought to ground, as is detailed more fully in the Chapters.

This English squire duly came and arrived in the city of Bruges and dismounted at the lodgings arranged for him. Sir Jacques's heart was filled

---

[254] In his *Mémoires* Olivier de la Marche, recalling the same episode, identified him more fully as '*ung escuyer anglois nommé Thomas Qué, qui venoit de Galles*' ('an English squire…who came from Wales'), and his editors Beaune and d'Arbaumont suggested, though with no apparent conviction, that the name might be interpreted as Thomas Keith. Olivier de la Marche, *Mémoires*, vol. 2 (Paris, 1884), p. 110.

with joy at the news of his arrival, yearning as he was to ensure that he and his illustrious deeds might be remembered and stand as an example for all noble men. So he sent a request to his lord the duke, asking permission to engage in arms with the English squire according to the terms of his Chapters, this Englishman having come from his land in response to his challenge. The duke freely gave him leave and promised to be their arbiter; and he assigned a date and gave orders for the lists to be erected in the place where they would engage in fine and honourable combat.

When the appointed day arrived, the two champions both made ready to perform their deed of arms. Quite rightly Sir Jacques de Lalaing was first to enter the lists, for it was in answer to his challenge that the Englishman had come to fight. The duke, with a splendid following, mounted the stand erected and prepared for him. He was accompanied by numerous great lords, knights and squires, and alongside, next to his own stand, were the Duchess of Cleves,[255] the Countess of Étampes[256] and a host of other great ladies and damsels; and a good number of foreigners were in the stands and at the windows of the houses surrounding the lists. Shortly afterwards Sir Jacques, hearing that the duke had arrived, entered the lists with a grand escort of knights and squires, both those of the duke's court and others, notably his two uncles the lord of Créquy and Sir Simon de Lalaing, lord of Montignies, by whom he was advised along with other distinguished lords. As he made his entrance he passed before the duke's stand and bowed to him and to the ladies and damsels present before moving on to his pavilion to arm. It wasn't long before the English squire arrived; he likewise bowed to the duke and ladies as he passed before the stands, and then marched on and entered his pavilion with some of his men, accompanied by two knights the duke had given to counsel him, as has long been the custom.

Once they were armed and equipped as they wished, the lists were set in final order and men stationed to guard the field; and to intervene when the time came and need arose several noble men were appointed, some of whom had fought and engaged in arms before and seen much in their time, such as Hervé de Mériadec. The appropriate announcements and regulations were proclaimed, and then the champions' weapons were inspected. There was an issue with the English squire's axe: it was not of the kind usually carried in the lists; it incorporated a blade and a hammer and was topped with a long, broad spike, and the blade of the axe, too, was long and sharp. Sir Jacques sent an objection via men of rank, but the Englishman refused to set it aside and accept one like Sir Jacques's. The matter was referred to the duke their

---

[255] Marie of Burgundy, mother of John 'the young duke of Cleves' who had earlier taken Jacques under his wing.

[256] Jacqueline d'Ailly, whose daughter Elizabeth was later to marry 'the young duke of Cleves'.

arbiter; it was duly discussed and all were agreed that the English squire should fight with the same kind of axe as Lalaing. But still the Englishman asked to keep it. The duke would not agree without the consent of all parties, and when Sir Jacques saw the squire begging so insistently to fight with the axe that he said he'd brought from England, he generously agreed to let him use it, being as he was more courteous than any man. This, as you'll hear, was a rash mistake. [f. 113v]

60

How Sir Jacques de Lalaing fought the Englishman before the Duke of Burgundy, and brought him to the ground

Once agreement had been reached about the axe, and the announcements and regulations had been proclaimed as said above, Sir Jacques de Lalaing stepped forth from his pavilion, which was beautiful, superb: adorned with thirty-two banners bearing the coats of arms of the lords from whom he was descended on both his father's and his mother's side, a glorious sight to behold. He was fully armed and clad in his coat of arms, but had a sallet on his head with no gorget or bevor,[257] and the only weapon that he carried was his axe. Then forth came the Englishman from his pavilion, fully armed, wearing a great bascinet with a bevor and with visor closed, clad in his coat of arms, with axe in hand and sword in belt. They looked and took the measure of each other and then strode to meet, and as they started striking blows their combat brought them before the duke's stand. Sir Jacques de Lalaing, comfortably armed and able to breathe freely, began raining mighty axe-blows on the English squire's head, so thick and fast that he drove him hither and thither at will; in all honesty he was close to being beaten to the ground: all he could do was concentrate on parrying Lalaing's axe-blows. But Dame Fortune, who gives to one and takes from another, turned at that moment against Sir Jacques; for in dealing one of his own blows he caught the point of his opponent's axe: it went clean through his left arm between vambrace[258] and gauntlet, cutting through vein and sinew, for the axe's spike was long and sharp. Finding himself thus wounded, Sir Jacques, with his mighty will and noble courage, strove to carry on fighting with his axe. But his hand was failing him. He gripped the butt of the shaft beneath his left arm and tried to wield the weapon with his right, but did little good; and seeing this he fiercely threw it to the ground and seized hold of the Englishman, grabbing his bascinet with one hand and

---

[257] i.e. he was lightly helmeted (a sallet is a simple, light helmet), with no visor or protection for his neck and lower face.

[258] The armour protecting the forearm.

his left arm with the other. He hauled him to the ground with such force that he fell face down, so heavily that the bascinet's visor plunged into the sand, leaving the back of the head upward and exposed: had he wanted, Sir Jacques with just a little knife could have killed and finished him; but on no account would his noble heart permit it. Without further hesitation the arbiter threw down his baton, whereupon the appointed guards came swift and straight to the Englishman, still lying full length on the ground, and lifted him up and brought him before their arbiter the duke. Sir Jacques was already standing there, for as soon as he'd brought his opponent to the ground he'd left him lying in the sand and touched him no more. When they were both before the duke their judge he said to them:

'Your deed of arms is accomplished; be brothers and friends and place your hands together.'[259]

And so they did, and with that the combat ended and each returned to his lodgings. Later that day the Duke of Burgundy grandly entertained the English squire, but Sir Jacques couldn't be there because of the wound to his arm, which went on to give him much trouble and pain.

We now need to speak of Sir Jacques de Lalaing's Chapters. They'd clearly stated that if in the course of the combat he brought a knight or squire to the ground, the defeated man would be obliged to send his gauntlet wherever Sir Jacques pleased, via an officer of arms who would be given due direction. But the Englishman now declared that this was not required of him because he hadn't fallen fully to the ground; he said it was true he'd had his head and hands and legs on the ground, but not the rest of his body: he claimed his hands had held him up. So Sir Jacques sent a request to the duke, as arbiter, to pass judgement and settle the matter. The question was brought before an assembly including many of the eminent foreigners who'd seen the combat – Germans, Spaniards, Scots, Italians – as well as others who'd been present. And the judgement was that the English squire had fallen full length – head, belly, legs and arms. The matter thus settled and decided, the duke as arbiter sent the council's verdict to the Englishman. He didn't know how to reply, other than to say he was ready to do as he should. When Sir Jacques heard that the squire was judged to have fallen fully, and that he'd agreed to do as required by the terms of the Chapters, he let the matter drop and in noble, generous spirit he excused the squire the sending of the gauntlet, on which he could have insisted had he chosen. And when all was done he sent the Englishman a handsome, splendid diamond, saying he was obliged to do so because he'd thrown his axe down when he'd hauled him to the ground, as

[259] As before, literally 'touch together'.

described above.[260] But to tell the truth I don't know that he took it;[261] and he said he was very sorry about the wound to Sir Jacques, and spoke of him most honourably. I've since been told that Sir Jacques, so full of honour and courtesy, sent the English squire some splendid gifts: a handsome horse and a complete set of armour, for which he gave him fulsome thanks.

Following this deed of arms the Englishman stayed a week in the city of Bruges, during which he was richly fêted at the duke's court and also by the Duchess of Burgundy. He gave them humble thanks as he took his leave, and returned to his native kingdom of England. [*f. 116r*]

61

How Sir Jacques de Lalaing sought leave of the Duke of Burgundy to hold a passage of arms for a year against all noble men, according to the terms of his Chapters, at the Fountain of Tears, which request the duke granted

On the same day that the combat between the two champions was fought and accomplished, and before the duke left his stand, Sir Jacques de Lalaing asked his sovereign lord the duke for his gracious permission to issue in his presence the Chapters for the passage of arms of the Fountain of Tears. The duke granted this wholeheartedly and gladly. And so the Chapters, set down in writing in the document, were proclaimed there on the stand in the presence of the duke and the princes, lords, knights and squires and the great host of other people present. They were as follows: [*f. 116v*]

62

The Chapters for the passage of arms before the Fountain of Tears at Saint-Laurent in Burgundy, beside Chalon-sur-Saône

'In praise and in the name of God and the glorious Virgin Mary and my lord Saint James, my lady Saint Anne and my lord Saint George, prime movers of all good works, it has been the custom, as it is still, for worthy and valiant knights and squires to test and know each other by seeking ways and occasion to engage in the noble exercise of arms and thus to win enduring high renown. Thus it is that a knight, of noble descent in every

---

[260] Jacques is thus observing the terms of the sixth of his Chapters: 'if in the course of the combat one of us should lose his axe, the first to be so disarmed will be bound to give his opponent a diamond' (above, p. 92).

[261] Lefèvre in his letter to Jacques's father says: 'I believe the Englishman didn't take it'.

line and without reproach,[262] desiring with all his heart to experience noble deeds of arms, has undertaken the following with the aid of God and the Virgin Mary. In this, by worthy and honourable means, he has secured the approval of the most high, excellent, mighty prince, his redoubted sovereign lord Philip, Duke of Burgundy and Lothier,[263] of Brabant and Limburg, Count of Flanders, Artois, Palatine Burgundy, Hainaut, Holland, Zeeland and Namur, marquis of the Holy Empire, lord of Friesland, Salins and Mechelen, who has given his gracious and generous consent.

'This knight will for a full year, on the first day of every month, pitch a pavilion before the Fountain of Tears in the county of Auxonne in Burgundy, at Saint-Laurent beside Chalon-sur-Saône.[264] On each of these first days an officer of arms, a man of distinction and good repute, will be present to accompany a lady, who will be there at the pavilion holding a unicorn bearing three shields; these may be touched by any knights or squires (or touched on their behalf by a King of Arms, herald or pursuivant) who are noble in four lines of descent and without reproach. They will be required to prove their fulfilment of those conditions by the sealed testimony of a prince or knight or officer of arms worthy of trust. The first to touch a shield on one of the said days will be bound within the six days following – he will be informed of the day by the aforesaid officer of arms – to engage in, perform and accomplish the deeds of arms set down in the following Chapters. The second to touch a shield on that day will be bound to do combat on the seventh day or on another as he will likewise be informed. The third and the fourth will be bound to engage in the weeks thereafter: combats will take place each month to the number of four. In the event that on one of the first days of a month more than four were to touch a shield, they will be assumed in turn, and in order, to have touched on the first day of the following month. However, if the knight undertaking this passage of arms so pleased, he might choose to answer the challenge in that same month and not defer.

'To oversee the fulfilment of this passage of arms, the aforesaid illustrious prince will appoint a competent King of Arms as arbiter. At the same time, if the knights or squires who touch the shields (or have them touched on their behalf) so wish, they may on their days of combat bring a King of Arms or herald of their choice to be arbiter alongside the King of Arms appointed by the said redoubted and sovereign lord.

---

[262] See note 107 above, p. 80.

[263] Certain territories within the duchy of Lower Lotharingia governed by the dukes of Brabant.

[264] The Île Saint-Laurent lies in mid-river at Chalon. The Saône divided the duchy and the county of Burgundy; the island thus lay directly between the kingdom of France and the Holy Roman Empire.

'This will commence on the first day of November in the year 1449 and end on the last day of October in the following year, '50.

'Each knight or squire may touch, or order to be touched, only one shield of his choosing; and in the said year he may engage only once with the one who undertakes this passage of arms.

'There may be some knights or squires who would prefer to engage in this noble challenge without being recognised or giving their name; this they may do, provided they have the said sealed testimony and are accompanied by knights, squires or officers of arms who certify that they meet the stated conditions.

'It must also be understood that the knights or squires who come to engage may not be present to watch another knight or squire do combat until they themselves have fought their own. They will be required to swear that this is the case at the moment they enter the lists.

'The terms of this passage of arms are as follows: [*f. 118r*]

63

Here follow the provisions of the Chapters

' Firstly, the aforementioned shields will each be different. The first will be white, the second violet and the third will be black, and all will be emblazoned with a scatter[265] of white tears.

'The second Chapter is: if it is the white shield that is touched, the defender of the passage[266] will be required to accomplish in one day as many axe-blows as the one who has touched dictates. This will be without respite; so if either party is brought fully to the ground or – God forbid – loses his axe, the combat will be deemed to have ended.

'The third Chapter is: they will fight with axes with equal spikes;[267] the axes will be provided by the knight who is staging the passage of arms, and the challenger will choose the one he wishes.

'The fourth Chapter is: if one of the combatants (God forbid) is brought to the ground – fully, as described – while fighting, he will be obliged for a whole year to wear a golden bracelet, fastened with lock and key, and

---

[265] '*chergies et semees*'; as will become clear, the tears are not always white: they are white or blue depending on a shield's background colour.

[266] '*l'entrepreneur*': 'the one who undertakes'.

[267] Perhaps remembering the wound Lalaing had suffered when fighting the English squire, above, p. 140.

throughout that time will be unable to remove it or have it removed unless he finds the lady or damsel who has the key; he must ask her to unlock it if she will, and give her the bracelet and offer her his service.

'The fifth Chapter is: if in the course of the combat either party loses his axe, he must present himself to the lady who in his mind should be deemed the most beautiful in his land or kingdom, and give to her a diamond of his choosing.

'The sixth Chapter is: the challenger who in the defender's judgement has delivered the finest axe-blows will be given a golden axe: the defender will send it to him by an officer of arms.

'The seventh Chapter is: if the challenger touches the violet shield, the defender will be obliged to deliver in a day as many sword-blows as the challenger decrees, keeping a distance of three paces, with no pursuit permitted.

'The eighth Chapter is: they will fight with identical swords; they will be provided by the defender and the challenger will have the choice.

'The ninth Chapter is: if in the course of their combat with swords one party – God forbid – is brought fully to the ground, he must present himself to the lady or damsel of his vanquisher's choosing, and give her a ruby on behalf of the one who has sent him.

'The tenth Chapter is: the challenger who in the defender's judgement has delivered the finest sword-blow will be given a golden sword: the defender will send it to him by an officer of arms.

'The eleventh Chapter is: if the challenger touches the black shield, the defender will be required to accomplish twenty-five courses with the lance; if when the twenty-five are done the challenger wishes to do more that day, the defender will oblige him unless he has some injury.

'The twelfth Chapter is: they will run their courses with a tilt,[268] and will carry identical lances, using each until the shaft is broken or at least a finger's width of the head is lost; and they will joust in saddles of war, without being strapped in the saddle.

'The thirteenth Chapter is: in the event – God forbid – that one of them is brought to ground in a fair clash of lances, he must send by an able officer of arms a fine, stout lance to the sovereign lord of the one who unhorsed him.

[268] See note 113 above, p. 82.

'The fourteenth Chapter is: the challenger who in the defender's judgement delivers the finest lance-blow will be given a golden lance: the defender will send it to him by an officer of arms.

'The fifteenth Chapter is: each man, on foot and horseback alike, may wear armour of his choice, double or single,[269] provided it is of the kind customarily worn by noble men in the lists, in *champ clos*, and provided also it has no underhand or illicit device of any kind and no addition to the arret.[270]

'The sixteenth Chapter is: at their entrance to the lists, all knights or squires who touch the aforesaid shields will be given a golden ring[271] enamelled in the colour of the shield they have touched.

'The seventeenth Chapter is: in the event – God forbid – that the defender is brought to ground while fighting on foot, or has a wound, illness, injury or other reasonable impediment, he may appoint in his place a knight or squire of his choice, noble and without reproach, to accomplish the deed of arms.

'The eighteenth Chapter is: in the event that the illustrious, excellent and mighty prince his redoubted sovereign lord Duke Philip of Burgundy should be engaged in any war preventing the completion of the stated period of a year, the defender declares to all that, if it please his sovereign lord, he will go where the war is taking place and on each of the aforesaid days will have his pavilion pitched and the shields displayed in the nearest suitable city, there to accept, perform and accomplish the challenges as described.

'The nineteenth Chapter is: in the event that his said redoubted lord has no war at that time but the most excellent Christian king of France or any princes of his blood should be engaged in war in the kingdom requiring them to secure their borders or to take the field in person, in that case the defender declares to all that, if it please his redoubted lord, he will go to the city nearest to the place of the said war and, if given permission, will have his pavilion pitched and shields displayed, there to accomplish his passage of arms.

'The twentieth Chapter is: so that all who come to accomplish this passage of arms may know where to find the defender in the event of such war, he will station an officer of arms at Saint-Laurent to give reliable direction.

---

[269] See note 110 above, p. 81.

[270] See note 111 above, p. 81.

[271] '*verge*'. It is unclear what this gift, which is to be mentioned several times in the account of the passage of arms, actually is. The word '*verge*' usually implies a rod, which is conceivably the case here, but it can also mean the band of a ring, and when used earlier with reference to a gift made to Jacques by the Duchess of Orléans (above, p. 61), the '*verge*' is clearly a ring.

'The twenty-first Chapter is: if in the fulfilling of these Chapters a question should arise about any of their terms, requiring interpretation or clarification, the matter will be resolved by deputies commissioned and appointed by the aforesaid mighty prince the Duke of Burgundy.

'The twenty-second Chapter is: with it being a Jubilee Year[272] and the site of the challenge on a busy route,[273] should any knights or squires happen to pass the Fountain of Tears and be without horses and therefore feel obliged to forgo touching the shields, the defender declares to all that the officer of arms guarding the pavilion will have ample horses and arms to hand, for combat both on foot and mounted, to lend to those in need. However, to avoid any difficulty arising from the lack of horses – since the horses or arms provided might not be as good as the borrower would wish – the defender asks all challengers to come equipped with all they need.

'The twenty-third Chapter is: in the event that so many knights or squires touch the shields that the defender cannot engage with them all in the manner described, and some are left at the year's end without having fought, he declares to all that he will stay and continue the challenge and meet them step by step, that is to say week by week, one each week, until all who have touched the shield of their choice have had their challenge answered as is laid down in these Chapters.

'The twenty-fourth Chapter is: the knight who has undertaken this passage of arms prays all princes and princesses, ladies and damsels, knights and squires who see or hear these Chapters not to be offended or displeased by his enterprise, or by his failure to give his name. For, before God, his motivation and intentions are only good, prompted not by hatred, envy or ill will toward any man, and he prays that no one will imagine otherwise. His aim in undertaking this is to do all in his power to elevate and enhance the noble estate of chivalry. It is also to keep himself engaged in knightly endeavour at a time when, by God's grace, we hereabouts have respite from the business of war. And also to have better knowledge and acquaintance of the good and valiant knights and squires of other lands, in the hope thereby of being of ever greater worth.

272 '*alors seront les pardons de Rome*'. The coming year 1450 was due to be a Jubilee, a year of universal pardon and remission of sins, involving pilgrimages especially to Rome. (In the 1450 Jubilee such numbers gathered in Rome that hundreds were trampled to death on the Ponte Sant'Angelo.)

273 The chronicler Olivier de la Marche wrote that Lalaing told him he had chosen to stage his passage of arms at Chalon-sur-Saône, firstly, because Burgundy was 'full of noble men eager to show their nobility and courage' and, secondly, because it would be at a busy point, being 'situated on the route from France, England, Spain and Scotland to Rome, with the holy pardons and Jubilee of the year '50 approaching', and 'he wanted to have fought in the lists against thirty men before he reached the age of thirty'. De la Marche, *Mémoires*, ed. Petitot, M. (Paris, 1820), Vol. X, p. 3.

'The twenty-fifth Chapter is: so that all may be assured that the one who undertakes this passage of arms means to fulfil and accomplish each and all of the terms laid down above, I have asked Sir Jacques de Lalaing to set his seal on these Chapters and to sign them by his own hand, which he has generously agreed to do.

'And I, Sir Jacques de Lalaing, knight, councillor and chamberlain to the most high and mighty prince, my redoubted sovereign lord the Duke of Burgundy, Brabant and Limburg, etc., at the request of the said defender of the passage of arms and for the fuller endorsement of each and all of the terms above, have signed these Chapters by my own hand and attached the seal bearing my coat of arms, on the twenty-seventh day of December in the year 1448.'[274] [*f. 122r*]

64

How Sir Jacques de Lalaing, after issuing his Chapters in the presence of good Duke Philip, took leave and returned to Lalaing, where he likewise took leave of the lord his father and the lady his mother, and journeyed on till he came to Burgundy

These Chapters were announced and proclaimed on high, upon the Duke of Burgundy's stand, before he descended or anyone had left: they were heard by everyone. You may be sure there were few who didn't guess they sprang from the high and virtuous courage of the noble knight Sir Jacques de Lalaing, though for the moment he didn't wish to name himself. And there was no one unconcerned about the wound he'd suffered in his arm in the course of the combat – though despite it he'd prevailed to his very great honour, as everyone had clearly seen that day.

After the Chapters had been issued and the duke had returned to his palace, and after the feasting and giving of gifts by the duke and Sir Jacques to the English squire who then returned to his native land of England, Sir Jacques was tended so diligently by the duke's doctors that he was soon fully healed and recovered. This was much to the joy of the Duke of Burgundy and the princes, princesses, ladies, damsels, knights and squires, for all who knew him – and even those who'd never seen him and knew him only by the renown of his noble deeds – were worried and distressed about his wound. All rejoiced at the news that he was fit and healed – above all, of course, his father and mother the lord and lady of Lalaing, and also, not to be forgotten, his two uncles the lord of Créquy and Sir Simon de Lalaing, by whom he was dearly loved and rightly so.

---

[274] These Chapters for the *pas d'armes* at the Fountain of Tears were, therefore, prepared not only before the combat with the English squire at Bruges, but before the journey to meet James Douglas in Scotland.

He was elated when he felt his arm was healed, and gave praise to Our Lord and the Virgin Mary. And he now prepared and planned for the fulfilling of the Chapters he had issued at Duke Philip's stand. His preparations were impeccable; and when he saw that he was ready for departure and equipped with all he needed, he took leave of the duke and duchess and the princes, barons, knights, ladies and damsels. And you may be sure that as he left the duke he was given such generous gifts of gold, horses, arms and gear to add to what he'd received from his father the lord of Lalaing that he was thoroughly, amply supplied with all he would need for his venture. Moreover, the most noble and virtuous prince his sovereign lord Duke Philip of Burgundy gave him as arbiter on his behalf the noble King of Arms of the Fleece, known by all as Golden-Fleece, who was deemed throughout his life to be the most expert, upright, trustworthy King of Arms then living, without rival: because of his integrity and wisdom he was councillor to the duke. Sir Jacques had known him for a long time, and was delighted when he heard that his sovereign lord the duke had chosen him as his arbiter. He took leave then of the duke, thanking him most humbly for the honours and gifts he had bestowed on him so generously, and praying that Our Lord would grant him grace to perform some service pleasing to him.

'Sir Jacques,' the duke replied, 'God grant indeed that you acquire renown that will redound to the glory of yourself and all your friends and kin.' And the duke took him by the hand and said: 'May God bring you perfect accomplishment, Sir Jacques, for in your beginning you have excelled.'

And with that the gentle knight departed, and came to the castle of Lalaing where he stayed for several days at the request of the lord and lady. Then, after all due feasting and celebration, he took leave of his father the lord of Lalaing and the lady his mother, not forgetting his two uncles. Ready for his venture, with everything in order and all farewells made, he left the castle of Lalaing accompanied by a number of gentlemen and rode on day by day till he came to Burgundy. [*f. 123v*]

65

How Sir Jacques, having left the castle of Lalaing and arrived in Burgundy, pitched his pavilion at the site of his passage of arms, and what he did there

On reaching the duchy of Burgundy, Sir Jacques de Lalaing pressed ahead to undertake his deed of arms and arrived at Saint-Laurent beside the city of Chalon in the region of Auxonne. There he had a pavilion pitched,[275]

---

[275] According to Olivier de la Marche, the lists were on the Île Saint-Laurent in a field on the site of the Franciscan convent built there by Duke Philip in 1452, and the pavilion was 'at the end of the great bridge, on the Saint-Laurent side'. De la Marche, *op. cit.,* pp. 4–5.

on top of which was a most beautiful image of Our Lady. Below, to the left, was a lady dressed in a gown lined with marten fur and patterned with white teardrops, and around her waist was a broad girdle of a gorgeous cloth. Her body was beautifully shaped and proportioned. As for adornments, her hair was lovely and long, tumbling over her shoulders and right down to her heels, but was covered by a simple veil; one end of this was held in her right hand to dab at her eyes to wipe away the great blue tears that were streaming forth and falling into a fountain. The fountain sent great gushes from three spouts to fall upon three shields that hung from the neck of a unicorn. These shields were of different colours: the first was white, the second violet and the third black, and all were blazoned with a scatter of blue tears, as described more fully in the Chapters above.[276] Guarding the pavilion was an eminent herald named Charolais; he guarded it for a whole year on the days and at the hours prescribed: that is to say on the first day of each month of the stated year. He began on the first day of that November, and finished at the pavilion on the last day of October in the year '50, as you're about to hear.

But the truth is that on the first days of November, December and January, no one touched a shield or had one touched on his behalf. [*f. 124v*]

66

How a young squire from Burgundy named Pierre de Chandio was the first to come and touch the white shield

It so happened that, with everything in place and ready, the first gentleman to order a shield to be touched was a young squire, about twenty-five years of age, one of the finest young men in the duchy and county of Burgundy and considered one of the strongest in all the region at that time. His name was Pierre de Chandio, son of the lord of Chandio and nephew of the Count of Charny.[277] [On the first day of February in the aforesaid year he sent Charny's pursuivant of arms, Montfort by name, to touch the shield,][278] and the herald Charolais gave him as the day of combat the seventh of that month, which was a Saturday. It was the white shield that Chandio ordered to be touched, signifying combat with the axe, and the number of blows that he set was twenty-one.

---

[276] To be precise, the tears were described there as white rather than blue; the contradiction may perhaps be explained by the improbability of having white tears on the white shield: they would presumably have been blue tears on the white and white tears on the violet and the black.

[277] The count was Pierre de Bauffremont, notable for having led the defence of the first major *pas d'armes* in Burgundy: the 'Tree of Charlemagne' at Marsannay-la-Côte near Dijon in 1443.

[278] These phrases are accidentally omitted in MS 16830, the scribe's eye probably having slipped down the page to a repetition of 'Charny'.

The seventh of the month came, and at about eleven o'clock the knight defending the passage[279] left the church of the Carmelites,[280] boarded a boat along with his men and crossed the river Saône to a little island where he'd had lists laid out and built in splendid style, and a fine house appointed for the arbiter. He entered the lists unarmed and dressed in a rich and full-length robe of cloth of gold lined with marten fur, accompanied by his men and with his officers of arms before him. He presented himself to Golden-Fleece, the duke's councillor and King of Arms, commissioned to be arbiter on his behalf for the deeds of arms the knight was to undertake, be they on foot or horseback. As the defender of the passage came before this appointed arbiter Golden-Fleece, he said:

'Noble King of Arms of the Golden Fleece, I present myself before you, as arbiter commissioned by my redoubted sovereign lord, to perform and accomplish the deed of arms laid down in the Chapters I have issued, asking you to give fair and proper judgement.'

In reply the arbiter bade him welcome and said he would do so willingly. Then the knight withdrew to his pavilion, where he armed and disarmed each time he fought on foot. This was the procedure he followed all year long in entering the lists and presenting himself to Golden-Fleece, except when the combat was on horseback. Even then, in going to fight he would always leave the said church of the Carmelites, board his boat and cross the Saône to the island as described; but then there was a tent outside the lists where he would arm and mount before going to make his presentation to the arbiter, saying the words given above. [*f. 125v*]

67

How Pierre de Chandio came on the given day to where the defending knight awaited him, and how they engaged in combat

When Pierre de Chandio was informed that the knight defending the passage had crossed the Saône and arrived at the lists and was awaiting him to do battle, he mounted, clad in a robe of black satin and already wearing his leg armour, with his horse's caparison displaying his coat of arms. Behind him rode a page on a horse draped in satin with patterning of velvet, and he was accompanied by a host of noblemen from Burgundy, fully six hundred knights and squires. They included a number of very great lords, foremost among them the bishop of Langres, duke and peer of France; the lord of

---

[279] See note 70 above, pp. 59–60. It is very noticeable that Jacques's feigned anonymity, as proclaimed in the closing Chapters (above, p. 148), is maintained throughout this entire account of the *pas d'armes* of the Fountain of Tears.

[280] The Carmelites had established a monastery in Chalon in the early 14th century; their chapel is now the town's library.

Arguel, son of the Prince of Orange;[281] the lord of Couches; Sir Jehan de Vergy, lord of Autrey; the Count of Charny; the lord of Buissy, son of the lord of Saint-Georges; the lord of Étrabonne; the lord of Pesmes; the lord of Toulongeon; the lord of Champdivers; the brothers Sir Claude and Sir Tristan de Toulongeon; the lord of Belle-Isle; the lord of Bellesaulx; the lord of La Marche and a good many more, too numerous to name.

When this noble squire de Chandio arrived at the lists, Charolais Herald came before him at the entrance and presented him with a golden ring enamelled in the colour of the shield he'd touched; and having received this ring he entered the lists and went straight to present himself to the arbiter. His uncle the Count of Charny spoke on his behalf, saying:

'King of Arms of the Golden Fleece, you see before you Pierre de Chandio, who presents himself to you as arbiter commissioned by my redoubted sovereign lord the Duke of Burgundy. Though the Chapters permit us to place another arbiter alongside you, he asks you alone, in light of the wisdom, loyalty and integrity he feels to be in you, to oversee proceedings justly and to give him due protection.'

In reply the arbiter said he would do so willingly and bade him welcome. Then Chandio withdrew to his pavilion to arm.

When the arbiter knew both champions were ready to do their duty, he had proclamations delivered on the duke's behalf and the other required procedures followed. Then the knight defending the passage stepped forth, clad in white with a pattern of blue teardrops, the same as adorned his pavilion. He took hold of an axe given to him by a knight named Pedro Vásquez;[282] for head-armour he wore a sallet and a small neck-protector:[283] that was how he fought.

Over his armour the squire Chandio wore a surcoat quartered with the arms of Chandio and Bauffremont, those of Chandio being ermine with a red fess and those of Bauffremont vairy red and gold.[284] On his head he wore a bascinet. His uncle the Count of Charny handed him his axe and took two steps forward with him before closing the visor on his bascinet and leaving him. Almost instantly the champions engaged. They fought most bravely, ferociously, dealing great and awesome blows with all their might, intent on achieving what they'd come for, and continued thus till their twenty-one blows were done. Then the arbiter,

---

[281] The Principality of Orange was an area north of Avignon.

[282] See note 44 above, p. 55. According to Olivier de la Marche, 'he was an impressively built and skilful fighter … and if Sir Jacques had been suffering any illness or injury I believe he intended to have Sir Pietre Vasque take his place' (as the Chapters permitted). De la Marche, *op. cit.*, p. 4.

[283] '*houscout*' or '*hausse-col*'; Olivier de la Marche specifies that this was of mail. As in his combat against the English squire above (p. 140), Lalaing is lightly helmeted and has no visor.

[284] 'Ermine' is white with a black pattern representing the winter coat of stoats; the 'fess' is a horizontal band; 'vairy' is a pattern of alternating colours.

seeing the deed of arms complete, threw down his baton and the appointed guards separated them at once. The arbiter called them both before him, and declared they'd accomplished their deed of arms well and honourably, and bade them touch hands and be good friends. They did as the arbiter had bidden and each returned by the way he'd made his entrance; and each time he fought, whether on foot or mounted, the knight defending the passage returned to his boat and crossed the Saône and went back to the Carmelite church.

That same day Pierre de Chandio gave a splendid supper attended by most of the knights and squires who'd accompanied him; notably present too was the knight defending the passage, likewise the arbiter Golden-Fleece and the officers of arms and a good many more. After supper and a time spent conversing they took leave of one another and returned to their various lodgings or wherever else they chose, till the following day when most departed. And so the first passage of arms at the Fountain of Tears was completed to the honour of both parties. [f. 127v]

68

How the Sicilian knight Sir Jehan de Boniface, who had previously fought Sir Jacques de Lalaing at Ghent, came and touched two shields, the black and the white

On the first day of March, the following month, a knight from the kingdom of Sicily, Sir Jehan de Boniface by name,[285] came in person and touched two shields, though the Chapters stated that no one could touch more than one. But the knight defending the passage in courteous, generous spirit gave him leave. He first touched the black, signifying combat on horseback, and he called for twenty-five courses; and on that same day he touched the white, signifying combat with the axe, and specified twenty-five blows. The date he was given by Charolais Herald was the sixth of the month, a Friday.

When the due day came, the knight defending the passage left the Carmelites, boarded his boat and crossed the river Saône and made his way to the lists just as before. After noon he entered his tent beside the lists, and then came to bow to the arbiter, presenting himself as was his custom. And then, straight after him, the Sicilian knight arrived at the lists fully armed astride a courser caparisoned with his coat of arms. Before him was a page on a horse with armour of boiled leather[286] bearing his coat of arms in the Lombard fashion;

---

[285] This is of course the 'Jehan Boniface' who arrived in Antwerp and met Lalaing in combat at Ghent, above, pp. 75–87.

[286] *Cuir bouilli* continued to be widely used for armour, especially for horses, and the phrasing suggests that it is probably the horse rather than the page wearing it here; the coat of arms would be carved into the leather while still soft.

on the page's head was an armet[287] with a crest consisting of a golden crescent with a peacock plume at each end and a spray of white peacock feathers in the middle, the whole being covered with a delicate veil.[288] He had three lances, of mighty length and girth, borne before him, on which were inscribed the following words:

'*Who has a fair lady, let him guard her well.*'

And before him, too, were two trumpeters and a drummer, and a herald sporting his coat of arms. In this manner he rode round the outside of the lists and then entered with all his company, and made a circuit of the tilt where the combat was to take place. Of Golden-Fleece the arbiter he asked leave to engage. This done, his men were sent from the lists, except those who were to provide him with lances and whatever else he needed for the combat. [*f. 128r*]

68a[289]

How Sir Jacques de Lalaing and the Sicilian knight fought on horseback

Once Boniface and the knight defending the passage were mounted, armed and ready in the lists, and their lances measured and approved by four squires in the arbiter's presence, and the announcements, regulations and due ceremonies complete, the defender of the pass was given his lance and the Sicilian knight likewise. Then they charged, and struck each other with such force that they smashed and destroyed the heads of their lances. On the third course they likewise landed blows, the Sicilian being struck on his armet – so hard that the mark was clearly visible – while he struck the Knight of the Passage on the gardebras[290] and broke his lance. On the fourth course, too, they struck each other, Boniface being caught on the head as before, and the Knight of the Passage on the body. On the fifth course they both landed blows to the body, so heavy that Boniface bent right back. On the sixth course again both found their target; Boniface was struck on the head right beside the two previous blows, and with such force that his horse turned about, and some said his armet's visor was dashed open. The Knight of the Passage rode on

---

[287] A helmet developed in the 15th century which fully enclosed the head.

[288] '*couvrechef de plaisance*'.

[289] With uncharacteristic carelessness, the scribe of MS 16830 omitted this chapter; in view of the phrase 'as you've heard' at the beginning of the next, this must have been unintentional. The translation here follows Lettenhove's edition (Chapter LIV, pp. 209–11).

[290] The armour covering the arm.

past to the end of the lists to complete his course as he'd done before, but it was fully half an hour before Boniface was ready to run another.

But then they ran their seventh course, and again both landed blows; Boniface bent back violently, and the Knight of the Passage's lance was split from the head right down to the arret. This gave rise to a hot debate: the Chapters had decreed that both must joust with the same lance, not changing it, till it was either broken across the shaft between head and arret or had lost at least a finger's breadth of the head, and despite the fact that the knight's lance was split right down its length and useless, Boniface's men insisted he must joust on with it because it wasn't broken. They came before the arbiter and showed the lance and asked him to pass judgement. He asked several knights and squires to see what they would say, and as he sought their opinions a knight came up named Pedro Vásquez who took the lance and went to Boniface and showed it to him and said it was useless and that to insist otherwise would not be to his honour. Boniface said he was satisfied and could see it was beyond further use.

So another was brought to the knight defending the passage to run the eighth course. But Boniface then said he was missing part of his armour and couldn't find a replacement, and knew his opponent wouldn't want to compete with him if he felt he wasn't properly equipped; so he sent to the arbiter affirming he couldn't replace the lost piece and asking him to adjudicate. The arbiter said it was clear to him that it wasn't a question of a failure of nerve on the part of the knight or his mount, and asked both parties to be satisfied, given that they were still due to do combat on foot. The two champions, informed of his reply, agreed, and rode off through the gates by which they'd entered, bringing an end to the mounted combat.

Each returned to his lodgings till the ninth day following, which was the twenty-fourth day of the month.[291]

69

Of the combat on foot between the two knights, that is to say the defender of the pass and the Sicilian knight

On the ninth day after the combat on horseback had been completed, as you've heard, it was time for the combat on foot. The knight defending the passage left his lodging and followed his custom of going to the church of the Carmelites and then boarding his boat and crossing the Saône and making his way to the lists. After crossing and arriving there, he came before his arbiter the King of Arms of the Golden Fleece and presented himself as described before, and then withdrew to his pavilion. Shortly afterwards the Sicilian

---

[291] Either the arithmetic is faulty or the date is wrong: unless there had been a delay, the date given for their first combat had been the sixth (above, p. 153).

knight arrived at the lists on horseback, his horse's caparison emblazoned with his arms and his men arrayed as they'd been for the mounted combat, except that they brought no lances. As he entered the lists Charolais Herald presented him with a golden ring enamelled in white to match the white shield – he'd done likewise at the combat on horseback, on that occasion the ring being enamelled in the colour of the black. That done, Boniface marched into the lists and went straight to present himself to the arbiter as described above, and then withdrew to his pavilion.

Soon afterwards, the customary announcements having been made, the knight defending the passage stepped forth from his pavilion, armed and clad in a white surcoat adorned with blue teardrops and with sallet on head as before. Then Boniface appeared, fully armed, with bascinet on head and clad in his coat of arms, which arms bore three red pales[292] and a silver border. All around his bascinet were sharp points about two inches long, and on the top was a little plume. With his visor closed, he marched to meet the defender of the passage, who strode fiercely to face him. And to it they went with their axes, exchanging weighty, mighty blows. They'd dealt each other some ten or a dozen when the Knight of the Passage seized Boniface's axe with his right hand; gripping his own with his left, he three times thrust the butt-spike into his visor, then let go of Boniface's axe and seized him instead by the crest atop his head, pulling him so forcefully that he brought him full-length to the ground. When the arbiter saw the Sicilian knight prostrate, he ordered the guards to lift him up and bring him to him, along with the defender. When they came before him, he told them the passage of arms was accomplished according to the Chapters. Boniface replied that he had no wish to go against the arbiter or the Chapters, and asked the arbiter kindly to reveal the identity of the knight he'd fought. The arbiter bade them touch hands and embrace, and they recognised each other very well, having met in combat previously in the fine city of Ghent. So the combat on foot was accomplished as you've heard, and they both returned to their lodgings.

Now, the Chapters had stated that whoever was brought fully to the ground would be obliged for a whole year to wear a golden bracelet, fastened with a lock, and throughout that time would be unable to remove it or have it removed unless he found the lady or damsel who had the key; she would unlock it if she chose, and he would have to give her the bracelet and offer her his service. Since that had befallen Boniface, the golden bracelet was presented to him on behalf of the Knight of the Passage, with the words:

'You will wear it as you please, under clothing or openly.'

Boniface received it willingly, and wore it as required. But who the lady or damsel was who unlocked it I have not discovered. [f. 129v]

---

[292] Vertical stripes.

70

How a squire from Burgundy named Gérard de Roussillon touched the white shield and fought the knight defending the passage

After these deeds of arms on horse and foot had been accomplished by the Knight of the Passage, on the first day of June in the said year,[293] a noble squire named Gérard de Roussillon sent Valois, pursuivant of arms of my lord of Pesmes, to touch the white shield, signifying combat with the axe. And although according to the Chapters the combat was meant to take place within a week of the shield being touched, the knight defending the Passage of the Fountain of Tears agreed to defer until the twenty-eighth day of the month.[294] Gérard de Roussillon asked for fifteen axe-blows to be exchanged that day.

When the day came, the knight defending the passage, as was his custom, left the Carmelite church at about eleven, boarded his boat and crossed the Saône and entered the lists, presenting himself at once to the arbiter before retiring to his pavilion to arm. It so happened that on that day Golden-Fleece, their arbiter, had left there at the duke's command on an embassy to the King of France; to replace him the duke had commissioned an eminent, wise and responsible squire by the name of Guillaume de Sercy, who was bailiff[295] of Chalon.

Returning to Roussillon: shortly after the Knight of the Passage entered, Roussillon arrived on horseback, bascinet on head and wearing his coat of arms. His arms were borne before him, too, on a banner and pennon: they were composed of gold and blue lozenges with a red label of three points.[296] He had the banner and pennon planted at two corners of his pavilion, then came and presented himself to the arbiter, saying:

'Noble squire, arbiter commissioned by my redoubted sovereign lord the Duke of Burgundy, I present myself before you to do combat against the knight defending the passage, according to the terms of his Chapters. And though they permit me to appoint another arbiter alongside you if I choose, the wisdom and honesty I know you to possess bid me forgo that right, while praying you give me due fair treatment.'

[293] i.e. 1450.

[294] According to Olivier de la Marche this was because Roussillon was unprepared and unequipped, and although 'a fine companion, tall and well built' he was young and did not yet have his father's permission. De la Marche, *op. cit.*, p. 19.

[295] The *bailli* was a king's (or in this case a duke's) administrative representative, responsible for administering justice and controlling finances in his *baillage* (bailiwick). Sercy, with its fine castle, is 15 miles south-west of Chalon.

[296] Lozenges are diamond shapes; the label (or lambel) is a heraldic charge denoting the eldest son in his father's lifetime.

That said, he withdrew to his pavilion. He was there from around half past eleven until two hours after noon. The reason for the long delay, they said, was that the armourer had failed properly to rivet his leg armour. Meanwhile the Knight of the Passage was in his pavilion armed and ready for fully three hours or so.

When Roussillon at last was ready, the knight defending the passage stepped forth from his pavilion, sallet on head and, as always, wearing over his armour his white surcoat patterned with blue tears. In his hand was his axe, which had no spike upon it. Gérard de Roussillon, seeing him leave his tent, left his own likewise, wearing his coat of arms and with his head protected by an old-style iron cap specially acquired, and with a mail neck-protector:[297] that was how he fought. They engaged in vigorous and valiant combat. It brought them before the arbiter, where they dealt each other mighty, awesome axe-blows. Both were young and full of strength and noble courage, and on they fought till they'd accomplished fifteen or sixteen blows. Then the Knight of the Passage, feeling it was taking too long to overcome his man, stepped in right close to Roussillon and seized his axe and struck him with the head-spike in the face, where he had already landed blows and drawn blood. Roussillon, realising he was wounded, grabbed the Knight of the Passage's axe, and when the arbiter saw they were clutching each other's weapons he threw down his baton, and they were parted by the men appointed. The arbiter declared they had both fought well and honourably and deemed their passage of arms accomplished; he bade them touch hands, and so they did. The combat over, they left the lists and each returned to the lodging from which he'd come.

Next day, Gérard de Roussillon gave a very fine dinner attended by the Knight of the Passage, the arbiter and a host of eminent lords. [f. 131v]

71

How on the first of October that year seven noble men had the shields touched to engage in arms with the knight defending the passage of the Fountain of Tears

When the first day of October came, the following arrived at the Fountain of Tears and touched the shields: first a squire named Claude Pitois, lord of Saint-Bonnet,[298] who had Valois, pursuivant of arms of the lord of Pesmes, touch the white shield. Toulongeon, herald to the lord of Toulongeon,

---

[297] '*houscot*': see note 283 above, p. 152. Olivier de la Marche wrote that Roussillon wore these 'because he'd been told that Sir Jacques always fought in a sallet and a mail *haussecol*': i.e. he wanted to fight on equal terms, without the advantage of a visor and better head protection. De la Marche, *op. cit.*, p. 20.

[298] Saint-Bonnet-en-Bresse is 20 miles north-east of Chalon.

was the second to touch the white shield, on behalf of a knight called the Unknown Knight who was later revealed to be the lord of Épiry.[299] Limburg, herald to the duke, was third to touch the white shield, on behalf of a squire named Jehan de Villeneuve,[300] known as Pasquoy. Next to touch the white shield, in person, was one by the name of Gaspart de Durtant:[301] he was the fourth. The fifth was Piedmont, herald to the Duke of Savoy, who touched the white, the violet and the black on behalf of one named Jacques d'Avanchy[302] – this was done with the permission of the knight defending the passage of the Fountain of Tears, otherwise he could have touched only one. [The sixth was Guillaume d'Amange, a squire from Burgundy,[303] for whom the black shield was touched.][304] The aforementioned pursuivant Valois touched the white again, this time for a squire named Jehan Pitois:[305] that was the seventh and last that day.

Returning to Claude Pitois, lord of Saint-Bonnet, who had been the first to touch: the knight defending the passage gave him the following day, the second of October, a Friday, for their combat. When the day came, the Knight of the Passage left the church of the Carmelites at about eleven in the morning, boarded his boat and made his way to the lists to present himself to the arbiter Golden-Fleece, now back from the mission on which he'd been sent by his lord the Duke of Burgundy. He was accompanied by his uncle the lord of Créquy, who was returning from the Holy Sepulchre in Jerusalem; he arrived there at the lists some two hours before the combat took place and was present then at all that followed.[306] Having presented himself to the arbiter, the Knight of

[299] On the western edge of Burgundy, some 70 miles north-west of Chalon. De la Marche says he withheld his identity because of the ruling in the Chapters that anyone who had seen others fighting at the Fountain of Tears would not be allowed to do so himself; eager to take part, he went incognito so that 'if he were refused, it would create less of a stir'. De la Marche, *op. cit.*, p. 28.

[300] Probably Villeneuve-sur-Yonne, in the north of Burgundy.

[301] De la Marche refers to him as 'Gaspart de Dourtain, a squire from the county of Burgundy, a strong man, well renowned'. *Op. cit.*, p. 45.

[302] 'Jaques d'Avanchies, a most noble squire from the duchy of Savoy.' *Ibid.*, p. 29. The name is rendered '*d'Avancier*' in the MS; it is probably the modern Vanchy, in Savoy west of Geneva, some 80 miles south-east of Chalon.

[303] Amange is beyond Dole, north-east of Chalon. De la Marche renders the name as 'Guillaume Basan'.

[304] This is another accidental omission by the scribe of MS 16830. The translation again follows Lettenhove's edition (p. 218).

[305] '*Pitoye*', but later spelt consistently 'Pitois'. De la Marche referred to him as 'Jehan Pietois, a squire from Burgundy, big and strong'. *Op. cit.*, p. 29.

[306] De la Marche says that Lalaing fought more often because of his uncle's presence: 'nine times in a fortnight and sometimes two combats in one day'. *Ibid.*, p. 37.

the Passage withdrew to his pavilion. Shortly afterwards Saint-Bonnet arrived at the lists on foot, unarmed and dressed in a long black robe; at the entrance to the lists he was presented with a ring of gold enamelled in the colour of the shield he had ordered to be touched. Then he entered and went straight to present himself to the arbiter, saying:

'Most noble King of Arms of the Golden Fleece, arbiter commissioned by my redoubted sovereign lord, I present myself before you to do combat against the knight defending the passage here in your presence. And though according to the Chapters I could appoint another arbiter alongside you, the wisdom and integrity I know you to possess bid me forgo that right, for I know you will protect the interests of both parties and show them equal justice.'

In reply the arbiter, preeminently able, bade him welcome and humbly thanked him for the honour he had paid him. Then Saint-Bonnet withdrew to his pavilion to arm. Soon after, the Knight of the Passage sent word to the arbiter that Saint-Bonnet hadn't specified a number of axe-blows as laid down in the Chapters: he wanted instead to fight on till one or other was brought full-length to the ground or had his axe removed from both hands. The arbiter sent to him at once, saying he could demand as many axe-blows as he wished but he had to give a number. Saint-Bonnet was content with this and asked for forty-three.[307]

As soon as the customary announcements and regulations had been proclaimed, the knight defending the passage came forth from his pavilion as he'd done before, that is in a white surcoat strewn with blue teardrops, sallet on head and axe in hand. Saint-Bonnet, too, was clad in his coat of arms and clutching his axe; on his head he had a sallet with a bevor. His arms were quartered, two quarters being blue with a gold cross ancred[308] and the others being chevronny[309] gold and blue with a red border. They marched to meet each other, right before the arbiter, and there they engaged and began their combat in mighty fashion – but not for long, for the Knight of the Passage, so adept and skilled in arms, seized Saint-Bonnet's axe with his right hand and with his own axe aimed to strike him in the face; Saint-Bonnet was forced to grab the knight's axe, whereupon the knight let go of Saint-Bonnet's and seized him by the neck; twice Saint-Bonnet broke free, but the third time the Knight of the Passage locked his head beneath his arm in the hold they call the Bagpipes, and with his mighty strength he hauled him to the ground, flat on his back: the knight then fell face-down, with half his body on Saint-Bonnet and the other half on the ground, but promptly he laid himself wholly on top of Saint-Bonnet, pinning him beneath him. Saint-Bonnet, finding the knight upon him, gripped him around the waist so hard that it was impossible for him to stand.

---

[307] Sixty-three (*lxiii* rather than *xliii*) according to Lefèvre's letter.
[308] A cross with all four ends bifurcated and curled.
[309] Divided into an even number of equal chevrons.

Seeing the two champions in this position, the arbiter threw down his baton and the guards stepped forward to bid them rise. When the knight stayed put on top of Saint-Bonnet, one of the guards, named Michault de Sardenne, said:

'Sir Jacques, that's enough – you must be satisfied.'

'It's not down to me!' he replied. 'He's holding me so tight I can't get up!'

The guards then looked and saw Saint-Bonnet had his arms locked round him, so they prised his hands apart and lifted the Knight of the Passage from him. But both were still clutching their axes: despite all that had happened, they'd never let them go. The arbiter called them before him and said:

'Your combat is accomplished according to the terms of the Chapters; I pray you touch hands and be friends.'

And so they did, and then made their way back to their lodgings.

But the fact was that the Chapters decreed that whoever was brought full length to the ground would have to wear a golden bracelet; so the Knight of the Passage sent an eminent knight named Pedro Vásquez to Saint-Bonnet to find out who he wished should take it to him. But Saint-Bonnet replied that in his view he shouldn't have to wear it: he hadn't fallen alone but with the Knight of the Passage, so shouldn't have to wear it any more than he – if he had fallen, so had the knight. He acknowledged that had their combat been *à outrance*[310] he would have had the worse of it, but in the context of their challenge he should not be obliged to wear the bracelet, and that was the end of the matter.

Seeing the stance taken by Saint-Bonnet, but knowing he had clearly been laid full-length on the ground as said above, the Knight of the Passage had the bracelet made ready to send him. Some of Saint-Bonnet's friends were made aware of this, and since it was the sure and proven case that he'd had his whole body on the ground while all that could be truly said of the Knight of the Passage was that he'd had his arms or legs down, they spoke to Saint-Bonnet and said that both he and the knight served the same prince and should protect each other's honour. It was resolved and decided that he should say the following words to the knight:

'Sir Jacques, I was eager to make your acquaintance. You know we have met in combat, since when you have sent Sir Pedro Vásquez to ask by whom I wished to have the bracelet brought to me. You are well aware that we serve the same lord and should desire each other's honour and look to protect it, so I pray you be content to have done with this. Moreover, I understand you have been told of things I am meant to have said of you; I assure you I would not wish to have said anything against your honour.'

That was how the matter then was left; for the time being it was spoken of no more. [*f. 134v*]

---

[310] See note 248 above, p. 134.

72

How the Knight of the Passage fought the lord of Épiry

After this combat had been accomplished as you've heard, the knight defending the passage of the Fountain of Tears was due to fight Jacques d'Avanchy,[311] lord of Épiry on the seventeenth[312] day of October; and so he did. At about nine in the morning he went to hear mass at the great church in Chalon, and there he found the lord of Saint-Bonnet. It had been agreed the previous evening that at ten o'clock that morning Saint-Bonnet would be at the Carmelite church in the suburbs of Chalon to say the aforementioned words to the Knight of the Passage; but though it was only nine the knight went to Saint-Bonnet and said:

'My lord of Saint-Bonnet, are you happy to pronounce the words in the little document[313] shown to you by Louis Sacet?'

Saint-Bonnet replied that he was ready to do so whenever he wished. The Knight of the Passage said he was pleased with his response, and released him from the wearing of the bracelet. So peace was made between them; they touched hands, and from that time forth it would have been hard to find two brothers who were such good friends.

Later that same day Jacques d'Avanchy[314] the lord of Épiry, calling himself the Unknown Knight, engaged in combat with the defender of the passage of the Fountain of Tears who, following his custom, left the Carmelite church, boarded his boat and crossed the Saône. He arrived at the lists and presented himself to the arbiter as previously, and then proceeded to his pavilion. Just a short while later the lord of Épiry arrived at the lists, and as he entered he was presented by Charolais with a golden ring enamelled in the colour of the shield he'd had touched. He rode into the lists on a horse caparisoned with his coat of arms, led by two officers of arms whose surcoats likewise displayed the arms of Épiry; the horse's head was draped with a veil of delicate fabric, somewhat like crêpe, fringed with green silk and golden thread. Épiry was

---

[311] The scribe curiously attaches this name to the lord of Épiry when it clearly belongs to a squire who is to fight later (below, pp. 166–8). But the error may in fact have been copied from a strange confusion in Lefèvre's Letter, which likewise refers here to '*Jaques Devanchier*' without at this point mentioning Épiry.

[312] To make consistent sense of the cited dates and days, this should be the third. Lefèvre's Letter refers to 'the second'.

[313] '*petite cedulle*' ('little schedule'): this has a distinctly legal sound, and was clearly intended to ensure that the form of words laid down and now to be uttered would safeguard the honour of both parties.

[314] See note 311 above; at this point Lefèvre in his letter refers to him as the lord of Épiry without giving the name Devanchier.

dressed in a long robe of white damask, bordered both top and bottom, with sleeves of crimson satin, and a vermilion chaperon with a green cornette.[315] There were four children around him, two of them his own and two his nephews, all dressed like him from head to foot and holding the four corners of his mount's caparison, and behind him rode a page dressed likewise, astride a horse draped in crimson velvet. Having dismounted at his pavilion he came straight to present himself to the arbiter, the four children before him, and declared out loud:

'Most noble King of Arms and arbiter here commissioned by my redoubted lord the Duke of Burgundy, this being the day assigned to me to do combat with the knight defending the passage, I present myself to you that I may with God's aid accomplish this deed of arms. And though the knight's Chapters declare that his challengers are entitled to choose an arbiter to join you, I for my part forgo that right; nor do I wish to ask that the rights of both parties be protected, for I think it unnecessary in light of your sagacity, discretion and reputation for sound judgement, which I believe to be such that the rights of both parties will be properly and justly observed in accordance with the laws of arms.'

In reply the arbiter bade him welcome and humbly thanked him for paying him such honour, and said he would do what he had asked to the best of his ability.

Then the lord of Épiry returned to his pavilion, which was white with a vermilion border at the top, matching the robes described above, and in the entrance, like a curtain, hung a rich golden drape. Inside this pavilion he armed; and while doing so he sent to the arbiter, asking if he would permit his four counsellors, in other words the four little children, to stay at his feet[316] to watch. The arbiter gladly and freely agreed: it was not a request to be refused. Then, after the required announcements and ceremonies, the axes were inspected: they had spikes at the head like all the others so far used.

That done, the Knight of the Passage stepped forth from his pavilion, armed and clad as previously. The lord of Épiry came forth likewise, wearing his coat of arms and with a sallet on his head which had a bevor and a visor; but hardly had he appeared before he threw his surcoat to the ground – his arms were quartered, two quarters being blue with a gold cross engrailed[317] and two being gold with four red points. As for the number of axe-blows demanded by Épiry, it was fifty-five. And truly, the Knight of the Passage and

315 The chaperon, a development from a simple hood, usually consisted at this time of a padded circular *bourrelet* from which hung a *cornette*, a long tail of fabric which could be wound around and over the head and/or left to hang loose.

316 Lefèvre's letter, from which this passage is copied, reads '*auprès de lui*' (beside him) rather than the MS's less probable '*aux piez de lui*'.

317 Its edges having semicircular indentations.

the lord of Épiry marched to confront each other and met before the arbiter and fought valiantly till they had delivered thirty blows; then the arbiter, seeing the courage and skill of both these knights and fearing the dreadful danger that might result, threw down his baton, whereupon the champions were separated by the appointed guards with honours declared even. As they were brought before him, the arbiter said:

'Sirs, I deem your deed of arms accomplished, and you have both fought well and valiantly.'

And he asked them to touch hands and to be good friends, which they freely did. Then they returned to their pavilions to disarm. Once they were disarmed they came to find each other in the lists, and embraced and gave mutual thanks for the honour they had paid one another. Then each returned to his lodgings and the day's engagement was done.

Next day, Sunday, the fourth of the month, the lord of Épiry gave a splendid dinner attended by the knight defending the passage and a host of knights and squires, the arbiter and many officers of arms and other men of note. [f. 137r]

73

How Jehan de Villeneuve, known as Pasquoy, fought the knight defending the passage

On the following day, a notable squire named Jehan de Villeneueve, known as Pasquoy, engaged in combat with the knight defending the passage of the Fountain of Tears, asking for the completion of seventy-five axe-blows. As was his custom, the knight set out that day from the Carmelite church at about eleven, and boarded his boat unarmed, wearing a long robe of cloth of gold; thus dressed he entered the lists and went to present himself to the arbiter in his usual fashion before withdrawing to his pavilion to arm. Shortly afterwards Pasquoy arrived, unarmed and wearing a long black robe. At the entrance to the lists he was presented by Charolais Herald with the gold ring enamelled in the colour of the shield he had touched; then he entered the lists, impressively accompanied, and presented himself to the arbiter with the same or similar words to those said by the others, and then went to his pavilion to arm.

Once the arbiter had inspected the axes, which had spikes at both head and butt, and the announcements had been made and ceremonies observed, they stepped forth from their pavilions. The Knight of the Passage fought in his usual armour, except that he had no leg armour on his right leg; Pasquoy fought with a sallet on his head and a high bevor, and was wearing his coat of arms, being black with five silver bezants in a saltire.[318] Armed thus and ready, with axes in hands, they marched from their pavilions and fiercely

---

[318] Bezants are roundels representing the Byzantine coins of the same name; a saltire is a diagonal cross.

advanced on one another, meeting and engaging right before the arbiter. The battle between these two was great, ferocious, with many a mighty axe-blow dealt, so thick and fast and fearsome that it delighted all those watching – it was easier to spectate than to be involved! The two champions fought till they'd delivered fifty-five blows or thereabouts; then the arbiter, in view of their great commitment and fine display, threw down his baton and had them separated to the honour of both parties. He summoned them before him and said he deemed their deed of arms accomplished and that both had fought well and valiantly, and asked them to touch hands and to be thenceforth good friends; and so they did. They went to their pavilions to disarm, and then returned to the lists where they embraced and exchanged thanks for the great honour they had paid each other. Then they both returned to their lodgings, the Knight of the Passage crossing back by boat as always to the church of the Carmelites from where he had set out. [*f. 138v*]

74

Gaspart de Durtant's combat against the knight defending the passage of the Fountain of Tears

The following Friday, the ninth of the month, it was the turn of a squire named Gaspart de Durtant. He was renowned and truly judged to be one of the mightiest men in all the duchy and county of Burgundy. That day the knight defending the passage of the Fountain of Tears left the Carmelite church at eleven, following his previous custom, boarded the boat with his company and, arriving at the lists, came straight to present himself to the arbiter before going to his pavilion to arm as he always did. Just a short time afterwards Gaspart arrived at the lists, and like the other challengers was presented at the entrance with a golden ring; then he entered his pavilion and armed. Meanwhile the axes were brought before the arbiter for inspection. The announcements were made and the other ceremonies performed, then out from their pavilions they came. The Knight of the Passage was armed and dressed as usual except he had no armour on his right leg; Gaspart was fully armed, with bascinet on head and wearing his coat of arms, being red with a silver fess and three roundels, likewise silver, and upon the fess a red star.

Seeing each other ready, they strode to meet at once, and engaged before the arbiter, Gaspart asking for sixty-four axe-blows. They fought most valiantly, but before they'd delivered ten blows the Knight of the Passage's axe was broken, the butt-spike and its ferrule falling to the ground. Nonetheless they completed the full sixty-four blows in fine and worthy fashion. The number achieved, the arbiter threw down his baton and called them before him, declaring they had accomplished their deed of arms according to the Chapters, well and valiantly, and asking them to touch hands and be good friends, and so they did. Then they went to disarm in their pavilions and returned to their lodgings, and thus the said combat was complete. [*f. 139r*]

75

How a squire from Savoy named Jacques d'Avanchy fought the knight
defending the passage

On the tenth, the following day, it was the turn of a notable squire from
Savoy to engage with the knight defending the passage of Our Lady of
Tears. At eleven o'clock that day the Knight of the Passage left the Carmelite
church and boarded his boat to go to the lists. Arriving there he presented
himself to the arbiter in his customary way and then entered his pavilion to
arm as he had always done. Shortly afterwards the Savoyard squire entered
the lists and, following the custom, was presented by Charolais Herald with
a gold ring enamelled in the colour of the shield he had touched. Unarmed
and dressed in a black robe, he came before the arbiter and spoke to him
with great humility and respect: he could have done no more in addressing a
mighty prince. Having made his presentation he entered his pavilion to arm.
The axes were inspected, the announcements and regulations issued, then they
stepped forth from their pavilions.

The Knight of the Passage was armed and dressed as he had always been
before, except he had no armour on his right leg and no gauntlet on his right
hand. Avanchy fought in a sallet and a gorget[319] of strong mail, and was wearing
his coat of arms: divided into pales of silver and red with a bend of gold.[320]
They came and engaged and fought before the arbiter. Avanchy had asked
for twenty-five axe-blows, and they'd fought well and valiantly to twelve or
fourteen when Avanchy stepped in close and grabbed the knight's axe with
one hand; then the Knight of the Passage promptly, smartly seized Avanchy
by the gorget and pulled him towards him three or four steps. In doing so he
made Avanchy lose his own axe – he held it with neither hand and it fell to
the ground. Thereupon the arbiter threw down his baton. They were stopped
at that point and called before him, and he declared they had fought well and
valiantly and asked them to touch hands and to be good friends; they did so,
and each returned to his lodgings. [*f. 140r*]

76

How this squire from Savoy fought on foot against the knight defending
the passage, this time with the sword

On the twelfth day of the month, this Savoyard squire fought with the
sword against the Knight of the Passage. They were both in the lists at
eleven o'clock, where they presented themselves to the arbiter as before and

[319] Protection for the throat.
[320] Pales are vertical sections, a bend a diagonal band.

then went to their pavilions to arm. Once the swords had been inspected and announcements and regulations issued, the Knight of the Passage stepped forth from his pavilion, bascinet on head[321] and so splendidly armed that he was a fine sight to behold. Over his armour he wore a robe of blood-red silk strewn with blue teardrops. The Savoyard squire wore an armet[322] on his head and over his armour his coat of arms. They marched from their pavilions towards each other, and met and engaged before the arbiter. The Savoyard asked for seven sword-blows, to be delivered in three steps, forward and back, and the guards were given clear instructions to set the combatants where they should be if they failed to observe this. But the Savoyard couldn't see well in his armet, so he never moved from his starting-point: he stood and awaited the Knight of the Passage and the blows he struck on each advance, which he made in fine, grand steps as he attacked the unmoving squire. Seeing the seven blows delivered, the arbiter threw down his baton and declared the combat well and honourably accomplished. They touched hands and returned to their pavilions to disarm. [*f. 140v*]

77

How Jacques d'Avanchy fought on horseback against the knight defending the passage of the Fountain of Tears

On the same day, two hours after noon, Avanchy engaged in his mounted combat against the knight defending the passage of the Fountain of Tears. But while Avanchy went to arm and mount at his lodgings, the Knight of the Passage stayed at the lists, arming and mounting in a tent close by. When they were both ready they entered the lists and presented themselves to the arbiter; then they were given their lances. Avanchy had asked for twenty-five courses but they ran only six, in which the Savoyard broke two lances; the Knight of the Passage broke one, with which he dealt the squire a fearsome blow to the head which seemed to have hurt and somewhat stunned him. He changed to a new armet, but in it he couldn't see well, and the arbiter, observing this, sent to him saying he was not well helmeted and asking him to forgo further action. The Savoyard replied that he was ready to do whatever the arbiter decreed. Hearing the squire's response the arbiter sent to the Knight of the Passage asking him to be content to do no more; but the knight replied that his opponent had broken two lances and he had broken only one, and so

---

[321] This would incorporate a visor, and Olivier de la Marche observed that 'it was the first and only time Sir Jacques ever fought with his face covered', adding that it was necessary to protect the face because they were using tucks (*estocs*: see above, p. 135 and note 251), swords designed for stabs and thrusts, the blows being struck unparried. *Op. cit.,* p. 40.

[322] See note 287 above, p. 154.

asked the arbiter to let them complete their challenge. He was told that the Savoyard had agreed to do whatever the arbiter decreed, and he repeated his request that the knight comply, assuring him his honour was safe. The Knight of the Passage, ever courteous and good-natured, acceded to the request, and the arbiter called them straight before him and spoke to the Savoyard, saying this or very like:

'I have asked that you be satisfied.'

The squire Avanchy replied that he was ready to do as he pleased, as he was his judge. The arbiter thanked him, and then called the Knight of the Passage to him and likewise asked him to be satisfied. The knight replied most courteously, saying he was ready to do whatever he pleased, whereupon the arbiter bade them touch hands. And with that they parted and returned to their lodgings.

That evening the Savoyard squire gave a very fine supper; the knight defending the passage was present, along with a host of other knights and squires, the arbiter and officers of arms and many other notables. There Avanchy in a spirit of friendship made generous offers to the Knight of the Passage, who responded in like fashion with many grand offers of his own; and so they parted in fine and brotherly love. [*f. 142r*]

78

Here follows the combat between one named Guillaume d'Amange and the knight defending the passage

The following day, the thirteenth, a squire by the name of Guillaume d'Amange fought on horseback against the knight defending the passage. He asked for the standard number of courses with the lance: twenty-five. They met in the lists that day at the customary hour, and having presented themselves to the arbiter, and their lances having been measured and the announcements made, they ran their twenty-five courses. Guillaume landed only two blows and failed to break a lance, but the Knight of the Passage struck him many times and broke two lances. Their twenty-five courses run, the arbiter called them before him and bade them touch hands, and with that they parted. [*f. 142r*]

79

How one named Jehan Pitois fought against the Knight of the Passage

On Thursday the fifteenth of that month, a squire named Jehan Pitois engaged in combat with the axe against the knight defending the passage of the Fountain of Tears. At eleven that day the Knight of the Passage boarded his boat and crossed the river and entered the lists in the form and manner he had done on previous occasions, and presented himself to the arbiter before going to his pavilion to arm. Shortly afterwards Jehan Pitois arrived at the lists, unarmed and dressed in a long black robe, and received a golden ring at the entrance. He passed through and came before the arbiter and presented himself in fine, distinguished fashion. Then he entered his pavilion to arm; in the meantime the axes were brought to the arbiter and inspected, and the announcements and regulations were issued and all due ceremonies performed.

When the two champions were ready they came forth from their pavilions. The Knight of the Passage was armed as had become his custom, without armour on his right leg. Pitois on his head had neither bascinet nor sallet, but something in the manner of a kettle hat,[323] specially forged for the occasion, with a high bevor, so that nothing of his face was visible but the eyes. Over his armour he wore his coat of arms, which were quartered, two quarters being blue with a gold cross ancred and the others being lozengy gold and blue.[324] He asked for sixty-three axe-blows to be delivered. They marched from their pavilions and came and joined in combat before the arbiter. There they both fought well and valiantly; and as they neared the end of their sixty-three blows, the Knight of the Passage struck Pitois beneath the eye with the butt-spike of his axe and wounded him; a moment later they seized hold of each other's axe, and as they did so Pitois aimed three blows at the knight's face with his gauntleted hand. Then the arbiter, seeing the sixty-three blows had been completed, threw down his baton and summoned them before him. As they arrived the Knight of the Passage said to Pitois, calling him by his first name:

'Jehan, I can't help saying it's a bit womanish to start hitting with a gauntlet when you've a perfectly fit weapon in your hand!'

The arbiter heard this; he declared their combat had been well and fully accomplished to the honour of them both, and asked them to touch hands and to be good friends, and so they did. Then Pitois went to his pavilion to disarm. [f. 143v]

But the Knight of the Passage stayed with the arbiter. A great number of nobles and gentlemen were there, and a crowd of other people had gathered, too, because it had been the final combat of that passage of arms: the time for the noble defender of the passage of the Fountain of Tears to be there at Saint-Laurent by Chalon had expired, the appointed days were now passed. And so it was that many a knight and squire and a great number of others had assembled to see how the Knight of the Passage would take leave of his arbiter, appointed by his sovereign lord the Duke of Burgundy. The moment to take leave having arrived, the valiant knight said the following words:

'Noble King of Arms of the Golden Fleece, arbiter here commissioned

---

[323] '*capel de fer*': a simple open helmet – literally an 'iron hat' – with a broad brim to protect from blows from above.

[324] For 'ancred' see note 308 above, p. 160; 'lozengy' is entirely composed of lozenges of alternate colours.

by my redoubted sovereign lord, I present myself before you now so that if anything remains to be done regarding this passage of arms and the terms of my Chapters, you may tell and command me accordingly; for I am ready, with God's aid, to accomplish what I am bound and required to do.'

The arbiter then replied most decorously, addressing the knight with the following words:

'Sir, according to what is laid down in your Chapters, I know of nothing you have failed to accomplish honourably and chivalrously in all respects. The time you were due to spend here you have fulfilled, thanks be to God, to your very great honour, praise and high renown.' Then Golden-Fleece, arbiter at this passage of arms as said, continued thus: 'Sir, I very humbly thank you and all the noble men who have engaged in arms with you for the great honour you have shown me, and ask them all, both present and absent, to forgive my slight and limited discernment and graciously accept such service as I have been able to render; for truly, any failing there has been is due to ignorance, not ill intent.'

After these exchanges the gentle knight withdrew to his pavilion to disarm as he had always done; then he returned to the church of the Carmelites to give thanks to our blessed Creator and His sweet mother.

After the good knight had spoken to Golden-Fleece and departed, a wise and eminent doctor of medicine, a native of the kingdom of Sicily named master Gonzalo,[325] came to Golden-Fleece followed by a servant carrying a most rich and handsome robe of cloth of gold, long and lined with marten fur, and said:

'Noble King of Arms of the Golden Fleece, the Lady of the Fountain of Tears sends you this robe, praying that you wear it out of love for her, and thanking you for the pains you have taken in her service.'

Then the King of Arms of the Golden Fleece took the robe, thanking the Lady of the Fountain of Tears, and donned it. And wearing it he attended the splendid supper given later that same day by the Knight of the Passage. To this he had invited the noble knights and squires who'd fought with him and a great number of others. The supper was held in the house of the bishop of Chalon, and a lavish banquet was served with a great array of dishes of many kinds. And displayed on a table was an *entremets*[326] some eight feet long and six or seven feet wide. To one side was a model of the city of Chalon with its churches, the clock-tower, the houses, the walls and the tower that stands on the bridge between Chalon and Saint-Laurent, the river Saône flowing beneath. And there at the end of the bridge was the pavilion, the selfsame colour and shape as that of the knight who'd defended the passage of the Fountain of

[325] '*Gonsalle*'. A Portuguese doctor, his name variously rendered as Gondessales or Gonzalve de Verges or Vargas, is recorded as serving both Duke Philip and his successor Charles the Bold.

[326] See note 12 above, p. 40.

Tears. And right before the pavilion stood the Lady of the Fountain of Tears, along with all the people and figures involved. The Lady's garments, hair and headgear were exactly as they'd been at the pavilion, and close beside her was the unicorn carrying the three shields, held by the herald Charolais; for the moment the image of the Virgin Mary was inside the pavilion. The gentle knight, defender of the Fountain of Tears, went to address Her most humbly with the following prayer: [*f. 145r*]

80

Here begins the knight's prayer

'Thou, chosen for the honour of the Earth,
Mother of God, who to the True Fruit gave birth,
At the pavilion here I come to pray to thee,
Where for a full year thou hast succoured me,
Giving courage to my heart most faithfully
To set and hold my passage in this place;
And now complete, I thank thee for thy grace.'

Then, after his prayer to the glorious Virgin Mary, the knight came to the Lady and said:

'Lady, my inspiration dear:[327]
Golden-Fleece, noble King of Arms,
Declares complete the passage of arms
Of the Fountain of Tears.'

81

The Lady's reply to the knight

'Since such has been the will of God
We must give Him thanks indeed;
Let us go and worship the cross
On which He was willing to die for us.'

But before the knight and lady went to worship the cross, the Virgin Mary emerged from the pavilion in a long silk gown, her hair flowing over her shoulders, and came before the cross and made her own prayer as follows: [*f. 145v*]

---

[327] Literally 'in whom I have all my recourse'.

82

The Virgin Mary's prayer

'O glorious Jesus crucified,
My son, my father and my lord,
For those who to this passage came
I thank you for all that you have done:
Their bodies and their honour safe
Through every challenge undergone,
Thanks to the care that you have shown.'

After the Virgin Mary had offered her prayer the Lady offered hers, saying:

'True cross, redemption of the world,
In the shade of which is safety and joy,
Foundation of the deepest faith,
The path and way to Paradise,
I yield to you, wherever I be,
And thank you for the blessings great
Bestowed by you upon this knight.'

The knight's prayer

'O cross, redeemer of human kind,
Death's conqueror, eternal life,
Allow your love to grow in me
Ever more strongly, that I pray;
For in your grace so bounteous
My strength finds greater sustenance
Than in any power of nature.'

83

A Portrayal

On the other side of the *entremets* was portrayed the town of Saint-Laurent
and the lists at the end of the bridge that crossed from Saint-Laurent to
Saint-Marcel.[328] The Lady of the Fountain of Tears was there on horseback,
accompanied by three women richly attired in the French fashion; her baggage-
train with her chests and coffers had already crossed the bridge; and beside
the Lady was Charolais Herald leading the unicorn that bore the three shields
as you've heard: he was leaving with the Lady. And as the hackney ridden

---

[328] Saint-Marcel is the town on the opposite bank of the Saône to Chalon, Saint-
Laurent being the island in mid-river.

by the Lady took its first step on to the bridge, the knight-defender of the passage came before the Lady and said these words:

> 'Lady, I come to ask of thee
> If you wish any more of me,
> For your command, if it be God's will,
> It shall be my duty to fulfil.'

84

The Lady's reply to the knight

> ' I wish no more of what has passed,
> But go to your challengers, first to last,
> And humbly thank them, every one,
> For the honour that they to you have done.' [*f. 146r*]

85

The knight's thanks

After these words had been exchanged, the Knight of the Passage found himself in the lists, and finely, beautifully modelled they were; for in the middle was the arbiter's house with the arbiter inside, and at one end of the lists as many pavilions as there had been noble challengers, all of whom were armed and clad in their coats of arms with their various devices and colours, each with axe in hand and wearing the headgear he'd worn in his combat. And behind their tents were their horses, all covered as they'd been for their deeds of arms, with either armour or caparison. Those who'd fought on horseback had a serving-man beside them holding a lance; the one who'd fought combats with both axe and sword had a sword in his belt as well as his axe. At the other end of the lists were two pavilions in the colours of the knight who'd defended the passage, and beside them was a horse which a serving-man was holding, along with a lance. And in the middle of the lists was the Knight of the Passage, armed and dressed as he'd always been for his combats on foot, with sword in belt and axe in hand. And he spoke now to all his aforesaid challengers, saying:

> 'My lords and my companions all,
> As humbly as I ever may
> I thank you for the honour all
> Have paid me by competing here.
> In no way can it be repaid,
> Save that you deem me from this day
> To be a knight at your command.' [*f. 147r*]

86

How the prizes were presented

On either side of the table where this *entremets* was displayed were eight banners, being the banners of the eight lines of the knight's family – that's to say, four on his father's side and four on his mother's. The *entremets* was altogether magnificent, much admired by everyone present: at that time no one had seen any more splendid or better crafted.

After supper, when everyone had risen from table with its glorious spread and viewed and examined the wondrous artwork on display, the Knight of the Passage retired to a great hall along with all the rest. There the prizes were presented. Gérard de Roussillon received the golden axe, the Knight of the Passage deeming him to have dealt him the finest axe-blow; Jacques d'Avanchy, the Savoyard squire, had the golden sword; and the Knight of the Passage bade that the golden lance be sent to Jehan de Boniface as the one who'd dealt him the finest blows with the lance: Boniface was said to be then in Lombardy, and the golden lance was sent to him there.

When all this was done there was much cheer and celebration among them all: that's to say, all who'd engaged in arms with the knight defending the passage of the Fountain of Tears, whose name was Sir Jacques de Lalaing – not that he'd ever hidden his identity except in his Chapters; but because he hadn't named himself therein, his name has not been mentioned in this account except at the very outset and the end.

And to assure you that the account is true, it was recorded and written by Golden-Fleece by order of the Duke of Burgundy, his prince and sovereign lord. He did it to the best of his ability, though not with the thoroughness he would have wished and that the matter demands, for it was a truly noble, glorious enterprise, honourably conducted from first to last and well worthy of remembrance: such a notable undertaking should not be hidden or kept quiet.

But, as is always said, even the greatest feasting and joy must finally come to an end, and after all the celebration and merriment they took their leave of each other, all together, in a spirit of love mixed with sorrow, as if they had all been brothers.

Following this supper and banquet where the prizes were awarded, Sir Jacques de Lalaing invited the ladies and damsels of Chalon to another splendid banquet where, once they'd supped, they rose from table and dancing and festivities began; and when the time came to retire, wine and cordials were served and all drank as they pleased. Then Sir Jacques took leave of them, preparing as he was to make his way to the holy city of Rome for the universal pardon.[329] To this banquet the Lady of the Fountain of Tears sent eminent messengers with a letter to the ladies and damsels present, which read as follows: [*f. 148r*]

87

The Lady's letter

'Honoured ladies and damsels, with all the love in my heart I commend myself to you. Knowing of the noble gathering at this joyous, delightful banquet, but not knowing whether all, or even most of you, would be together again soon, I send this message to the assembly, for three main reasons.

'Firstly, to bid the adventurous knight, who on account of my piteous tears has held and defended the passage at this noble city of Chalon, to fulfil and accomplish, with God's aid, his vowed commitment to the journey to the holy pardons in Rome.

'Secondly, to thank you sincerely for the honour and favour you have shown the said knight.

'Thirdly, to pray and entreat you on his behalf that, if he has wronged you or failed to honour you in any way, you will forgive him at my request; for I am assured that if he has transgressed it has been purely through that most minor sin of ignorance, which can be effaced simply by the knowledge, which I confirm, that he would not for all the gold in the world wish to think, say, do or countenance anything to offend you in the least: he would rather be no longer on the Earth. So I ask and pray you once more, in view of the above, to excuse any failing of the knight. In return for which, by the power and authority I have over him, I oblige him to be your most humble servant in arms forever more. To verify and testify to this obligation, I have sealed these letters with the shields of the holy Fountain of Tears, praying to Our Lord to convert it to a fountain of joy and grant you continuous delight, endless happiness and riches immortal.

'Written in such haste that I have not had time to append the name or date.'

At the top of the letter was written: 'On behalf of the Lady of Tears.' And the address on the back was: 'To my very dear and honoured ladies and damsels residing in the noble city of Chalon.' [*f. 148v*]

---

[329] See note 272 above, p. 147.

88

How, after accomplishing the passage of arms at the Fountain of Tears,
Sir Jacques de Lalaing went to Rome and then to the King of Aragon at
Naples, where he found the Duke of Cleves returning from Jerusalem

After the banquet at which the aforesaid letter from the Lady of Tears
was read, Sir Jacques de Lalaing set out on his journey to Rome for the
universal pardons. Having spent a time in deep devotion there, fulfilling the
duties of a faithful and devout pilgrim to that holy city, he made preparations
to leave and go to Naples.

In residence there was the most excellent and victorious prince Alfonso,
king of Aragon, who received him with great honour. But because of the
alliance and brotherly love between himself and the Duke of Burgundy, he
would not permit Sir Jacques to wear his token of challenge as he'd done in
other kingdoms; nor did he wish any man of his court, realms or dominions
to engage in combat with him.

But as happy chance would have it, on the day he came to the King of
Aragon's court, there Sir Jacques found the Duke of Cleves, newly arrived
on his way back from the Holy Sepulchre at Jerusalem. It was, Sir Jacques
felt, one of the most joyous things that could have happened, for in his youth
he'd been raised with the Duke of Cleves at the court of his uncle the Duke of
Burgundy; he'd been very close and dear to him, as if they'd been brothers,
and they'd always dressed alike in every detail, just as the Duke of Cleves
chose, such was his affection for Sir Jacques. The joy and long-standing love
between them was now redoubled and renewed.

The King of Aragon was delighted by the duke's arrival, and also by Sir
Jacques de Lalaing's, and seeing the way the duke welcomed him he gave Sir
Jacques a grand and warm reception. And with the duke being the nephew of
Duke Philip of Burgundy, and Sir Jacques's renown spreading far and wide
through every realm and province, he feasted them both so lavishly and with
such honour – so I, the author of this book, have been told – that he could
have done no more for any prince, no matter how close of kin. I would have
my work cut out to describe in full how they were fêted and honoured by the
king – I shall move on quickly!

After staying there a while, the Duke of Cleves and Sir Jacques took their
leave of the king, who presented them with splendid gifts for which they
thanked him deeply. Then they departed, and rode together right through
Italy; Sir Jacques wore his token of challenge constantly, but nowhere as they
journeyed did he find anyone who would touch it.

On they rode through Lombardy, Savoy and Burgundy, and came to the
land of Hainaut. It was now the year '51. The Duke of Cleves set out then
for his own land, while Sir Jacques, having taken leave of him, went straight
to Mons to the court of the duke his sovereign lord, from which he had long

been absent. And truly, the duke was overjoyed and received him with great reverence and honour, as did all the princes, counts and barons of the court. At that time, there in the city of Mons, the duke was holding the feast and ceremonies of his Order of the Golden Fleece; I, the author of this book, was present and witnessed all the solemnities. In the course of them the gentle knight Sir Jacques de Lalaing was elected to be a brother and companion of the order, for he was truly worthy of that high honour.

When the feast was done, before the brothers and knights of the order departed, a number of weighty matters were debated and discussed before the duke – the head of the order – and the knights brothers and companions; and it was decided that a great and distinguished embassy should be sent to our holy father the Pope[330] with a view to countering the designs of Mahomet, the grand emperor of Turkey,[331] so that plans might be made in good time, urgently. At the head of this mission were sent Sir Jehan de Croÿ, lord of Chimay,[332] Sir Jacques de Lalaing and Golden-Fleece, along with a noble abbot,[333] an eminent cleric who was a doctor of theology.

When they reached Rome they devoted themselves to the pressing matters that had brought them to our holy father the Pope. They were received and entertained with great reverence and honour out of love for the Duke of Burgundy and respect for their clear eminence.

They departed then, and rode on day by day through Italy, Lombardy, Savoy and Burgundy and made their way to the King of France. In the course of these journeys and embassies Sir Jacques de Lalaing behaved with such worth and dignity that he earned much honour and praise; and truly, with no disrespect to others, honour was due to him above any knight I ever saw or knew.

When they came to the King of France's court they were received and entertained, but the business on which they had come was lightly passed over by the king, and they did not stay many days.[334]

They departed then and rode so hard that in just a few days they found the Duke of Burgundy in his fine city of Brussels, and there before him and his son the Count of Charolais and his great council they reported the response

---

[330] Nicholas V, pope 1447–55.

[331] The Ottoman sultan Mehmed II, 'the Conqueror', ascended the throne for a second time early in 1451 and began strengthening his navy and planning the conquest of Constantinople.

[332] Jehan II de Croÿ (c. 1390–1473), Count of Chimay, a major figure at the Burgundian court and one of the first members of the Order of the Golden Fleece.

[333] The abbot of Averbode in Brabant.

[334] The business may have involved the threat from the Ottoman sultan, but may well have concerned also the uneasy relations between the king and duke over the Somme towns – the territory around Amiens, Abbeville and the county of Ponthieu – which Charles VII had mortgaged to Duke Philip in 1435 and was eager to reclaim.

of the Holy Father and the King of Aragon[335] and also what had transpired with the King of France. The duke was very satisfied, and bade his embassy most welcome back, as did his son the Count of Charolais and the lords and barons of the court. [*f. 151r*]

89

How the Ghenters rebelled against their lord the Duke of Burgundy, for which in the end they paid dearly

At this time, towards the end of 1451,[336] on account of certain demands made by the Duke of Burgundy of the people of his city of Ghent and the land of Flanders,[337] the Ghenters were stirred by great pride and presumption: they declared that before they would accede to the request made by the Duke of Burgundy – the Count of Flanders, their lord – they would resist till the last man in Flanders was left standing. And indeed, they several times attacked men and officers of the duke, which the duke took very ill. Their disloyal and damnable actions, their faithlessness and disobedience, intensified: they were stealing, robbing and pillaging, and murdering the duke's servants and officers.

Informed of this, he summoned his great council without delay, along with all his knights, barons and captains,[338] for guidance and advice on how to respond. And while these discussions were taking place in the city of Brussels, some notable men of Ghent brought together the deans of the guilds and the captains[339] in their city in the hope of finding an amicable path. They gently

---

[335] In MS 16830 there has been no reference to the King of Aragon in relation to this embassy; the scribe transposed and accidentally omitted some phrases regarding their visit to the pope. The following sentence, however, appears in Lettenhove's edition, p. 250: 'And after taking leave of the Holy Father, they returned from Rome having first sought out the King of Aragon and explained their mission to his high majesty.' i.e. they presumably tried to gain his support in opposing the Ottoman sultan.

[336] In the modern calendar the first months of 1452; as noted previously (pp. 82–3), a year was then counted as running from Easter to Easter.

[337] In particular, a tax on salt. The demands had been made a good deal earlier, starting in 1447, but tensions escalated in the autumn of 1451 and reached a head the following spring. An excellent account is given in Richard Vaughan, *Philip the Good* (rev. ed. Woodbridge, 2002), pp. 306–17. Vaughan points to the extreme importance to Philip of the salt tax: he 'evidently hoped, by enlisting the cooperation of Ghent, to establish the tax in Flanders and, by invoking the example of Flanders, to impose it throughout his other territories' (*Ibid.*, p. 307).

[338] The heads of his bodyguard.

[339] '*haulx mans*', a rendering of '*hoofdmannen*', elected captains who had replaced the existing civic government during the escalating crisis in December 1451.

tried to explain to the people the danger, the peril they were running in thus assaulting and killing the prince's officers and, worse still, wishing to burn and destroy his land of Flanders and wage undeclared war on him. They could have done no worse, they said, and they implored them in God's name to go no further and to cease such offences against their good prince; they would find a way to have them pardoned for what they'd done so far, if only they would desist from further outrage. These distinguished burghers with their fine, persuasive words won their agreement; all the people promised not to continue, provided the prince's pardon was secured for what had already been committed. They asked that certain worthy men be chosen and sent to the duke to appease him and persuade him to forgive them for what had been done; they promised to make amends in whatever way those chosen thought best. Hearing the people's willing assent, these burghers wept with relief and joy.

To carry out this mission they straightway appointed a distinguished embassy: the prior of the Charterhouse of Ghent, the Three Members of Flanders,[340] deputies from the main towns and county of Flanders, along with a number of other eminent men. Together they set out from Ghent and came to Brussels in Holy Week, arriving on Good Friday. The prior and the other deputies came and knelt before the Duke of Burgundy. The prior was their spokesman, and he tearfully implored the duke that, out of reverence for the Passion of Our Lord Jesus Christ, he might have pity on the city of Ghent; if he would graciously go there, all his poor subjects and inhabitants of the city were ready to come and meet him at the gate with the churchmen in their vestments bearing crosses and banners, as the clergy rightly should to welcome him, and the captains and civic officials and all the people would come bare-headed and barefoot to crave his mercy, begging him to pardon all, officials and people alike, for their misdeeds. The Duke of Burgundy replied that, although they had behaved badly and committed grave offences against him and his lordship, he still had as much mercy in him to forgive them as he had ever had: he had always been ready to pardon. But he feared their true feelings didn't tally with their words, for he had often witnessed and experienced their malign intent. Nonetheless he was ready to listen to all pleas and proposals honourable to him; his decision would be conveyed to them by appointed councillors, but in view of the current holy days the matter would not be dealt with till the following Wednesday.

Yet in spite of all this, on that very day, Good Friday, while the people of Ghent had their ambassadors making their piteous plea to their prince, they were sending men to seize the castle of Gavere, three leagues from the city of Ghent;[341] and on the fifth day after Easter, while the duke's deputies and

---

[340] Representatives of the towns of Bruges, Ghent and Ypres.
[341] Gavere is some 12 miles to the south.

the ambassadors were busy negotiating in their interest, the Ghenters, true to their wicked and treacherous nature, marched from their city in force and went to lay siege to the city of Oudenaarde[342] from both sides, expecting to find it devoid of troops and armaments. But God, who ever watches over his friends, had sent a gentle knight named Sir Simon de Lalaing to Oudenaarde; he had gone there at the duke's command for a number of reasons which will be made clear, and there, as you will hear, he behaved so finely and with such honour that it will be remembered forever more. [f. 153r]

90

Of the fine leadership shown by Sir Simon de Lalaing at Oudenaarde, and how the Ghenters laid siege to the city

A s you have heard, the Duke of Burgundy knew the Ghenters all too well, and to counter their damnable schemes and abounding wickedness he had posted captains, noble lords of the land, in certain Flemish towns to ensure their safety. Among them he ordered to Oudenaarde the lord of Gruuthuse[343] and the lord of Escornay.[344] But some time in the week before Palm Sunday, because the people of Bruges were asking to have the lord of Gruuthuse as their captain (and also because the lord of Escornay had returned home as he and Gruuthuse could not get on), the Duke of Burgundy sent Gruuthuse to be captain of Bruges; and knowing Sir Simon de Lalaing to be a wise and valiant knight, he ordered him to go to Oudenaarde and see to it that Escornay and his men returned there, and to settle any disputes that there might be. Lalaing duly did so, and the lord of Escornay and his companions went back.

But there was much discord in the city of Oudenaarde: they had been given to understand that a great garrison of Picards and other foreigners was about to be planted there, which none of them would tolerate at any price, and to prevent it they had issued a proclamation ordering all the people of the suburbs to withdraw inside the city with their belongings. Then Sir Simon de Lalaing, with his shrewd intelligence, foreseeing that it would be the ruin of the city, assembled the civic leaders, prominent men and deans of the guilds, and argued that if the people of the suburbs were summoned inside, fully two thousand peasants would follow from all around Ghent, and would have no provisions to bring with them. Furthermore, if the Ghenters, Oudenaarde's enemies, came to besiege the city, some of these country folk, in fear that the

---

[342] About 7 miles south-west of Gavere.

[343] Louis de Bruges, lord of Gruuthuse (c. 1427–92), a major figure at the Burgundian court and a member of the Golden Fleece.

[344] Arnould VII de Gavre, lord of Escornay (Escornaix – 'Schorisse' in Flemish – south-east of Oudenaarde).

Ghenters would burn their homes – and in any case likely to side with the Ghenters rather than their prince, and more inclined through their poverty to pillage Oudenaarde than defend it – might well make efforts to deliver the city to their besiegers. Lalaing also argued that they had strength enough to defend the city, and it was neither wise nor necessary to garrison it with people from outside unless they were people of wealth and power and brought plenty of supplies to support themselves: they could take such people in, but not lesser folk.

'As for those,' he said, 'who've led you to believe that you're about to be garrisoned with strangers, they are wrong: my lord the Duke of Burgundy has never had any such thought. It's a ploy to deceive you and undermine your confidence in your prince. Rest assured, my lord the duke has ordered here only the lord of Escornay and myself, who are your neighbours and friends.'

The good and the noble realised at once that Sir Simon was telling them the truth; but the common folk – and some of the more prominent, too – were not convinced, and told him they were sure he had no intention of staying and if trouble came he would be off to Sluis, where he was governor. Sir Simon responded by insisting he had come to stay with them, and by way of assurance said he would send for his wife and eldest son, and so he did. Thus he reassured them and kept them sweet as best he could, and kept insisting they needed no garrison, to stop them bringing in anyone from other towns.

And it was as well that he did; for when on the Thursday after Easter, as mentioned above, the Ghenters marched from the city of Ghent and the surrounding villages to lay siege to Oudenaarde, the aforesaid people of other towns showed their treachery all too clearly: they entered the city under the pretext that it was a market day, but had armed themselves as secretly as could be; they were planning to take control of the market-place, hoping that the people would side with them. But Sir Simon, alerted to the wicked intent of these false-hearted, treacherous rebels, launched sudden raids from house to house and drove them out and took control of the gates. The townsfolk now realised that the outsiders had been planning to betray them, and from that point on were all united in support of their prince. But a small number fled: they may have been colluding with the outsiders, planning to let them stay that day and to lodge that night in the suburbs; they went now and joined forces with the people of the surrounding villages. Had he wished, Sir Simon could have had these people banished, but he didn't want it said that he'd caused or instigated anything so critical.

That very night the Ghenters advanced in mighty numbers with a great train of artillery, and around noon made camp before Oudenaarde, on the side towards the county of Aalst. They sent a letter to the citizens saying they hadn't come to do any harm, but had heard that foreigners meant to come to the land and they wanted to prevent this, and asked that they might have food in return for payment and be received as allies if the need arose. Sir Simon de Lalaing, hearing the messenger and the Ghenters' request to the citizens, answered him loud and clear, saying they were strong enough to defend their own city, and as for the request for food, there was none but for the people of Oudenaarde. He told the messenger furthermore that he knew very well they had come thinking there was a rift among the citizens and that they could thereby take the city; he told him to go and inform his masters that from the highest to the lowest they were all united and resolved to defend the city for their prince.

As soon as they were given this reply the Ghenters declared war on the people of Oudenaarde, laying siege by land and water all around. Those inside the city could send no one out or receive any news from the Duke of Burgundy or from anyone outside.

Four days after the Ghenters began the siege, pressing in close on every side, the people of the city sallied forth in two places and set fire to all the suburbs, forcing the besiegers further back. The Ghenters now opened fire upon the city with their bombards, cannons and veuglaires,[345] and their shot included balls of red-hot iron, about the size of silver cups, with which they aimed to set the town ablaze. And it was indeed a dire hazard: had they landed in dry wood or straw the city would have been in danger of burning. But Sir Simon de Lalaing, shrewd, resourceful and experienced in war, set watches in two bell towers who called and pointed to where any of these balls fell, and to deal with them he had great barrels of water positioned all around the streets. Women were deployed to stand watch, too, and when they saw where the balls were falling they would quickly run with pails of brass or iron in which they placed the balls and took them out of harm's way, while everyone hurried to quench the fire.

It now happened one morning that Sir Simon de Lalaing, returning from the watch, fell into the river Scheldt with his sword at his belt, a little chaperon[346] round his neck, and a gown and mantle over mail.[347] He was in grave danger of drowning, as he couldn't swim at all. But the speed of the current swept him right to the portcullis where he was able to hang on. It seemed a miracle that he escaped death, but God, knowing the people of Oudenaarde still had urgent need of him, saved and protected him, as He did all the people of the city. The loss of such a knight would have been a great shame and pity, for he and the citizens behaved so honourably and bravely that the Ghenters could

---

[345] The veuglaire, sometimes rendered as 'fowler' in English, was a long-barrelled wrought iron cannon. According to a chronicler of Tournai the bombardment began 'on Sunday 16 April 1452 ... The sound of the cannons and bombards could be heard from the city of Tournai.' Tournai is some 20 miles away.

[346] See note 315 above, p. 163.

[347] 'gouches a armer', the sections of mail covering parts of the body unprotected by plate armour.

inflict no harm, and to the Duke of Burgundy they gave a fine account of themselves and of their city, as you're about to hear. [*f. 156r*]

91

How news came to the Duke of Burgundy that the Ghenters had come in force and laid siege to Oudenaarde

News of the siege reached the Duke of Burgundy in Brussels, where the Ghentish ambassadors were busy working in the cause of peace. They were behaving in honest, godly fashion, knowing nothing of the treacherous, wicked actions of the people who'd sent them there – and who had put them in grave danger: had they been dealing with a prince of unbridled fury he would have had them all killed. But the duke informed them of what had happened and they were utterly aghast, not without cause; they didn't know what to say, other than to place themselves entirely at his mercy and to say it was the most dreadful thing that could have befallen them, and that they'd been foully betrayed. Matters had taken a sudden and dangerous turn! But the duke could clearly see they disapproved and had known nothing of the Ghenters' treachery, for, as mentioned above, among the ambassadors were a number of eminent men from Oudenaarde,[348] who couldn't now return to their homes because of the siege, as the Ghenters strove to seize their city at the same time that they were suing for peace. And indeed, the fact is that several of the ambassadors didn't return to Ghent either, because of the dishonesty and disloyalty they saw now in their people.

The Duke of Burgundy, roused to great anger towards the Ghenters, now issued an urgent command to go to the aid of Oudenaarde. He left Brussels in person on the fifteenth day of April, after Easter 1452,[349] stopping en route at Notre Dame in Halle and next day lodging at Ath in Hainaut, where he stayed till the twenty-first, waiting for his troops. From there he advanced to Grammont,[350] which had been taken and sacked because they'd committed themselves to the Ghenters and appointed a Ghenter as their captain; it had been taken by Sir Jehan de Croÿ, bailiff[351] of Hainaut, and Sir Jacques de Lalaing. There at Grammont in the Duke of Burgundy's company were his

---

[348] The embassy included 'deputies from the main towns and county of Flanders' (above, p. 179).

[349] MSS give the date as 1451, the confusion caused perhaps by the Old Style calendar.

[350] 'Grammont' is the French name for Geraardsbergen, north of Ath and south-east of Oudenaarde.

[351] See note 295 above, p. 157.

son the Count of Charolais, Adolph the son of the duke of Cleves,[352] João lord of Coimbra, cousin of the King of Portugal,[353] Corneille the Bastard of Burgundy,[354] the lord of Croÿ,[355] the lord of Buchan,[356] the lord of Créquy, the lord of Montaigu,[357] the lord of Auxy,[358] the lord of Aumont,[359] the lord of Humières,[360] and many other knights and squires usually at the duke's court. With them also were the Count of Saint-Pol and two of his brothers, that is the lord of Fiennes[361] and my lord Jacques of Saint-Pol,[362] and Sir Jehan de Croÿ, all of whom had men at arms at their command. In their company were a good two thousand troops, in addition to those of the Duke of Burgundy's court. [*f. 157v*]

92

How Sir Jehan de Bourgogne, Count of Étampes, won the bridge at Espierres from the Ghenters, and went from there to Oudenaarde; and of the great deeds of valour of Sir Jacques de Lalaing

Now we shall tell of the Count of Étampes,[363] the Duke of Burgundy's cousin, who at the duke's bidding and direction had raised a very fine army in Picardy. It included some great lords: the lord of Moreuil, the lord

---

[352] Adolph, lord of Ravenstein (1425–92) was the youngest son of Adolph I, Duke of Cleves.

[353] João of Coimbra, Prince of Antioch (1431–57), was in exile at the Burgundian court following his father's failed rebellion against the Portuguese king. He was later made a knight of the Golden Fleece.

[354] See above, p. 57.

[355] Antoine I 'the Great', lord of Croÿ and count of Porcien (c. 1385–1475) was a major figure at the Burgundian court, and in 1452 was appointed Governor-General of the Netherlands and Luxembourg.

[356] '*Bocquem*'; Wolfert VI of Borselen (c. 1433–86) became Earl of Buchan through his marriage in 1444 to Mary, fifth daughter of James I of Scotland. He later became stadtholder of Holland and Zeeland, and a knight of the Golden Fleece.

[357] Jehan II de Neufchâtel (c. 1417–89), chamberlain of Duke Philip.

[358] Jehan IV d'Auxy (c. 1396–1474), likewise chamberlain of Duke Philip and a member of the Golden Fleece.

[359] Another of Duke Philip's chamberlains, Jacques d'Aumont, lord of Méru and Chappes.

[360] Dreux II de Humières, Duke Philip's chamberlain and a member of the Golden Fleece.

[361] See above, p. 83.

[362] Jacques de Luxembourg (c.1420–87), lord of Richebourg.

[363] Jehan II (1415–91), who previously appeared in the attack on Luxembourg, above, pp. 56–7.

of Roye, the lord of Wavrin, the lord of Rochefort, the lord of Lannoy,[364] the lord of Fosseux son of the baron of Montmorency, the lord of Harne, the lord of Saveuse, the lord of Noyelle, the Bastard of Burgundy,[365] Sir Jehan bastard of Saint-Pol,[366] the lord of Dompierre, Sir Philippe de Hornes,[367] the lord du Bos,[368] the lord of Neufville, the lord of Haplincourt, the lord of Humières, the lord of Beauvoir, the lord of Jaucourt, the lord of Bazentin, the lord of Cohem, the lord of Dreuil[369] and many other knights and squires numbering two or three thousand fighting men.

The Duke of Burgundy, having mustered his army, ordered his battalions: he commissioned the Count of Saint-Pol with his two brothers and Sir Jehan de Croÿ to form his vanguard, while he and some of his blood, accompanied by several great lords, formed the main battalion. The Count of Étampes was to lead the rearguard, and once all was in order he commanded him to take his force straight to a crossing from Picardy to Oudenaarde called the bridge of Espierres;[370] the Ghenters were guarding it in substantial numbers, and had done all they could to fortify the town's church. When Sir Jacques de Lalaing, having been ordered by the duke to join the main battalion, heard that the count had been commanded to head for this bridge at Espierres, he realised it was right on the road to Oudenaarde where his uncle Sir Simon de Lalaing, whom he dearly loved, was besieged, so he asked leave of the duke to let him join the count. The duke granted him permission, and Sir Jacques, overjoyed, set out and went to the Count of Étampes who was delighted by his coming.

The count, following the duke's command, now led his forces towards the bridge at Espierres, with a great train of artillery including culverins and veuglaires as well as crossbows, brought by the lord of Lannoy from his fortress not far from the bridge.[371] As soon as the count drew near, he deployed

[364] Jehan II de Lannoy (1410–93), a prominent figure in the Low Countries; Duke Philip had appointed him stadtholder of Holland and Zeeland in 1448 and made him a knight of the Golden Fleece in 1451.

[365] Anthoine de Bourgogne (1421–1504), son of Duke Philip and his mistress Jeanne de Presle. Along with Corneille (above, pp. 57, 184) he was one of the duke's favourite illegitimate sons.

[366] Jehan (c. 1400–66), lord of Haubourdin, called the Bastard of Saint-Pol, was the illegitimate son of Waléran of Luxembourg, Count of Saint-Pol. He was cousin of the Count of Saint-Pol who appeared above, pp. 59–74, 83, and was a member of Duke Philip's council and a knight of the Golden Fleece.

[367] Philippe I de Hornes (1421–88), lord of Bassignies and Gaasbeek. Hornes was an important noble house in the Low Countries; the name refers to Horn in Limburg.

[368] Jean III Bois d'Annequin, lord of Bos.

[369] Gauvain Quiéret, mentioned above, p. 55.

[370] Espierres-Helchin is the French name for Spiere-Helkijn, on the Scheldt south-west of Oudenaarde.

[371] Lannoy is about 10 miles away.

his force and in fine order launched an assault on the bridge and crossing. The artillery opened fire, the archers and the crossbowmen advanced, and some noble men leapt into the river: Sir Jacques de Lalaing and a number of others went in up to their necks to take and secure the crossing. The bridge was vigorously assailed, and when the Ghenters saw the Picards attacking with such force and courage their hearts failed them, and they abandoned the bridge and retreated to the church. There they were attacked from every side and by force of arms were trapped. Great valour and great feats of arms were seen, for the Ghenters, with death staring them in the face, mounted a brave defence, and hurt and wounded a fair number of noble, worthy Picards, among them the lord of Roye and Anthoine de Rochefort, gentleman, and one named Lanselot from Portugal, and several more. As for the Ghenters, some seven- or eight-score[372] men were slain, in addition to all the prisoners.

After the taking of the bridge at Espierres, the Count of Étampes advanced with his whole force and camped three leagues from Oudenaarde. This city, besieged by the men of Ghent, stands on the River Scheldt; the Duke of Burgundy was lodged at Grammont, on the Brussels side of the river, but the Count of Étampes was now camped on the other bank, the side towards Bruges. So the river was between them, and they couldn't support or aid each other.

To return to the Count of Étampes: having taken the bridge at Espierres and camped three leagues from the siege lines, he sent ahead some thirty lances[373] of brave, experienced knights and squires accompanied by sixty archers. They were led by Sir Jacques de Lalaing, and with him were Philippe de Hornes, the lord of Dreuil, Robert de Miraumont, Hue de Mailly and others. They went as close as they could to reconnoitre, to see what lay between the Count of Étampes's camp and the Ghenters, and to gain the best possible sight of their positions – and of their skirmishing, to see how they were conducting themselves when it came to action in the field. Once Sir Jacques had taken stock and assessed them as fully as he could, he and his company returned to the count, who straightway sent for the lords and captains to hear the report from Sir Jacques and those who'd gone with him.

That same day the count received a letter from the Duke of Burgundy instructing him, the moment he'd read it, to go with his whole force and join him at Grammont, and to advance no closer to the Ghenters; he'd received reports that they had fully thirty thousand besieging Oudenaarde, and he didn't want the count to confront them with so small a force: he had only two or three thousand, too few to engage so great an army as the Ghenters were said to be. The count assembled all his captains and put the matter to them, and there was much debate before it was resolved: some were of the

---

[372] MS 16830 appears to read 'seven to eight thousand'; Lettenhove's edition gives the more modest and reasonable figure.

[373] A 'lance' is a unit comprising a knight or squire and his attendants.

view that the count should follow the duke's command, but others agreed with Sir Jacques de Lalaing that they couldn't be so close to the Ghenters without paying them a visit.

'We're mounted,' they said, 'and the Ghenters are on foot. They can't do us any damage, but we can do them plenty! And what will the people of Oudenaarde say if they hear we were so near and didn't show ourselves? Let's engage the Ghenters in skirmishes while Sir Jacques de Lalaing rides into the city to give strength and cheer to his good uncle Sir Simon and all the people. That's what we should do; then, God willing, Sir Jacques will enter the city or die in the attempt: that's why he's come!'

The matter thoroughly debated, the Count of Étampes decided to go next day and take a closer look at how the Ghenters were conducting the siege, and if the best he could do was get Sir Jacques inside the city, so be it: it would still be a fine deed. Such was the count's decision, taken with the advice and backing of the great lords and captains of his company.

So that night he ordered his forces – scouts, vanguard, main battalion, rearguard – and made all necessary preparation. And it was planned that two men who knew those parts and the local tongue and were strong swimmers would go by night and try to find a way into Oudenaarde and inform Sir Simon de Lalaing of the count's approach. The plan was duly followed: the two men – one of them, named Jonesse, was a servant of the lord of Haubourdin[374] and previously of the lord of Roubaix[375] – entered the city by swimming across the river and told Sir Simon that the count was on his way. Mightily cheered, Sir Simon spent the night unblocking the city's gates, preparing for a sortie against the Ghenters to coincide with the count's arrival.

Next morning, the twenty-fourth of April, the good Count of Étampes left camp and advanced in fine order towards the siege. The vanguard was led by Sir Anthoine, bastard of Burgundy, accompanied by the lord of Saveuse, Philippe de Hornes, Sir Jacques de Lalaing and a number of other great lords. The Ghenters, informed of the count's advance, armed themselves and mounted guard on all the approaches to their siege lines. They sent six hundred troops to defend a bridge a quarter of a league away – it crossed a small river directly on the count's line of approach – and made every preparation to defend themselves and their camp. The Picards rode on till they reached the crossing guarded by these six hundred, some of whom had gone beyond the bridge and seemed to be drawn up in the open field: the lord of Saveuse was sent ahead to reconnoitre their position, and he went up close and saw that a section of the Ghenters' force had crossed the river on to what appeared to be open ground. He pointed this out to Sir Jacques de Lalaing and others

[374] Jehan bastard of Saint-Pol – see note 366 above, p. 185.
[375] Haubourdin and Roubaix are both near Lille.

who'd been sent forward from the vanguard and numbered twenty-five lances of noble, valiant men.

'Look!' he said. 'A party of Ghenters are on our side of the river – they're in the open field.'

When they heard the lord of Saveuse say this, Sir Jacques and those who were drawn up with him spurred their horses forward instantly. With great courage and valour they headed straight for the Ghenters, aiming to charge into their midst, but found a deep gully between themselves and the foe, uncrossable. Then Sir Jacques de Lalaing, desperate to get at them, rode with seven other lances right along this gully and at the very end found a narrow way across. With, as said, just seven others, he charged into the Ghenters: along with Sir Jacques the eight were Philippe de Hornes, the lord of Crèvecoeur,[376] the lord of Bos, Arnoul de Hérimez and Jehan d'Athies,[377] the two others being gentlemen of Sir Jacques's household. When these eight brave men found themselves in among the foe, they performed all possible deeds of courage and skill at arms. Anyone seeing Sir Jacques de Lalaing charge into their midst and scatter them would have thought they'd been hit by a thunderbolt: he struck them down, he cut them down, they all made way before him. The truth is that those eight brave men performed such feats that were I to recount them in full they would not be believed. But the Ghenters met them and struck back fiercely, too, and one of the eight, named Jehan d'Athies, was killed when his saddle turned on his horse's back: it was a grave pity, for he was a valiant man. And the lord of Crèvecoeur, who fought bravely that day, was wounded, and would have been slain but for the courage and daring of Sir Jacques de Lalaing and his gentlemen, aided by the lord of Saveuse, who now came galloping up behind. Thus reinforced, they routed the six hundred Ghenters who'd been sent to defend the bridge, and few of them escaped alive.

The Count of Étampes, eager to attack the foe, pressed forward now towards the siege lines, riding on in splendid order. When he caught sight of the Ghenters he called for Sir Jehan, bastard of Saint-Pol, and asked of him the order of chivalry; he was knighted there by the bastard of Saint-Pol's hand. This done, several noble men came to the count and requested the order of chivalry of him, and a good number were knighted that day by the count's hand; others were knighted also by the hand of other great lords present. But I shan't name them; I'll pass on, as I wish to continue with the matter in hand, which I mean to complete to the best of my ability. [*f. 162r*]

---

[376] Philippe de Crèvecoeur, lord of Esquerdes (1418–94), a knight of the Golden Fleece. Crèvecoeur-le-Grand is between Beauvais and Amiens; Esquerdes is south-east of Calais.

[377] Just east of Arras.

93

How the siege of Oudenaarde was raised by the Count of Étampes; and of the fine feats of arms performed there by Sir Jacques de Lalaing

Now we must speak of the valiant knight Sir Simon de Lalaing, besieged by the Ghenters in the city of Oudenaarde. As you've heard, he spent the night unblocking the city gates in preparation for a sortie against the Ghenters with his troops – and with the townsmen, too: they were all armed, and dearly hoping for aid, as all people under siege are bound to be. The moment they saw the count's forces approaching, they threw open the gates and began to sally forth, and the Ghenters raised the alarm. The Count of Étampes's men were now nearing the siege lines, and the lord of Saveuse and Sir Jacques de Lalaing, passionately eager to see his good uncle Sir Simon, were right out in front with about a hundred troops. They charged into the Ghenters, cutting down and killing all in their path. From the other direction rose a mighty roar from the men of the city as they inflicted terrible slaughter on the Ghenters. Nothing could be seen but men butchering and slaying, and the Ghenters fled in total disarray, abandoning their camp and their artillery, great and small, and all their provisions and their baggage, intent on saving nothing but their skins. They fled to a bridge they'd built across the Scheldt; some leapt into boats, in such numbers that the whole lot went to the bottom. The Ghenters had been lodging in and around a church, and a great many were slaughtered there.

Truly, before the count's main force arrived to confront them, fewer than a hundred men had routed them through the prowess and valiant conduct of Sir Jacques de Lalaing and his companions, who crushed the Ghenters by their mighty feats of arms. The besiegers on that side of the city were destroyed and put to flight. Some were slain and some were drowned; those who managed to escape went to join the besiegers on the other side of Oudenaarde, where their numbers were greatest. In this engagement[378] Sir Simon de Lalaing and the townsmen likewise showed their mettle and their courage, winning most of the Ghenters' artillery.

The Count of Étampes, still in fine, impressive order, advanced towards the Ghentish host but, as said above, they didn't wait to face him: they took to flight. Witnessing the rout, with all the besiegers on that side of the city dead or drowned or having fled across the Scheldt, the count rode into Oudenaarde

---

[378] There is ambiguity here. I have translated as 'in this engagement' but the MSS say 'there', which, given the sequence of sentences, might suggest that it refers to the siege-lines 'on the other side of Oudenaarde'. But it seems unlikely that the townsmen would have launched an attack there independently, especially given the passage that follows in which they advise the count to stay put. It seems far more probable that they made their sortie on the same side as the count's attack, and captured the artillery while Lalaing and the others were putting the Ghenters to flight.

where he was greeted with the utmost joy by the citizens, being held in high esteem there.

He was advised to stay and lodge in the city: they told him that the Ghenters on the further side were camped in huge numbers, that their camp was strongly fortified and they had plenty of artillery; they were there in all their pride, and among them were the captains[379] and governing body of Ghent. It would be best, they said, to let the Duke of Burgundy know what had happened and how things stood so that he could order matters as he chose, and the count decided to follow this advice. But I've heard it said since that if the count and his men, after the first line of besiegers had been routed and driven across the river, had gone on to attack those on the other side, it would have been the end of the Ghenters' war, for they wouldn't have dared stand and face him. But that's not what was done. The count billeted all his troops in the city of Oudenaarde.

And then, just as they were preparing to eat, news reached the count that the Ghenters had raised their siege some time before and were withdrawing in good order with their artillery, cannons and other gear. So the Count of Étampes sent his pursuivant of arms, Dourdan[380] by name, to inform the Duke of Burgundy at Grammont. When the duke received the news he ordered trumpets to sound and everyone to horse, intending to pursue the Ghenters.

Meanwhile, the count already knowing of their retreat, a good number of noble, valiant men mounted and rode from Oudenaarde and headed in pursuit. Sir Jacques de Lalaing and his men were the first to mount, followed by the lord of Moreuil, the lord of Rochefort, the lord of Lannoy, Robert de Miraumont and many more nobles and gentlemen. They rode off after the Ghenters, and through the valour of Sir Jacques and his company they made them abandon all their baggage and transport; they attacked at every narrow pass, and took the lives of many.

While this chase was under way, Allard de Rabodenghe,[381] Guiot de Béthune[382] and twenty troops had left the Duke of Burgundy's camp and ridden across country in search of adventure. They heard the commotion and saw the Ghenters on the move and headed after them. They found the valiant knight Sir Jacques de Lalaing leading the pursuit, and joined him. At one point the Ghenters stopped and made a stand with banner unfurled, whereupon the said Allard de Rabodenghe and Guiot de Béthune asked Sir Jacques to confer on them the order of knighthood, which he did, and they then performed most valiantly and chased the Ghenters to within a league

---

[379] '*haulx mans*': see note 339 above, p. 178.

[380] A name presumably referring to the castle of Dourdan, a few miles north-west of Étampes; one of the count's many titles was lord of Dourda(i)n.

[381] Lord of Moulle in Picardy, chamberlain of Duke Philip.

[382] '*Bectun*'.

and a half of the city of Ghent until their horses were blown. Several times the pursuers put themselves in grave danger, given how few they were: in all they numbered less than a hundred. [*f. 164r*]

94

How the Duke of Burgundy left Grammont in great haste to pursue the
Ghenters who had raised their siege

To return now to the Duke of Burgundy: as said above, when he was informed of the Ghenters' retreat, he and his men mounted and rode hard to catch them up; they carried on in hot pursuit, as fast as their horses could go, but couldn't catch them before they were almost at the city of Ghent. But Sir Jehan de Croÿ, determined to overtake them, kept pressing on with his company, and found a large number of the Ghenters resting, thinking they were clear of danger. Their main force was already back inside the city. When these Ghenters, resting, saw Sir Jehan de Croÿ coming, they drew up for battle, with a banner and two pennons, in a fine position near a windmill; and Sir Jehan, seeing the enemy in battle order, sent word to the Duke of Burgundy so that he would hurry. The duke, delighted by the news, thrust in his spurs and headed for the enemy with all speed, and when the Ghenters saw the size of the approaching force they broke and took to flight, running into woods and marshes and down to the river. Their banner and pennons were captured, and a good hundred or six-score of those who'd drawn up for battle were slain or drowned. The duke was sorry they'd so quickly fled, as there were several young squires in his company who dearly wished to be knighted and now feared the chance had gone; but they were to find the time and place soon enough.

Following this rout and chase, the duke withdrew and lodged that night in the town of Gavere, where the castle's garrison was firmly hostile.[383] Then he left next morning and returned to Grammont.

Regarding those killed and drowned at the lifting of the siege of Oudenaarde, the true numbers were never known; but it was said that from Ghent and the surrounding villages at least two thousand men were lost. If people had behaved properly the whole business would have been over and there would have been an end to the war which was to cost the lives of many valiant men.

Following this there was a good deal of action around Ghent and elsewhere which I'll pass over; I wish to move on and tell of the encounters involving that valiant knight Sir Jacques de Lalaing, whose story I wish to tell until his end – which was fast approaching, as you'll hear, and a great pity and loss it was. [*f. 165r*]

---

[383] The castle was in enemy hands: it had been taken by the Ghenters, above, p. 179.

95

How the lord of Lannoy, the lord of Humières and Sir Jacques de Lalaing made a foray to Lokeren, how Sir Jacques escaped from grave danger by his mighty prowess, and of the fine feats of arms he performed there

On the eighteenth day of the month, which was Ascension Day, the lord of Lannoy, the lord of Humières and Sir Jacques de Lalaing, all three of them knights of the Order of the Golden Fleece, mounted a foray into enemy territory; with them were the lord of Fretin,[384] Sir Jehan bastard of Renty[385] and Morelet de Renty[386] and around four hundred troops.

They rode to a village on the edge of the Waasland called Lokeren,[387] held by a very large body of men who were siding with the Ghenters. They had fortified the village with extensive bulwarks, and in several places had broken up the approach roads, digging ditches. Because of that – and concerned in any case about the heavy, difficult ground thereabouts – the aforenamed knights had brought with them ten pioneers[388] to repair the roads. They rode on till they found themselves at the first of the defences, but the Ghenters didn't hold the first earthwork or the second or the third or the fourth: they took to flight and fell back into Lokeren, well fortified as said above by ditches and ramparts; it also had a very fine church, where most of the Ghenters took refuge. The knights pressed on to the village and attacked the bulwark at the entrance. The moment the Ghenters saw them coming they fled, some into the church and others to the bridge over a great river called the Durme that runs out of the Waasland. They were determined to hold this bridge: they'd broken it down and over it laid a narrow plank, which even men on foot could cross only at great peril; and they had two boats below with crossbowmen on board, ready to guard the crossing and the bridge, now raised. It was one of the routes into the Waasland, an area the Ghenters were especially keen to hold: it was their main source of food and aid and support, so they were very concerned and afraid of losing it.

When Sir Jacques de Lalaing and the other nobles with him saw the Ghenters abandoning the entrance to this village of Lokeren, they crossed a ditch – a foul and dangerous passage – and followed them, both on foot and horse, as they fled, some to the church and others to the bridge. There at the

---

[384] Just south of Lille.

[385] In Picardy, west of Béthune.

[386] Morelet was captain of archers in Duke Philip's household.

[387] About 15 miles east of Ghent; the Waasland is an area of East Flanders stretching towards Antwerp.

[388] In military terms, a pioneer is a member of the infantry preparing ground for the main body.

bridge a fierce skirmish began between the Ghenters on the further bank and the Duke of Burgundy's men who, seeing them ready to mount a defence, launched an assault upon the bridge. The first to attack was a squire from Brittany named Jehan de la Forest.[389] While the assault was under way – and dangerous it was indeed – a trumpeter who was with them found a ford across the river Durme; Sir Jacques de Lalaing crossed there with a good hundred men, and when the Ghenters saw them coming they all turned tail and fled into the woods and marshes.

We'll now turn back and explain the division of troops made by the three knights leading this foray. This is how it was: Sir Jacques de Lalaing and Morelet de Renty were in charge of the scouts, riding ahead and prepared to fight on foot if need be; Sir Jehan bastard of Renty commanded the archers; the lord of Humières and the lord of Lannoy led the main battalion.

Returning now to the village of Lokeren: when Sir Jacques de Lalaing and Morelet de Renty had broken into the village and gone after the Ghenters, chasing some to the church and others to the bridge as said above, Sir Jehan de Renty headed with a number of his archers to a crossroads where one path led to the church and one of the others ran down to the river. He held that position for the time being, well placed to deal with any sortie by the three or four hundred Ghenters who'd retreated to the church. As for the lord of Humières and the lord of Lannoy, they didn't cross the difficult passage at the entrance to the village, and the colours stayed there with them and the main battalion.

So, returning to Sir Jacques de Lalaing: he forded the river and chased the Ghenters as they fled to the woods as fast as they could run with the Picards in pursuit killing all they overtook; then he went back across the river and into the village of Lokeren. There he found Sir Jehan bastard of Renty at the crossroads where the path led to the church. He started telling him what had happened at the river and how they'd found the ford. While they were talking the lord of Fretin came up and said that the lord of Humières and the lord of Lannoy had sent him to say it was best to withdraw, for there was more likelihood of loss than gain. Sir Jacques replied that there were three or four hundred Ghenters in the church, and that he should tell this to the lords of Lannoy and Humières; if they wanted to attack them, they should come on through with the main battalion, but if they wanted to withdraw without further action they should send word to that effect. Then he said to Sir Jehan bastard of Renty:

'Stay here and guard against any sortie from the church. I'm going to fetch our men who're still on the other side of the river and bring them back to join us in whatever's decided: to attack the church or withdraw.'

Then Sir Jacques, eager to see this action through, rode swiftly down to the river with just seven of his men, and crossed and then returned, heading

---

[389] Hervé de Mériadec's nephew.

briskly back to where he'd left Sir Jehan. Sir Jacques was riding a little horse without using the stirrups because he'd been a long time on his feet. And as he returned to the bridge he saw that fire had been newly started in two houses at the bridge's end and also in one of the boats. He didn't know who'd done this. He had with him only seven men, as said above: the rest were following after. They were expecting to find Sir Jehan bastard of Renty at the crossroads where the Ghenters could break out from the church, but he'd left and returned to the two lords – Lannoy and Humières, that is – to find out what their decision was and what they wished to do. His men had gone with him, and because there was the difficult passage to negotiate, in their eagerness to get ahead and be the first across they were in total disarray and many of their horses were stuck in the mud. They abandoned them in their haste to get away, as if they were men fleeing from a rout, without waiting for each other or seeing anyone in pursuit. They'd no idea why they were doing this, except that the cowards among them were yelling:

'There are six thousand coming to cut us off!'

Because of these cries, and with the roads being broken up and riven with ditches, and so overgrown with trees and bulky hedges that the battalion couldn't see the vanguard, nor the vanguard the scouts, nor the scouts their foremost riders, many were so stricken with fear that the brave couldn't reassure them. And thanks to this disorder – and because Sir Jehan bastard of Renty had not stayed put at the crossroads – the noble knight Sir Jacques de Lalaing and his men were all in grave danger of being captured or slain. If only Sir Jehan the bastard had sent one of his men to the two knights none of this would have happened. Shepherdless sheep, as the saying goes, are hopeless.

But the good knight Sir Jacques de Lalaing knew nothing of this shambles. He rode smartly back from the river with his seven men, and the others following behind, expecting to find Sir Jehan bastard of Renty at the crossroads where he'd left him. But a pursuivant of arms named Talent[390] appeared and told him to beware, for the enemy were coming to cut him off: they were out of the church and already at the crossroads – Sir Jehan and his men had retreated over the passage back out of the village. When Sir Jacques heard this and realised the peril he was in, he dismounted and, with great courage and daring, fearless of mortal danger, and seeing the enemy at hand, exhorted his men to fight well. He and his men drove into the enemy, and by force of arms and the mighty prowess he possessed, he sent them reeling back, killing and felling them before him, cutting off legs and arms; his men did likewise. Truly, so many dead and wounded lay around them that it would be hardly credible had it not been seen by worthy men who reliably reported to the Duke of Burgundy. Sir Jacques de Lalaing performed so many fine deeds of arms

[390] Gilles Gobet: see Introduction, p. 2. '*Talent*' in medieval French implies 'keenness', 'ardour', rather than its English sense.

that he forced the enemy blocking his path to fall back and rejoin the main body of the Ghenters' army. Thanks to this, his brother Sir Philippe de Lalaing and other noble men and archers returning from across the river were able to make it past the crossroads where the Ghenters had tried to cut them off. Sir Jacques, now with just three others, fought off the Ghenters until all his troops and the rest had managed to get past. They went as far as the entrance to the village but didn't cross the passage: they waited for Sir Jacques who, once he was sure there was no one left behind, retreated in great danger to the passage, where he found his brother Sir Philippe, Arnoul de Hérimez, Jacques de Gouÿ and others. Beyond the passage the lord of Humières, Sir Pedro Vásquez, the lord of Fretin and five or six others were waiting for him: they'd returned to find out what had happened to him, for those who'd fled had gone around bawling that he and all his men were dead, and when the lord of Humières realised that Sir Jacques was still in grave peril, and that the Ghenters had sallied from the church in force and were attacking Sir Jacques and his fellows with all their might, he'd gone and called back some of his men to go to his aid. On the way he'd met the lord of Lannoy and the lord of Fretin, valiant knights both, who'd readily returned to help and support Sir Jacques, the lord of Lannoy saying to Humières:

'That worthy knight Sir Jacques de Lalaing must not be left behind! Others can be gone if they wish, but for my part, I'm staying for him!'

The lords of Humières and Fretin said the same, and tried to rally men to go to his aid; but none would stay: most were setting off in disorder. They found one of Sir Jacques's men, his standard-bearer, who hadn't in the first place crossed the passage; he diligently went to join his good master now, and never thereafter left his side and fought with him most bravely.

Returning now to Sir Jacques de Lalaing, who by his valour and courage had saved those left behind, as he reached the foul passage he said to his brother Sir Philippe:

'Go on, brother! You must get across! Here come the Ghenters, pursuing us in force!'

So Sir Philippe set about crossing, but was so bogged down in the mire that no one could reach him – and he wasn't alone: no one could get across save in mortal danger because of the crowd of horses stuck there, abandoned by their masters who'd fled. And when the Ghenters saw Sir Jacques with so few men they rushed to the attack, and he had an even harder time now than before. But by his bravery and mighty prowess he saved them all, except four archers who were slain there. And at least twenty horses were lost, either killed or captured. There at the passage courage and daring had to be shown, or it was death; for most of the main battalion and the rest were already far away from this foul and perilous passage – all except the aforenamed lords of Humières and Lannoy, Sir Pedro Vásquez and the lord of Fretin and just a handful of men. As for the passage, it was so bad that hardly any men or horses had crossed without falling in, and many were so plastered with filth that they looked as if they'd been dragged right through a vat of cream.[391] In winter it's one of the worst places to get through in the whole of Flanders. Two valiant noblemen from Portugal were present, and having witnessed all the fighting their comment was:

'The courage and daring of a single knight, Sir Jacques de Lalaing, have saved the lives of more than three hundred men this day, and preserved the whole company from dire shame.'

They also said they'd heard that this Sir Jacques had fought eighteen combats in the lists, and emerged with honour all eighteen times, but in their view he'd fought as honourably that day, and won as much honour, as he'd done in his whole life previously – though it was a fine thing that so young a knight, only thirty or so, had fought eighteen contests in the lists.

Once Sir Jacques and his companions had managed to cross the passage, and the action described above was over, they headed back towards Dendermonde.[392] Sir Jacques provided the rearguard with just a very few men, and Ghenters launched an attack on him, but he valiantly drove them back to their bulwarks with two Ghenters being slain. They didn't try to come after him again – except one man on his own: he came up unexpectedly and they asked him:

'Who goes there?'

And he answered: 'Ghent!' – which was, I believe, the last word he ever uttered.

And that was how the battle at Lokeren ended. [f. 170r]

96

Of the Ghenters' boasts after their return to Ghent, and of the attack on Overmere, where Sir Jacques de Lalaing performed many brave deeds

Mention must be made of the Ghenters' boasts next day: back in the city of Ghent they bragged to the people that in the village of Lokeren they'd killed two or three hundred of the Duke of Burgundy's men. They'd done nothing of the kind: the truth was that the only losses were those given above.

It was not long after the battle that the duke held council in his fine town of Dendermonde. Present that day were the Count of Saint-Pol, the lord of Croÿ, the lord of Créquy, Sir Jehan de Croÿ, the lord of Montaigu, the lord of

---

[391] '*tout au long du pot a la crayme*': the definite rather than indefinite article ('*du*' rather than '*d'un*') suggests the possibility that this refers not to a vat of cream (evocative though the image is) but to the nickname at that time of a notoriously foul stretch of land in Flanders. I've left it as the former.

[392] About 7 miles south-east of Lokeren.

Lannoy, the lord of Humières, the lord of Ternant[393] and the lord of Pissy.[394] After much discussion and debate it was decided that an assault should be made upon a strong fort held by the Ghenters near a village called Overmere, about halfway between Dendermonde and Ghent.[395] It was ordered thus: the lord of Croÿ would guard the Duke of Burgundy's standard and lead the men of the duke's court to form the vanguard; Sir Jacques de Lalaing would take charge of the scouts, accompanied by Sir Anthoine de Vaudrey and his brother Sir Guillaume,[396] the lord of Aumont and Sir François the Aragonese;[397] Sir Jacques had about twenty-five lances and eighty archers. A gentleman from Burgundy named Anthoine de Laviron[398] was to lead an advance scouting party of seven or eight lances.

This Sir Anthoine went ahead of Sir Jacques; after Sir Jacques went Sir Daviot de Poix,[399] governor and master of the duke's artillery, leading the pioneers and infantry carrying axes, bill-hooks, saws and drills to break down barricades, fill in ditches and remake roads where needed. After Sir Daviot de Poix went the lord of Lannoy and the lord of Bassignies[400] at the head of some hundred troops to support and reinforce Sir Jacques if the need arose. After the lord of Lannoy went the lord of Créquy, and with him the lord of Contay[401] and Morelet de Renty, leading the archers of the duke's guard. After the lord of Créquy was the lord of Croÿ with the Duke of Burgundy's standard, and accompanying the standard were my lord Adolph of Cleves, my lord the bastard of Burgundy, the lord of Montaigu, the lord of Arcis,[402] the lord of Ternant, the lord of Berzé,[403] the lord of Pernes,[404] Philippe de Bergues[405] and a great many other knights and squires. After the lord of Croÿ came the Count of Saint-Pol and his brothers the lord of Fiennes and Jacques de Saint-Pol,

---

[393] Philippe de Ternant, a councillor of Duke Philip and member of the Order of the Golden Fleece. Ternant is in Burgundy, west of Chalon-sur-Saône.

[394] This is probably a rendering of Pisy (in Burgundy), as lord of Pisy was one of the titles of 'François the Aragonese', who is about to be mentioned below.

[395] Overmere is about 12 miles east of Ghent.

[396] Two prominent courtiers; Vaudrey was a family of note in the Franche-Comté.

[397] This is François de Surienne (c.1398–1462), a mercenary from Aragon noted for his expertise with artillery and military engineering. He had fought for both the English and the French before entering Duke Philip's service.

[398] East of Besançon.

[399] David de Poix, lord of La Verrière, an experienced campaigner but, to be precise, not appointed master of the artillery until 1453.

[400] Philippe I de Hornes, mentioned above, pp. 185, 186, 187.

[401] North-east of Amiens.

[402] Jean de Poitiers, lord of Arcis, mentioned above, p. 78.

[403] In Burgundy, north-west of Mâcon.

[404] In Artois, west of Béthune.

[405] Lord of Grimbergen, north of Brussels.

and other great lords with knights and squires in great numbers; the count was commanding the main battalion. After him, leading the rearguard, came Sir Jehan de Croÿ with a splendid company of knights, squires and bowmen.

And so it was that on Wednesday the twenty-fourth of May all the above-named companies set out from Dendermonde to attack the fort at Overmere, with orders given to return by way of the village of Lokeren mentioned above. But it so happened that after the lord of Croÿ had crossed the bridge from Dendermonde with about four or five hundred archers and six-score men at arms, a break appeared in the bridge. It looked as if it wouldn't be possible to repair it in less than four or five hours, so the Duke of Burgundy told the lord of Croÿ to press on with all who had already crossed and go and attack the said fort. The lord of Croÿ was pleased to do so and set off, but thanks to the duke's personal diligence and the great efforts of the people of Dendermonde, the bridge was repaired in less than an hour, so that the Count of Saint-Pol, Sir Jehan de Croÿ and all the others who were ready to go could now cross. They numbered a good two thousand, and the aforesaid lords advanced in the order given above.

The scouts rode ahead until they caught sight of the Ghenters emerging from their fort and marching with pennons unfurled as if to do battle. They were reckoned to number between eight hundred and a thousand. But they were coming only to defend a deep ditch about a bowshot ahead of their earthworks. When Sir Jacques de Lalaing and the noble knights and squires with him saw them advancing, they dismounted and drew up in fine order. Following behind came the next battalion with Sir Daviot de Poix. At this point Golden-Fleece, King of Arms of the Fleece, was right at the front with Sir Jacques; seeing the Ghenters marching forward in battle order with trumpets sounding and apparently intending to engage, he went to find those leading the vanguard, the main battalion and the rearguard, and proclaimed for all to hear:

'If any squire or other man wishes to be knighted, I'll take them to a fine place for it: right before the enemy!'

This he said to the lord of Croÿ, who was overjoyed, as were many of the lords and nobles present who greatly desired to be knights. The lord of Croÿ replied:

'Go, Golden-Fleece, and lead us to the place you say, where you've seen our foes the Ghenters!'

Hearing this news of the enemy from Golden-Fleece, all the lords rode on eagerly with their divisions, preparing to attack the foe as planned. But they couldn't advance in battalion because of the roads, which were so very narrow that they could only proceed in companies.

When the lord of Croÿ came to where Golden-Fleece now led him, several great lords came before him and requested the order of chivalry. The following were knighted there, some by the hand of the lord of Croÿ and some by Adolph of Cleves once he himself had received the order of knighthood by the hand of the valiant knight Corneille, bastard of Burgundy: first to be knighted were Sir Adolph of Cleves and Corneille, bastard of Burgundy; the Earl of Buchan;[406] Sir Philippe de Wavrin, lord of Saint-Venant; Sir Charles de Chalon; Sir Philippe de Croÿ; Sir Charles de Ternant; the lord of Pernes; Sir Philippe de Bergues; the lord of Arcis; Sir Michel de Chaugy; Sir Friedrich von Mengerstreut; Sir Baudoin d'Oignies, governor of Lille; Sir Claude de Rochebaron; Sir Philibert de Jaucourt; Sir Crestien de Digoine; the lord of Humbercourt; Sir Watier de Renolt; Sir Colard Baillet; Sir Louis de la Viefville; Sir Yvain de Mol; Sir Henri de Ophem; Sir Philippe Hinckaert; Sir Warnier de Linsmeau; Jehan de la Trémoïlle, lord of Daours.[407]

The above-named having been knighted, the lord of Croÿ and all of them dismounted and marched towards the enemy, who had a great ditch in front of them and looked fiercely determined to defend it. These Ghenters were attacked most valiantly: archers began to shoot upon them, and the assault then began with a mighty roar from our men. The Count of Saint-Pol, leading the main battalion, joined the vanguard diligently. So did Sir Jehan de Croÿ, who had command of the rearguard; but the plan was to hold his troops together in case the Ghenters had men behind or to the side: the land round about was so thick with bushes that you couldn't see further than half a bowshot, so the Ghenters could manoeuvre and rally with more speed and stealth than would have been possible in open country. So Sir Jehan ordered a noble knight to take charge of his troops while he for his part rode to join the others as said above.

The attack upon the Ghenters was ferocious, and at the very forefront was Sir Jacques de Lalaing. And as soon as the Ghenters saw the might of the assault, they broke and took to flight. The lords, men at arms and archers, keeping excellent order and array, followed and chased them all the way to their bulwark. It was strong and could well have been held, but the Ghenters abandoned it without attempting to resist, despite the fact that the ditch before it was too deep to cross, which is why they were able to escape and flee into the thickets, marshes and alder woods.[408]

The lords, thinking they would have retreated to the church in Overmere, some half a French league beyond the bulwark, headed towards it on foot and horseback, expecting to find the Ghenters there. But they found no one:

[406] 'le conte de Bouquam': see note 356 above, p. 184.

[407] Of those not previously noted, the newly knighted figures listed here come from Picardy (Humbercourt, Oignies, Saint-Venant, Daours), Champagne (Jaucourt), Burgundy (Chalon, Chaugy, Digoine), Franconia (Mengerstreut), Limburg (Colard Baillet), Hainaut (Viefville), Brabant (Linsmeau) and Flanders (Ophem). Yvain de Mol was from Ledeberg, now part of Ghent. Almost all are recorded as having positions in the household of Duke Philip or of his third wife, Isabella of Portugal.

[408] Alder is mentioned specifically because it grows abundantly in wetlands such as there in Flanders.

they'd all run off to the woods and marshes. Sir Jehan de Croÿ, Sir Jacques de Lalaing, Sir François the Aragonese and a number of others halted there outside the church. Then Sir Jehan ordered the forest bailiff[409] of the county of Hainaut to lead a body of troops beyond Overmere and head towards Ghent; it had been reported that on the way there were two bulwarks manned by Ghenters: he was to reconnoitre and see if this was true. The bailiff went that way but found no one there, and returned to Sir Jehan de Croÿ and Sir Jacques de Lalaing, who were waiting for him outside Overmere church. [f. 173v]

97

More about this foray, in which a great many Ghenters were slain
and routed and put to flight

When Sir Jehan de Croÿ heard the bailiff's report that he had found no one, he asked a number of the lords present what they thought was the best next move. Sir Jacques de Lalaing, seeing no one reply, said:

'Sir, I think it would be best if I went to the Count of Saint-Pol and the lord of Croÿ to find out what's to be done.'

And so it was: Sir Jacques went to them and they discussed how to proceed. They decided to head to Lokeren where, as described above, the Ghenters were defending a great bulwark. They told Sir Jacques to gather his men and take the road to Lokeren, and so he did.

Wishing with all his heart to win praise and high renown, as soon as he had his men together he set out smartly for Lokeren. He had almost all his company except Sir François the Aragonese: he stayed behind with Sir Jehan de Croÿ, and they were both informed of what had been planned.

And then, as soon as Sir Jacques and his company started marching towards Lokeren, which was about a league and a half from Overmere, they saw at least a thousand Ghenters heading straight towards them. These Ghenters hadn't been able to see the fighting that had happened, but they'd heard the noise quite clearly, not to mention the bells sounding the alarm to the surrounding country. That's why they'd rallied together; and now they were aiming to attack and rout the forces of the Duke of Burgundy, their natural lord. They were marching with fierce intent, in battle order and with colours flying. Seeing them advancing so, Sir Jacques de Lalaing told Sir Anthoine and Sir Guillaume de Vaudrey, the lord of Aumont, Sir Pedro Vásquez and five or six others to remain on horseback while he dismounted, which he

---

[409] '*le bailli des bois*': the officer in medieval Hainaut responsible for protecting comital / ducal rights over woodland and for guarding against illicit hunting, gathering of wood, etc. At this time the office was held by Jacques de Harchies (west of Mons).

did straightway, crying a loud alarm and bidding the trumpets sound, and a mighty blast it was indeed. The Ghenters, it's fair to suppose, had no idea of the numbers present, but were trusting in the rough, restricting nature of their land and thinking they could take the duke's men by surprise and in disorder; for it was a wide expanse of heather-strewn terrain, and the ditches that lay between them made it very hard for the duke's men to attack.

The Count of Saint-Pol and the lord of Croÿ and the fine battalion of nobles and knights were soon there and all arrayed for battle; but the trouble was that they could see no way to attack the enemy, and they all sought separately to right and left. It was on the right, where Sir Jacques had gone, that the Ghenters were first broken: there the two Vaudrey brothers fought most valiantly on horseback, along with the lord of Aumont, Sir Pedro Vásquez, Chaumergy[410] and a number of other noble knights and squires, charging into the Ghenters. At the far end of that right flank Sir Jacques, with his men and others on foot, performed with very great valour. As for the left, it was impossible for any horse to pass, but those who attacked on foot did splendidly. In the centre no one could get through at all, so deep and foul were the ditches, but in several other places they strove to force a passage. Without a doubt, had there been a clear line of attack no Ghenter would have escaped death or capture. As it was, it wasn't long before their pride was crushed and they were routed and put to flight. In all, four or five hundred of the Ghenters were slain, both there and in the ditches and alder woods where they tried to flee – including those Sir Jehan de Croÿ ran into as he rode back from the church at Overmere – and also in the earlier assault upon the fort. Some thirty prisoners were taken, too, who were later all beheaded at the duke's command in the town of Dendermonde.

Following this last encounter, the planned advance to Lokeren was abandoned for that day for two reasons: firstly because it was where the captured men had come from and they told them they would find no one there; and secondly because the Count of Saint-Pol and Sir Jehan de Croÿ had their lodgings in Aalst, a good four leagues from the place where they'd beaten the Ghenters.[411] The decision was made to return to Dendermonde without going on to Lokeren, and so they did. On the way Sir Jehan de Croÿ led the vanguard, and behind him came the Count of Saint-Pol and then the lord of Croÿ, and Sir Jacques de Lalaing and his company formed the rearguard. In places many houses were set afire that day. [*f. 175v*]

---

410 Olivier de la Marche refers to Jehan de Chaumergy as 'first esquire of the stable' at Duke Philip's court. Chaumergy is in Burgundy, to the east of Chalon.

411 And it would have been even further back if they'd gone on to Lokeren: i.e. they had a longer return journey than those lodged with the duke at Dendermonde.

98

How the Count of Étampes by force of arms twice took the town of
Nevele from the Ghenters, who were slain and routed and put to flight

Now we shall return to that noble, gentle knight Jehan de Bourgogne, Count of Étampes.[412] On the twenty-fourth day of May he left the city of Oudenaarde accompanied by several great lords, with men at arms and crossbowmen and archers, having heard that the Ghenters had marched from their city in mighty force, heading in the direction of Tielt;[413] some said they meant to lay siege to the town of Ingelmunster.[414] He set up camp that day at a village called Harelbeke,[415] ready to advance on the Ghenters, and there he ordered his battalions: he gave charge of the vanguard to Sir Anthoine, bastard of Burgundy; the lord of Saveuse, Sir Gauvain Quiéret, lord of Dreuil and others were to ride ahead as scouts; the Count of Étampes would command the main battalion, and there would be no rearguard.

The count was then informed that the Ghenters had occupied a town called Nevele,[416] which was enclosed with gates and ditches, and they were manning a strong bulwark in front of the gate on the Courtrai side. The roads leading to this bulwark had been broken up and pitted, and in the cornfields they'd fixed crossed stakes in the ground so that horses couldn't pass.

The party of scouts and the vanguard dismounted to attack this bulwark, while men at arms and archers crossed the ditches outside the town, the water coming up to their chins. Then the archers started shooting at the Ghenters from the flanks and sides, so fiercely that they broke and took to flight in disarray. By force of arms and valour Nevele was taken as the Ghenters abandoned the town and fled, desperate to escape, for there was no question of ransom or mercy: anyone who was caught would be put to the sword. The fugitives headed for the city of Ghent, except some from the surrounding villages who hid in the hedges and bushes.

The Count of Étampes, seeing the town was taken, ordered some of his captains to hunt down the fleeing Ghenters; Sir Anthoine bastard of Burgundy went in pursuit, carrying his standard, as did the lord of Wavrin, the lord of Rubempré,[417] Sir Gauvain Quiéret and others. Those who stayed in Nevele started searching and foraging and taking everything they could find.

---

[412] Last seen at the raising of the siege of Oudenaarde, above, pp. 184–91.

[413] Tielt is some 20 miles west of Ghent and the same distance north-west of Oudenaarde.

[414] About 7 miles beyond Tielt to the south-west.

[415] 5 miles south of Ingelmunster.

[416] Halfway between Ghent and Tielt.

[417] Anthoine II, lord of Rubempré, chamberlain of Duke Philip; Rubempré is in Picardy, just north of Amiens.

It wasn't long before the surrounding land was filled with the clamour of the fugitives and the pursuing lords. Then bells began to peal in the towns and villages round about, and such was the alarm that every last man began to arm. Some grabbed their pikes, others clubs or swords; fully five hundred peasants now assembled. Those pursuing the Ghenters were unaware of this, and carried on, intent on hunting them down, and caught a good many and put them to death.

Meanwhile the band of peasants who'd gathered were told by some of those escaping from Nevele that very few troops had stayed behind in the town, and that if they wanted they could easily win it back. The peasants, rejoicing at this news, not imagining what was to befall them, rushed ahead till they were nearing Nevele. The troops inside the town heard the racket and commotion that they made as they came, and some twenty men at arms and archers, foremost among them Sir Anthoine de Hérin, set off and headed to where they could hear the approaching Ghenters. They opened the barrier and crossed the bridge and marched to meet the enemy without knowing their strength: they couldn't get a clear sight of them as they were advancing down a narrow lane. They gave a cry and attacked the Ghenters and drove them back; but the Ghenters, seeing the count's men in such small numbers, took heart, and without more ado they fell upon them and forced [Sir Anthoine and his company back to the bridge beside the barrier. And there they slew][418] Sir Anthoine de Hérin, which was a grievous pity, for he was deemed to be a valiant knight. And with him died a gentleman from the Dauphiné named Cibois Pelerin, Charles de Moroges from Burgundy, Rollequin le Prévost, Rouely and Oudart Hatterel from Picardy and two other gentlemen whose names I don't know.[419]

The Count of Étampes was most displeased when he heard that they'd been killed, for the fact is that if Sir Anthoine and his company had kept the barrier closed and not thrown it open the Ghenters would never have got through: the count had been there on the other side of the town, knowing nothing of the attack, keeping his men in battle order, waiting for the scouts and vanguard to return from their pursuit. As the saying goes: act in haste, repent at leisure.[420] Had Sir Anthoine de Hérin and his men not been so hasty and rushed out to meet the Ghenters without any sight or knowledge of their numbers, the fate you've heard would not have befallen him. [*f. 178v*]

---

[418] Accidentally omitted in MS 16830 because of the repetition of the name; translated from Lettenhove's edition, p. 273.

[419] Anthoine de Hérin and Cibois Pelerin were both members of the ducal court, Charles de Moroges was from the Count of Étampes's household, but the identities of Rollequin and the Hatterels are uncertain.

[420] Literally 'great haste always brings repentance in its wake'.

99

How the Count of Étampes recaptured the town of Nevele from the Ghenters

So the Count of Étampes was outside Nevele with his battalion, waiting for those who'd ridden in pursuit; and when he heard that the Ghenters had won the town back from his men, having broken in and slain those who'd gone to face them, he was greatly troubled, and not without cause. He called Sir Simon de Lalaing, that noble knight entrusted with his standard, and sought his advice on what to do. Sir Simon replied, saying:

'Sir, the town must be won back from these rogues immediately, without delay. If we dally at all before we attack, my fear is the word will quickly spread and the peasants will rise on all sides and come flocking to support their men. What's more, those of yours who've gone in pursuit know nothing of this and won't be able to return to you without great danger, and they're the flower, the most acclaimed of all your company.'

Then the Count of Étampes commanded that everyone dismount, and that his standard be given to a gentleman from the Nivernais named Philibert Bourgoing, reputed to be a most valiant man, brave and bold in arms; and indeed, he was to show his worth that day. Then he gave orders for the trumpets to sound the attack, and Sir Simon de Lalaing and his men at arms and archers launched a fierce assault, and the Ghenters started fighting back.

It was now, as the attack was under way, that the scouts and vanguard returned: that's to say, Sir Anthoine bastard of Burgundy with his standard, the lord of Wavrin, the lord of Rubempré and Sir Gauvain Quiéret. They arrived at the town expecting to ride straight in, but as they drew near they heard the clamour and din of the assault and realised the Ghenters had retaken Nevele. So they went and joined the count and his men in attacking from every side, until at last the town of Nevele was reconquered and won back from the Ghenters. The Bastard of Burgundy and the other lords broke into the town from two directions, as did the Count of Étampes's forces. Most of the Ghenters were slaughtered on the spot. Those who fled and tried to get away took refuge on a motte surrounded by water; they were attacked there and all put to death: not a single one escaped.

The battle over, the Count of Étampes and his company set out and returned to the village of Harelbeke where he'd spent the previous night. On the way back, at certain narrow points along the route, he found trees newly felled since he'd passed that way that morning. Here bands of peasants lay in ambush, bent on inflicting damage on the count and his men on their return; and they did indeed attack, these peasants or Ghenters springing from the trees and corn and alder clumps where they were hidden. Three of the count's men were slain, two of them being noblemen, one by the name of Jehan de Inde and the other Charles de Héronval. As for the Ghenters or peasants, between three and four hundred were struck down and killed. That day, inside Nevele, during the pursuit and on the motte and including this final fighting, the Ghenters lost a good thousand men and more, as those who were present testified.

When all was over, the count returned to Harelbeke and next day to the city of Oudenaarde where he was garrisoned. [*f. 180r*]

100

How the nations of merchants in Bruges[421] and ambassadors of the King of France came to the duke in an attempt to make a treaty between the duke and the Ghenters, but without success; and of the expedition to Rupelmonde where the Ghenters were routed

In the course of all this, the nations of merchants had gone from Bruges to Ghent in the hope of forging some kind of treaty between the prince and the Ghenters. But no terms discussed for any truce or cessation of hostilities would they observe; the more favourable the terms, the less they kept their promises. Nonetheless the King of France, to try to secure a sound agreement between the Duke of Burgundy and the people of Ghent, sent an embassy – but they achieved nothing; talks were held for many days at Lille, in Brussels and elsewhere, but to no avail, and the war continued, more bitter and more deadly than before.

For the duke, enraged by the great disloyalty and malice of the Ghenters, marched from the city of Dendermonde on the thirteenth day of the month,[422] and with all the forces he then had with him headed to cross the river Scheldt at Rupelmonde.[423] With him went his only son the Count of Charolais,[424] the Duke of Cleves and his brother Adolph, Sir Corneille bastard of Burgundy, the lord of Croÿ, count of Porcien, the Count of Horn, the lord of Créquy, the lord of Montaigu, the lord of Lalaing,[425] the lord of Ternant, the lord of Humières, Sir Jacques de Lalaing, the lord of Wavrin, the lord of Bassignies, the lord of Arcis, Sir Charles de Chalon and many other great lords.

At Rupelmonde was a large village which the Ghenters had razed to the ground, but because the place where the village had stood was surrounded by ditches it was decided to station eight hundred or a thousand troops in the ruins

[421] Foreign merchants in Bruges were organised into 'nations' according to their countries of origin.

[422] June (1452). The compiler of *The Book of the Deeds* accidentally fails to include the name of the month; in the preceding paragraph he has briefly summarised a lengthy passage in the chronicle from which he has taken this section which details the failed peace negotiations.

[423] About 15 miles north-east of Dendermonde on the road to Antwerp.

[424] i.e. his only legitimate son and heir, Charles.

[425] i.e. Jacques's father.

before the Ghenters could occupy the place – if they did they could block the crossing of the duke and his men at Rupelmonde. Two notable knights, Sir François the Aragonese and the lord of Contay, had been sent to secure this position a day before the duke set out. Sir François went by river,[426] taking several boats, barges and ferry-craft, and passed on the way a good number of the enemy who attacked and assaulted him fiercely several times. But in spite of them he led his fleet to Rupelmonde while the lord of Contay rode there, and they made camp and guarded the position till the duke arrived. That same day, after the Count of Saint-Pol and Sir Jehan de Croÿ had crossed the river at Rupelmonde, they camped there in the open, everything having been burnt by the Ghenters.

The Duke of Burgundy now crossed the Scheldt, accompanied by those of his blood and the main battalion of men at arms and archers, and encamped there likewise at Rupelmonde. Their numbers being so great, two notable men were instructed to see that the crossing was made in due order; all the men under the duke's standard went first, then Sir Jacques de Lalaing and his company, followed by the others; behind them came Sir Daviot de Poix, master of the artillery, who was also in charge of the train of carts of the merchants supplying provisions followed by more of the baggage train organised by the provost marshal; finally came the rearguard. And they all made camp there in the fields.

It wasn't long before news reached the duke that his enemies the Ghenters had entered the village of Bazel, just a quarter of a league from where he was camped at Rupelmonde.[427] The Count of Saint-Pol and Sir Jehan de Croÿ took to horse, and found the Ghenters arrayed for battle, with artillery and pavises[428] before them; but the Ghenters were quickly broken, some fleeing to the church there in Bazel, others into hedges and bushes, and some to a fort nearby. They couldn't hold the church and it was taken by force; then the fort was attacked and they surrendered to the Count of Saint-Pol on behalf and in the name of the Duke of Burgundy.

But while this assault on the fort was under way, some Ghenters had gathered and attacked the men guarding the assailants' horses. Sir Jehan de Croÿ and the Count of Saint-Pol's brother the lord of Fiennes were mounted with some forty lances, and took the brunt of the attack, holding their ground till the rest of their force reassembled. The alarm was raised on all sides, and was heard by the Duke of Burgundy. He'd only just arrived at Rupelmonde and hadn't eaten or drunk that day though it was at least four in the afternoon. But it was his custom to fast on bread and water on four days of the week:

---

[426] Rupelmonde, like Dendermonde, stands on the Scheldt.

[427] Bazel is about a mile and a half to the north.

[428] The pavise was a large shield, usually body-length, used especially by crossbowmen and archers.

Monday, Wednesday, Friday and Saturday; and as soon as he heard the alarm he set off towards it, accompanied by the lord of Croÿ and a number of others, to aid and support the Count of Saint-Pol and Sir Jehan de Croÿ. But even before they arrived, Fiennes and Sir Jehan had overcome the Ghenters: those lords had performed most valiantly, Sir Jehan being wounded in the right foot by a crossbow bolt.[429]

So the Ghenters were defeated and put to flight twice that day and lost around two hundred men; they would have lost still more had the country round about not been thick with hedges and riven with ditches so that they couldn't be quickly caught when they started fleeing: because of that they were able to escape. [*f. 182r*]

101

Of the battle fought near Rupelmonde called the battle of Bazel where the Ghenters were slaughtered in great numbers, and of the danger faced by Sir Jacques de Saint-Pol[430] and how he was rescued from the Ghenters

On the Friday following, the duke ordered the burial of the dead. He entrusted the task to Louis de Masmines[431] and the King of Arms of Flanders with forty or fifty pioneers.

And while they were in the middle of the burying, into view at that very place came an army of Ghenters, thirteen or fourteen thousand strong, with banners, wagons, pavises, culverins and artillery; and about a quarter of a league from Rupelmonde they drew up in order of battle in a strong position, enclosing themselves with their wagons and pavises, and there they stood for more than an hour. Throughout the duke's army came the call to arms, and the Count of Saint-Pol and Sir Jehan de Croÿ, commanding the vanguard, left camp and set their men in battle order, in fine array. A little behind and to the side of the vanguard was the Duke of Burgundy with his main battalion. The Duke of Cleves was sent to guard an approach that the Ghenters might take to the camp at Rupelmonde; he'd come straight from his land of Cleves, most diligently, to join and serve his uncle the duke in the Waasland where he expected there'd be a battle, as indeed there was. He was sent to guard this approach as said, accompanied by his brother Sir Adolph of Cleves, the Count of Horn, the lord of Lalaing, the lord of Ternant, Sir Simon de Lalaing, charged with the Count of Étampes's standard, and a number of others.

[429] Specifically a '*vireton*', a bolt with feathers set at an angle to make it spin in flight.

[430] i.e. the lord of Fiennes.

[431] Lord of Grammene (west of Ghent), a squire of the duke's household.

While the duke's battalions were being deployed, several noble men rode ahead to view the enemy position. The Ghenters were drawn up in such tight-packed ranks that it was hard to assess their number, but the men sent to reconnoitre were experienced in war: the lord of Saveuse, Sir Guillaume de Vaudrey, Simon du Chasteler[432] and Jehan de Chaumergy.

The Ghenters stayed where they were, not moving, for a good hour or more. Seeing them hold their strong position, the Duke of Burgundy's battalion pretended to be in retreat, whereupon the Ghenters came streaming after them in huge numbers, one behind the other, yelling and bawling as if they'd routed them. They found themselves in a fine open field with a windmill; they set fire to the mill before marching on to where the duke's vanguard was positioned – but they couldn't see them behind a screen of big trees. The Count of Saint-Pol now sent word to the duke that it would be a good move to send forward a hundred mounted men at arms. This was done: they included Sir Jehan bastard of Saint-Pol, the lord of Wavrin, Sir Jacques de Lalaing and fifteen or sixteen lances from the lord of Croÿ's men; they numbered fifty lances all together. And as the lord of Wavrin, the bastard of Saint-Pol and Sir Jacques de Lalaing advanced towards their enemies, they ran into them in a narrow pass. The Ghenters were marching forward smartly, and could now see the vanguard very close, less than a bowshot away. The cry went up from the vanguard, and men at arms and archers advanced to meet the foe on foot and horseback; and when the Ghenters saw the Duke of Burgundy's men attacking with such clear intent and courage, they broke and took to flight. But those at the front rallied at a strong point where others of their force came up and joined them. There they gave battle and tried to mount a vigorous defence, but the valiant knights and squires on horseback – Sir Jacques de Lalaing and others – charged into them so bravely that they couldn't hold their ground. Some seven hundred Ghenters were killed. It wasn't long before they took to flight again, using their long pikes to vault across great ditches, and those valiant men went after them, pursuing them over ditches so deep that they had to be seen to be believed. Once beyond the ditches the Ghenters turned to fight again, but men at arms and archers engaged with them so bravely that they couldn't resist. Sir Jacques de Lalaing and Sir Jacques de Foucquesolles were there, and both performed such feats of arms that had they not been witnessed they would have defied belief.

The valiant knights and squires who were sent to pursue the Ghenters, and others who went without being ordered, chased them for a full French league in a constant slaughter. The Count of Étampes was one of those pursuing independently, and without any device to distinguish him, accompanied by only five or six others including, I understand, the lords of Roye and Chaumergy; as for

---

[432] Maître d'hôtel in Duke Philip's household.

his troops, they were with the Duke of Cleves. Sir Jacques the brother of the Count of Saint-Pol had his horse killed under him[433] and for a moment he was in mortal danger, but that valiant knight Sir Jacques de Lalaing, who performed so many deeds of valour and skill at arms that day, arrived with the lord of Wavrin and Sir Jacques de Foucquesolles, and all three helped to rescue Sir Jacques de Saint-Pol. He was wounded and sorely hurt in several places, and would have died for sure had it not been for the good knight Sir Jacques de Lalaing, for the Ghenters, seeing him unhorsed, were all intent on nothing but his death, fiercely and boldly though he fought. But through the great prowess and courage of the three knights Lalaing, Wavrin and Foucquesolles his life was saved, and they rescued him from his perilous plight.

Many splendid feats of arms were performed that day by the lord of Wavrin, the bastard of Saint-Pol, the lord of Saveuse and the lord of Roye, and also by Sir Jehan de Croÿ, even though his foot had been pierced [by the crossbow bolt][434] the Tuesday before, and by Sir Anthoine and Sir Guillaume de Vaudrey, Simon du Chasteler, Jehan de Chaumergy, Le Bon de Saveuse[435] and many other knights and squires and a great number of brave archers. They carried out so much slaughter, putting to death so many Ghenters, that it was terrible to see.

The duke's battalions stayed in order, not moving except to advance a little after those who were pursuing the Ghenters, because no one really knew how many of the enemy there were, the area being so hostile to the Duke of Burgundy. And the land was so riven with earthworks, ditches and ambush-points that advancing on horseback was safe only in strength – it was impossible to tell what the Ghenters were planning; and there were reports that they had very great numbers, both from the city of Ghent and the surrounding country, and would be sending three armies at once against their lord the Duke of Burgundy, from three different directions. That was why the Count of Saint-Pol, as said above, remained in fine order, banner unfurled. As for the duke's battalion, they didn't unfurl his banner or pennon but were drawn up and ready, as were those guarding his banner and his person. His principal bodyguards were the lord of Montaigu, the lord of Créquy, the lord of Arcis, Sir Charles de Chalon, the lord of Humières, the Amman of Brussels,[436] Sir François the Aragonese, Sir Philibert de Jaucourt, the Count of San Martino[437]

---

[433] Some MSS specify that this was 'by a hand culverin', a very simple forerunner of the musket.

[434] Above, p. 207. The scribe misread the text and wrote 'a terre' rather than 'percé'.

[435] Brother of Philippe, lord of Saveuse.

[436] The Amman was an important post, effectively the Chief Justice, representing the duke.

[437] The Count of San Martino Canavese (in Piedmont, north of Turin), at this time a chamberlain of Duke Philip.

and a number of other knights and squires I'll refrain from naming for brevity's sake. The duke also had in his battalion his only son the Count of Charolais; the lord of Croÿ, count of Porcien; my lord João of Portugal, son of the Duke of Coimbra; the lord of Auxy; the lord of Lalaing; the lord of Bassignies and the lord of Rochefort: all the noble knights and squires of his guard and of his banner except the lord of Ternant who was with the Duke of Cleves.

This battle was called the Battle of Bazel by Rupelmonde, and was to the very great honour of the Duke of Burgundy, with little loss. He lost that day just a single man: Sir Corneille, his eldest bastard son, which was a grievous pity for he promised much and had as much valour as there can be in one of his youth. He was a fine figure of a man, endowed with many virtues and much loved by all, so he was greatly mourned – even by his enemies from the city of Ghent when they heard the news. He had been governor of the duchy and land of Luxembourg and was of true distinction, and his death was a grave sorrow to the duke his father, not without cause, for he had been set to be of great service to him and to his son the Count of Charolais. He had his body buried with all honour, carried to the city of Brussels and laid to rest in the church of Saint Gudula[438] close to the vault in which he laid his legitimate children when they passed from life to death. The Duke of Burgundy suffered no other loss that day, but it was a great one. As for the Ghenters, they lost a good six thousand men along with all their artillery, transport and baggage, and would have lost still more had it not been for the difficult terrain: had they been in open fields, not a single man would have escaped.

That day – Saturday – and the next, Sunday, the Duke of Burgundy stayed at Rupelmonde, but on the Monday he set out and took lodging in a town there in the Waasland called Waasmunster.[439] He went by way of a fortified village called Temse[440] where there was a fortress belonging to a gentleman by the name of Martin Vilain. Both the village and the fortress had been set ablaze, the reason being, as regards the fortress, that the said Martin Vilain had let it be lost when the Ghenters besieged it: the duke had offered him Flemish troops to defend it but he'd refused, thinking he could guard it well enough himself. The Ghenters had now abandoned the town and the fortress on hearing that the duke was approaching with his army, leaving them in flames as said above.

When the duke reached Waasmunster he stayed for a full week on account of the arrival of an embassy from the King of France, charged by the king to request that the duke make peace with the Ghenters, that he assuage his anger and restore them to his good grace. This embassy wished to act in the interests of the duke's honour, just as they would for the king: that was the king's express command. They set forth their commission to the duke in the

---

[438] Now the cathedral, Gudula being the patron saint of Brussels.
[439] Just east of Lokeren, and about 6 miles north of his base at Dendermonde.
[440] About 7 miles east of Waasmunster.

presence of several of his council. He replied by expressing his thanks to the king for choosing to send this appeal for peace but asking that he kindly refrain from intervening: he had no doubt he would deal successfully with the Ghenters, and if the king were properly informed and knew the truth about them and their wicked rebellion and disobedience he wouldn't wish to be involved. He asked the ambassadors to be content and to say no more on the matter: if they knew how greatly the Ghenters had offended him, they would not repeat their request, and neither would the king. They continued to debate the issue, however, until the duke agreed that they should go to Ghent. And so they did, but to little avail, for while they were there in negotiation with the Ghenters, the Ghenters were waging fiercer war than they'd done before. Not just once but several times, just as it seemed they'd found a way to peace and mediation, the Ghenters did the very worst they could. [*f. 186r*]

102

*How the Count of Charolais set out in force from Dendermonde
and advanced on the village of Moerbeke*

In the Waasland were a number of places fortified with great bulwarks and ditches, and all the roads were blocked with earthworks and trenches. Among these was a town called Moerbeke,[441] where it was said there were six thousand fighting men, both from Ghent and from the country round about. So it was decided that the Count of Étampes should take his company on a foray that way – some two thousand troops he had – and they set out on the twenty-third of June.

Into the Waasland they went, and as they ranged through the country they found fortifications in amazing numbers. They rode to within a league of Moerbeke, but such was the heat that day that the count returned to Waasmunster: in all truth it was so fiercely hot that one gentleman died of heatstroke and five or six other lords were in danger of dying likewise; some said they'd never seen so hot a day in Flanders in their lives.

Next day, the feast of Saint John,[442] plans were put in place for the Count of Charolais to go in force to this town of Moerbeke. There were several great lords in his company, and in all they were about two thousand strong. They ordered these troops into vanguard, main battalion and rearguard some half a league from Moerbeke between an abbey called Boudelo and a large village called Stekene. The scouts were sent ahead; they rode to within a quarter of a league of Moerbeke and found two strong bulwarks manned by Ghenters. They returned at once and reported to the Count of Charolais and the lords who were with him, saying that if they wanted to attack these fortifications

441 Moerbeke-Waas, north of Lokeren, about 15 miles from Dendermonde.
442 24 June.

they would have to send the vanguard. But for the time being no advance was made, because they feared for the safety of the Count of Charolais – and he gave them cause to worry indeed.[443] They turned back without any action at all, much to his rage and frustration; the lord of Créquy was angry, too: his view and insistent counsel had been that they should advance closer to the town of Moerbeke and, depending on what they encountered, press on or return to Waasmunster – which is what they did: they returned to base without venturing further for now. [*f. 187r*]

103

*How the duke's planned mission to Moerbeke was thwarted,
which angered him greatly*

Beyond the Waasland was a fine stretch of land known as the Quatre Métiers;[444] here lay a large and handsome town called Hulst which was loyal to the Duke of Burgundy. But the men there were few in number, so Sir Louis de Masmines was sent with about sixty troops as reinforcements, and they stayed there till the duke sent more.

Meanwhile the duke, knowing his son the Count of Charolais had achieved nothing in the mission entrusted to him, assembled his council to determine how to proceed regarding the town of Moerbeke, which at that point they were singularly set on taking. So certain knights were deputed with orders to draw up in writing an action plan for attacking Moerbeke. They included the lord of Créquy, the lord of Montaigu, the lord of Ternant, the lord of Humières, Sir David de Poix and Sir François the Aragonese. And they did indeed set down a detailed, written plan for the vanguard and the artillery to accompany it, the place where they would assemble to attack, who should be on foot and who on horseback, where the artillery of ribauldequins,[445] culverins and veuglaires would be placed, where to deploy the crossbowmen[446] and where to station provisions and wagons. Plans were drawn up in every detail, as well as could possibly be, and having been delivered to the duke in the presence of his great council, the day and hour of departure were set. But on the day when the duke expected to set forth, with all the provisions, transport, artillery and everything needed for the assault upon the town, a number of cautious knights, concerned about the potentially grave danger involved in attacking

---

[443] Charles was only 19 and the duke's only legitimate heir, and this was his first command. The duke had been doing his best to keep him out of harm's way, and his men evidently feared that he was rather too eager to leap into dangerous action.

[444] The area to the north of Ghent and the Waasland, centred on the towns of Boekhoute, Assenede, Axel and Hulst.

[445] A gun with multiple barrels to create volleys of iron shot.

[446] '*crennequiniers*', a reference to a particular crossbow mechanism, the cranequin.

Moerbeke, reportedly well fortified and defended by six thousand men, found a way of stopping the enterprise, so subtly that it was hard to see what had been done. But abandoned the mission was, much to the fury of the Duke of Burgundy, and he made his anger plain in words to all his council; and he had his standard, which was hung in the windows of his lodging, furled and taken inside, and railed that his mission had been thwarted and he didn't know by whom. But so things stayed for the moment.

Next day, the twenty-sixth of June, the King of France's ambassadors renewed their pleas to the duke to temper his wrath towards the Ghenters and, out of love and favour for the king, to listen to calls for peace. They requested a truce – without a suspension of war there was no hope of peace – and continued their entreaties until the duke agreed not to engage in war with the Ghenters for a full three days: Tuesday, Wednesday and Thursday the twenty-seventh, twenty-eighth and twenty-ninth of June.

But the Sunday before – the twenty-fifth – he had ordered his troops from Holland[447] to go by boat from Dendermonde to the town of Hulst, and so they did, setting out in fine array up the river Scheldt. They passed through the city of Antwerp and came to the sea, and then made their way to Hulst. And on the Tuesday, the twenty-seventh, the duke sent Sir Anthoine bastard of Burgundy and Sir Simon, Sir Jacques and Sir Sanche de Lalaing with about three hundred mounted troops to join them there.

Having arrived there that same day, they learned that night that fully six thousand Ghenters stationed at a fortified town called Axel[448] had marched forth, but it wasn't clear what they planned to do. So very early on the Wednesday Sir Jacques and Sir Simon de Lalaing left Hulst with sixty troops and headed straight for Axel to find news of the enemy. But they hadn't ridden far before they came upon a strong bulwark manned by Ghenters. It was well lined with powder artillery, and they opened fire on the Lalaings, even though they knew a three-day truce had been declared. When Sir Jacques and Sir Simon saw they were ignoring the truce they pressed on towards them and the Ghenters opened fire once more. Seeing this, Sir Jacques and Sir Simon ordered their archers to dismount. They marched straight to engage with the Ghenters who, seeing them advance so near, began to flee. Then Sir Jacques de Lalaing, with great courage and diligence, set off in pursuit with about fifty troops, while Sir Simon stood ready to rescue and aid his nephew if needed. That day the good knight Sir Jacques de Lalaing, by his mighty courage and prowess, conquered and won from the Ghenters seven or eight great bulwarks, and rode through two villages, one of them well entrenched and having a fine and fortified church, and with his small company of troops routed the enemy

---

[447] Jehan de Lannoy, as stadtholder of Holland (see note 364 above, p. 185), had raised some 3,000 troops who had sailed from Rotterdam to Dendermonde in the middle of the month.

[448] 7 miles west of Hulst.

and sent them fleeing all the way to Axel. Had he had a full contingent Sir Jacques would have carried on into Axel itself.

So, as you've heard, the valiant knight Sir Jacques de Lalaing was heavily involved that day, dealing and receiving many a blow. Through his courage and talent and skill at arms he earned such renown that Fortune was his friend wherever he went, not only that day but as long as he lived. That day only ten or a dozen Ghenters were killed and about twenty taken prisoner, for such was his reputation that the moment they saw him drawing near, none of them dared face him for fear of death.

When the action was complete Sir Jacques and Sir Simon de Lalaing returned to Hulst. As for the six thousand Ghenters who were said to have marched from Axel, reports arrived that they'd gone to set fire to two houses near the sea belonging to noble men who sided with the Duke of Burgundy. [f. 189v]

104

How the Ghenters at Axel went to lay siege to Hulst, and of the great and valiant actions of Sir Jacques de Lalaing

The following day, Saint Peter's Day at the end of June,[449] the Ghenters at Axel, reported to number seven thousand or more, marched out and headed straight for Hulst with a great train of transport and artillery including cannons and culverins along with pavises and everything needed by the said artillery. They planned to lay siege to Hulst or to take it by assault.

When the Ghenters were seen approaching in this array, the Hollanders were sent to guard one of the gates, Sir Sanche de Lalaing to another, and Sir Anthoine bastard of Burgundy was positioned with his men in the market-place, ready to reinforce wherever help was needed, while Sir Jacques de Lalaing would lead a sortie with a body of men at arms and Sir Georges de Rosimbos[450] leading the archers. Meanwhile Sir Simon de Lalaing had ridden to the Duke of Burgundy who was then at the town of Waasmunster as mentioned above. With forces marshalled thus, a party of Hollanders sallied from one of the gates, on the side from which the Ghenters were approaching. Sir Jacques de Lalaing and Sir Georges de Rosimbos had likewise sallied from the town; and when Sir Jacques saw the enemy advancing in their direction, he sent to Sir Anthoine the bastard for fifty or sixty more archers, who were duly dispatched. Thus reinforced, and seeing the Ghenters now ceasing to advance, he ordered a small party of archers to move to his left and forward so that they could shoot into the Ghenters' flank. Then he started marching smartly towards the enemy. When they saw him advancing, and felt the archers' volleys

[449] 29 June.
[450] From Picardy, a squire of the stables at Duke Philip's court.

start upon them, they broke and took to flight. They could only see our men in small numbers, but the valour and daring of the good knight Jacques de Lalaing were their undoing. A mighty cry went up as men at arms and archers now set off to pursue and slaughter Ghenters. And the Hollanders didn't shirk, for sure: they joined in the chase as fast as they could on foot.

Defending the town of Hulst were a number of knights and eminent lords from Holland, Picardy, Hainaut and elsewhere: the lord of Lannoy was there, the lord of Brederode,[451] the lord of Bassignies, the lord of Brederode's brother and Sir Sanche de Lalaing, all of them valiant knights. Some had joined the sortie and others stayed on guard, for the size of the Ghenters' force and all the transport and artillery they'd brought gave reason to fear that they meant to attack the town – which had indeed been their plan, but they found different men at Hulst than they'd expected.

Returning to the rout of the Ghenters: Sir Jacques de Lalaing pursued them on foot for a short while before running into a pursuivant named Talent; he took his horse and mounted, while others went to fetch horses from the town, both for him and for his men. A good few noble men were desperate for horses, and when they found them – but not many did, for there were only about fifty to be had – they went about their business of chasing and killing Ghenters till both they and the horses were exhausted. Sir Jacques de Lalaing was the very last to give up the pursuit; he had his horse killed under him and had to switch mounts three times that day. He had only five or six of his men with him, along with Josse de Halluin,[452] the bastard of Saveuse[453] and Plateau,[454] for by the end of the day there were only ten or twelve horses to be found that weren't blown. And mounted men alone were needed to pursue and kill the Ghenters, for their only self-defence was flight as they flung their pikes and armour to the ground, the better to escape. In the course of the pursuit some of them went to surrender to officers of arms,[455] begging for their lives to be spared. Four hundred Ghenters were killed that day, and at least a hundred taken captive, and they lost all their artillery, transport, pavises, provisions and other gear, and it was said they had a good forty carts and wagons.

Truly, the Duke of Burgundy had understood this to be a period of truce as requested by the king's ambassadors – as you've heard, he'd agreed to a suspension of war on the Tuesday, Wednesday and Thursday; and that Thursday, Saint Peter's Day, was the day of the said battle. The Ghenters had been planning to take the duke's men by surprise at Hulst, thinking they'd be off their guard because of the truce and suspension of war; and that was

---

[451] Reinoud II van Brederode, a knight of the Golden Fleece and governor of Utrecht. He was the husband of one of Jacques de Lalaing's sisters: see above, p. 41.

[452] Halewijn, in East Flanders.

[453] The illegitimate son of Le Bon de Saveuse who appeared above, p. 209.

[454] Jehan des Plateaux, a long-standing member of the duke's household.

[455] i.e. heralds or pursuivants.

always their way: whenever peace or a truce was discussed, or there was any break in hostilities, they would mount some underhand attack – and as you've heard, it backfired on them at Hulst.

The duke had given orders that on Saint Peter's Day, at about seven at night, he and his main battalion would set out, followed at nine by his rearguard, and head to the town of Axel[456] where it was reported the Ghenters had six or seven thousand men. Just as the marshal of the army was relaying the duke's commands to the provost marshal for the ordering of provisions and to the master of artillery to prepare the necessary, a pursuivant named Pavillon arrived with sure and certain news of the battle and rout of the Ghenters outside Hulst, just as you've heard. The duke continued preparing to set out from Waasmunster, where he'd long been based; and when ambassadors from the king asked him to delay his advance against the Ghenters at Axel, saying that one of their embassy was still in Ghent who might well return with news to make the move unnecessary, the duke replied that he was absolutely sure of the Ghenters' bad faith: it was constant, and they had made it plain that very day while both parties had agreed to a truce. So he intended to press on with his plan.

At seven that night the vanguard set out and after them the main battalion and the rearguard, followed by the train of provisions and other gear and a small number of lances to guard it. The transport was sent out last because of the roads, which were very narrow and the whole area riven with ditches: if any cart had broken down the whole road would have been blocked and the troops unable to go to each other's aid. Ordered thus, the duke and his army pressed on all night, heading straight for the town of Axel in the land of the Quatre Métiers, where he expected to find six or seven thousand Ghenters.

The route brought them right before the town of Hulst where the fighting had been the previous day. From the duke's base at Waasmunster to Hulst it was four long Flemish leagues,[457] and day had broken by the time they reached there; it was another long league from there to Axel, so fully five leagues from Waasmunster to Axel. As he came within half a league of Hulst the duke drew up in battle order and waited for the Hollanders, Picards, Flemings and Hainauters in the town to join him. The transport won from the Ghenters the previous day was a boon for the Hollanders: having gone to Hulst by boat they had no horses. But the duke was in battle order waiting for the Hollanders, whose captain and governor was the lord of Lannoy, for quite a while. They were almost all riding in carts and wagons, with some on foot.

Once they arrived the duke ordered all his forces to advance and attack the great, well-fortified town of Axel, strongly protected with bulwarks on every side. Sir Jacques and Sir Simon de Lalaing were sent ahead with their

---

[456] From where the Ghenters had mounted their attack on Hulst.
[457] It is about 14 miles.

men to reconnoitre the approaches and see how the Ghenters were positioned and prepared. The rest of the army would follow in order as arranged for the assault. But it was all for nothing: the Ghenters had fled the night before – every man, woman and child – and emptied the town of most of their possessions; they'd retreated to the city of Ghent a full four leagues away.[458]

Word reached the Duke of Burgundy that the Ghenters had fled in the night and no men, women or children were left in Axel – just five or six old women. The duke was most displeased: he'd ridden all night expecting to find those Ghenters; but they'd been so alarmed the day before by the rout at Hulst that they'd fled to Ghent without more ado.

As soon as this was known the duke ordered the marshal of the army to take the quartermasters to Axel and arrange billets. This was duly done, and the duke and his army lodged there. Then parties of men ventured beyond the town and found cattle in such numbers that a fine cow went for five sous. And later that same day, the last day of June, once men and horses had eaten, the duke sent troops to scour the Quatre Métiers towards the sea as far as Boekhoute.[459] The valiant knight Sir Jacques de Lalaing went, as did his uncle Sir Simon and a number of other knights and squires; but they found not a living soul in those parts, man, woman or child: all had retreated to the city of Ghent. The two lords, Sir Jacques and Sir Simon de Lalaing, following the duke's direction and command, had the town of Boekhoute set ablaze along with all the land they passed through. They fired a full three leagues of land, as those in the city of Ghent could clearly see. [*f. 193r*]

105

How the Duke of Burgundy ordered the burning of Moerbeke and many other towns

The following day, the first of July, the Duke of Burgundy sent Sir Louis de la Viefville and Sir Louis de Masmines to the town of Sluis in search of provisions, for bread had run short in the duke's army and was very expensive. He ordered them to bring supplies to a town called Wachtebeke, a fine town two leagues from Ghent.[460] The duke stayed at Axel for three full days; on the fourth – which was the third of July – he decamped and advanced to take lodging at Wachtebeke.

But before leaving he had sent a strong force on a foray to Moerbeke, a fortified town with well-defended approaches which was thought to be amply

---

[458] Ghent is about 17 miles from Axel.

[459] 8 miles west of Axel, and 15 miles due north of Ghent.

[460] Wachtebeke is roughly half way between Axel and Ghent, and just to the west of Moerbeke.

garrisoned. The mission was undertaken by Sir Jehan de Croÿ's men, along with the lord of Maingoval,[461] Sir Jehan de Rubempré, nephew of the lord of Croÿ, and many other knights and squires. But Moerbeke was deserted. They'd all fled to the city of Ghent or into the marshland thereabouts, for peat is cut from the Moerbeke marshes, making them very dangerous: no strangers can venture in without grave risk to life. Some did go in optimistically and were never seen again, but I understand it was only two or three. When Rubempré and Maingoval saw there was no progress to be made into these bogs, known in those parts as moures,[462] they set fire to the town of Moerbeke as they had been commanded. This foray took place on the first of July.

Returning to the good duke's departure: on the third of July he marched from the fine town of Axel; for the people of those parts consider it not a village but a proper town, having a coat of arms, municipality and town hall – not to mention two or three thousand houses, which were almost all set ablaze when the duke's army left, leaving little but a very fine church and the house of Sir Guy de Ghistelles. This was moated and so protected from the fire, and was spared from being burnt because the knight was on the side of his lord the duke.

So, as you've heard, the duke and all his army left the town. He proceeded in the best order he could in the circumstances, the land being so riven with ditches that riding was possible only on the roads. The roads had been blocked with earthworks, too, but these were breached and the roads remade, and the duke pressed on that day to Wachtebeke, mentioned above, and lodged there for two days; and supplies arrived in abundance there from Sluis, brought by Sir Louis de la Viefville and Sir Louis de Masmines as instructed: they'd fulfilled their mission well.

During the two days that the duke and his army were based at Wachtebeke, a number of troops ventured into the country thereabouts, and one party came upon an outpost held against them; they took it by force, and all inside were put to death. There was so much livestock found around Wachtebeke that they didn't know what to do with it all; they rounded up so many that anyone wishing to buy could have a hundred head for four écus.

Around the town, too, were great stretches of marshland with the river Durme running through them, and these marshes were foul and treacherous. But Sir Daviot de Poix and the lord of Contay reconnoitred, and orders were given for paths to be made across the bog in the hope that the duke's army would be able to get through. It was in fact attempted, and a good number made it across, both mounted and on foot; but the marshy ground sank underfoot so alarmingly that the plan had to be abandoned. The worst of it was that those

---

[461] Anthoine de Lannoy, son of Jehan II lord of Lannoy.

[462] The Dutch word for marshes or swamps is *moeren*, hence the name of the town, Moerbeke.

who'd crossed had to be called back, for if the Ghenters had attacked them there would have been no way of sending help, and on their return they were so sodden and befouled that it was piteous to see. So the duke's forces had to stay at Wachtebeke all that day and go and repair the roads and bridges at Moerbeke.[463]

The duke then decamped with all his army on the sixth of July. As they left they set everywhere ablaze; they'd fired other villages the day before, including Ertvelde[464] and elsewhere. On that sixth day of July the Duke of Burgundy crossed the Durme at a ford called Daknam,[465] and he and his army then made camp nearby. [f. 195r]

106

Of the foray to Ghent led by the Duke of Cleves, and what he did there

When morning came the duke left Daknam and moved on to make camp in the fields beside the Scheldt near a town called Wetteren, which stands on the river between Dendermonde and Ghent about a league and a half from the latter.[466] There the duke and his army encamped in tents, pavilions and shelters such as are made at a siege.

To this camp at Wetteren the king's ambassadors came once more – they'd stayed in Dendermonde while the duke had been in the Quatre Métiers and the Waasland; and once again they asked him to consider a peace treaty, which would be impossible to secure without a truce. But he wouldn't countenance it; he said the Ghenters' only aim was to have him disband his army. They did all they could to persuade him otherwise, and they had a fine way with words, but for the time being the duke was adamant, and the ambassadors returned to Dendermonde.

Then on the tenth of July he commanded the Duke of Cleves to lead a foray to the city of Ghent. He entrusted his standard to him, and gave him most of his knights and squires. Sir Jehan de Croÿ led the vanguard that day and the lord of Rubempré the scouts; many of the Count of Étampes's men went, too.

They advanced together in fine order till they found themselves right outside the Saint Bavo gate at Ghent. There was a small house just before the drawbridge; this they set afire, and the barricades they sawed through and broke down. The gate was hurriedly barred to them, and the alarm and terror inside the city were great. The Ghenters opened fire on the duke's men

---

[463] The significance of this is that the marshland is forcing the duke to take a circuitous route to the east and south before heading west again to Ghent.

[464] Just to the west of Wachtebeke.

[465] North of Lokeren.

[466] Wetteren is about 10 miles south-east of Ghent.

with crossbows, cannons and culverins, and an archer on the barrier outside the Saint Bavo gate was hit in the leg with a crossbow bolt, from which he died. Shortly after, the Ghenters assembled in great numbers and sallied forth, but the noble knight de Rubempré three times drove them back beyond their barricades, so fiercely that they were falling and tumbling over each other as they poured back into the city.

The skirmishes lasted long. At one point thirty or forty English made a sortie on horse and foot, for the Ghenters had some English with them who carried on the fight;[467] but whenever a charge was made at them they immediately fell back inside the range of the Ghenters' fire. So if some of the duke's men and horses were killed and wounded it's no wonder; for that day, I believe, there were three standards borne closer to the city of Ghent in battle than had ever been in the time of emperor, king or prince.[468] The first of the three, and the one borne nearest, was the standard of the lord of Rubempré: three or four times it was carried right to the barriers at the Saint Bavo gate. The second was the standard of Sir Jehan de Croÿ, who had a great body of men at his command as he led the vanguard that day; as in all engagements, he was accompanied by the Count of Saint-Pol. The third was the Duke of Burgundy's standard, guarded by the Duke of Cleves, who had it carried so near that if it were not within range of the cannon fire it could hardly have been closer.

The Duke of Cleves and all the duke's army were there for a good two hours; and truly, brave knights and squires skirmished constantly, trying to draw the enemy away from the city and out beyond the range of their fire. But the Ghenters wouldn't venture far, so the army had to withdraw. As they left they set fire to a windmill just outside the city; a fine house was also fired belonging to one by the name of Jacques de Fatre, and a number of other houses, too; and a great many sheep were taken that day, which they drove back with them to camp.

Now we should explain why this foray to Ghent was undertaken, and what the plan had been. The fact is that the duke had received reports that if he sent a force to Ghent, the Ghenters would mount a sortie and do battle. That's why he'd sent his nephew the Duke of Cleves to the city, accompanied as you've heard, thinking it would draw the Ghenters out. If they did sally forth, the plan was that the Duke of Cleves and all his forces would retreat smartly; for after his nephew and the others had gone, the Duke of Burgundy had secretly, without any fanfare, sent word throughout the camp to all the remaining troops to be saddled and ready to mount if need be. He'd given orders that he was to be informed at the gallop of the Ghenters' response,

---

[467] These were mercenaries from Calais who are known to have defected to the duke the following year, in all probability for better pay.

[468] A comment reflecting the number of times the city had rebelled against count or king.

especially if they came out to do battle in force, so that he and all the rest of the army could go to the aid of his nephew the Duke of Cleves. To ensure, without fail, that he was sent word in a flash if the Ghenters decided to offer battle, the duke ordered Golden-Fleece to take with him on the mission all the kings of arms, heralds and pursuivants of his court, to bring him reports of the Ghenters' response. This was duly done. But the Ghenters did not come out to fight, and nothing more was done that day, and they all returned to the duke's camp on the banks of the river Scheldt.

He was there from the seventh of July to the feast of the Magdalene, the twenty-second. And the King of France's ambassadors kept coming to talk about peace. They finally managed to secure a truce to last for six weeks; this was announced on the twenty-second of July, whereupon the duke dismissed his army. But he left men at arms and archers and crossbowmen in the cities of Courtrai, Oudenaarde, Aalst, Dendermonde and Biervliet.[469] It was arranged that the king's ambassadors, the duke's council and deputies, and representatives from the city of Ghent would meet in Lille on the twenty-ninth to discuss and negotiate peace terms.

On leaving his camp at Wetteren on the banks of the Scheldt, the duke made his way to Brussels, where his wife the duchess was. [f. 197r]

107

Of the assembly at Lille where the King of France's ambassadors negotiated peace between the Duke of Burgundy and his subjects the Ghenters

The day now came – the twenty-ninth of July – when the king's men arrived in the city of Lille: that's to say the Count of Saint-Pol, Sir Thomas de Beaumont, the archdeacon of Tours and the king's attorney-general. There too was the Ghentish delegation bearing the authority of their captains, aldermen and municipality;[470] they had also sent an advocate named Master Jehan de Popincourt[471] to Paris to plead on their behalf and to counsel them, knowing there were few men in the world who hated the Duke of Burgundy more. Shortly afterwards the duke arrived in Lille with a noble company of knights and wise counsellors.

The duke's men and the deputies from Ghent spent many days with those commissioned by the king to arbitrate the dispute, and a settlement was finally

---

469 Biervliet is near the coast north of Ghent.

470 '*haulx mans* [as above, p. 178], *eschevins et ceulx de la loy*'.

471 Jehan II de Popincourt, lord of Sarcelles and Liancourt in the Île de France, was one of a prominent family of Parisian magistrates and members of the Parlement of Paris.

reached. All the terms of the treaty were set down in writing, listing the fines and reparations honourable to the duke which the king's ambassadors condemned the Ghenters to pay their lord for their rebellion. With that the Ghenters' deputation left Lille and returned to Ghent, where they read and set forth the honourable and substantial fines they were required to pay to their prince the Duke of Burgundy, Count of Flanders. The Ghenters entirely disregarded the sentence and treaty, and started waging war again more fiercely than before.

With winter approaching, the duke kept his troops in place along the frontier, ready to oppose the Ghenters. The Marshal of Burgundy was stationed at Courtrai with a great body of knights and squires and excellent troops from Burgundy, Flanders and Artois. At Oudenaarde was Sir Jacques de Lalaing with a very fine company. Sir Anthoine bastard of Burgundy was at Dendermonde, likewise well accompanied by knights and squires. In the town of Aalst were Sir Anthoine de Wissocq[472] and Sir Louis de la Viefville with a large body of troops. Elsewhere, the lord of Gruuthuse was in the city of Bruges with a strong contingent, and in Sluis was Sir Simon de Lalaing with the captain of the Franc of Bruges.[473] As for the nobility of Flanders, they all sided with their prince in waging war against the Ghenters, both in their own immediate areas and in the cities loyal to the duke. At Ath in Hainaut and in the marches thereabouts was Sir Jehan de Croÿ, lord of Chimay, grand bailiff and governor of Hainaut, with a very fine company of knights and squires and other troops from Hainaut and Picardy.

All that winter and into the following summer the Ghenters continued waging war, burning villages and farms, inflicting all manner of harm in Flanders and Hainaut upon the obedient subjects of the duke their lord. In return the above-named lords stationed along the borders waged fierce war and inflicted heavy losses on them, with many Ghenters being struck down, killed and captured.

I'm not going to name them, except for the Bastard of Blancstain. He led a great horde of Ghentish lowlifes, a company calling themselves the Green Tent,[474] a host of outlaws, brigands and arsonists: two or three thousand kept banding together, sometimes more, sometimes fewer. And on the ninth of June 1453 this Bastard of Blancstain assembled some sixteen or eighteen hundred

[472] Chamberlain of Duke Philip. He was from Artois, his family taking their name from a hamlet near Calais.

[473] '*pays du Francq*'. This is the Brugse Vrije, a prosperous castellany in the area around Bruges which became part of the Four Members of Flanders along with the 'Three Members' mentioned above (p. 179) – the cities of Ghent, Bruges and Ypres. The implication is that the Ghenters were not supported by the 'Franc'.

[474] '*la verde tente*', so called because they wore green hoods rather than the white of the regular Ghent militia; the Bastard of Blancstain (the Dutch rendering of '*Blanche Estrain*') probably hailed from Zeeland.

fighting men to go and ravage Hainaut. Into the land he went and set fire to a village called Ellezelles.[475] The news reached the lord of Chimay, who was then at the town of Ath in Hainaut with many knights and squires brought by the lords of Lahamaide, Bossu, Harchies[476] and others; for as the duke had ordered payment for a hundred, so the land of Hainaut had paid for a hundred lances and for the archers, led and captained by Sir Jehan de Croÿ, lord of Chimay. As soon as he heard the news that Ellezelles had been set afire he bade a trumpeter call everyone to horse; his men were straightway armed and mounted, and seeing them ready he led them from Ath and headed straight to where they could see the flames and smoke.

On they rode till they came to Ellezelles, set ablaze by the Ghenters, where they found women who told them the Ghenters had headed back to their own parts and had a train of artillery with them. The lord of Chimay sent scouts ahead who followed the Ghenters' tracks; they found them in a wood, drawn up ready for battle. This wood was thick and the ways into it blocked, and the lord of Chimay and his men couldn't see how to attack, for the enemy had positioned culverins in the wood guarding the narrow entrances. Nonetheless, as was the will of God, the lord of Chimay ordered his archers to dismount, and they drew up along a narrow path and started shooting at the Ghenters, who returned fire with their culverins; right at the outset the Bastard of Blancstain was hit by an arrow in the leg, and the moment he saw he was wounded he called for a horse to be brought so that he could mount and make his escape, which he did. Seeing the Bastard of Blancstain take to flight, the lord of Chimay ordered his standard to advance, carried by a noble knight named – ;[477] and when the Ghenters saw their captain flee and the lord of Chimay's standard march towards them, and felt the archers' arrows on them, they all broke in disarray and took to flight. There was a great slaughter of the Ghenters: where they'd been in the woods, and in the cornfields where they tried to hide, around four hundred dead were found.

There were many fine encounters with the Ghenters – both by the aforesaid lords and captains in the border towns and castles and by the noble men of Flanders – before the duke set out in force to subjugate his Ghentish foes. But so he now did. He would have raised his army and moved against them sooner had it not been that the nations of foreign merchants once again[478] requested his permission to try to broker peace between him and the Ghenters; they asked

---

[475] About 10 miles north-west of Ath.

[476] All from close by in Hainaut, Bossu (Boussu) and Harchies being just south of Ath and Lahamaide being between Ath and Ellezelles. (Jacques de Harchies was the *bailli des bois* of Hainaut mentioned above, p. 200).

[477] The name is left blank in MS 16830 and almost all others except one where another hand has inserted 'Josse de Hamme' (a misreading of Halluin, as above, p. 215) and another which gives 'Crestien de Digoine', mentioned above, p. 199.

[478] i.e. as above, p. 205.

his leave to go to Ghent and attempt to find some kind of resolution. The duke gladly and graciously granted this: for his part all he wanted from the Ghenters was that they behave towards him as good subjects should to their good and natural lord and prince. These foreign merchants, most displeased about the Ghentish rebellion, made every effort, coming and going back and forth between the duke and the Ghenters, until the Ghenters sent their most eminent men to the duke and peace and agreement were finally reached.

But the details I'll pass over, because after the treaty and accord had been made between the two parties, the Ghentish deputation – thinking they'd done a fine job – returned to Ghent in joyful spirits and showed the city's captains, aldermen and commons the treaty made at Lille with their lord and prince the duke, but the Ghenters would have none of it: straight back to war they went, and set afire one of the finest towns in Flanders, Hulst by name. So the duke was forced to act, and he assembled his army once again. [f. 200r]

108

How the Duke of Burgundy set out from Lille and went to Flanders to lay siege to Schendelbeke

On the eighteenth of June 1453 the Duke of Burgundy left Lille and lodged at Courtrai, where he stayed for five days while his army and artillery made ready. Once his army was assembled – men at arms, archers, crossbowmen and artillery large and small – his bodyguard and banner-guard were ordered as they'd been the previous year, except that the lord of Ternant, who had then been charged with his banner, was now in Burgundy, so the commission was given instead to Sir Jehan bastard of Saint-Pol. As for the vanguard, in place of the Count of Saint-Pol, who at this time was with the King of France, it was entrusted to the Marshal of Burgundy and Sir Jehan de Croÿ, who was always at the forefront in these wars, along with Sir Simon de Lalaing and his nephew Sir Jacques. The Count of Étampes led and commanded the rearguard. As for the lord of Croÿ, Count of Porcien and governor of Luxembourg, he was sent to Luxembourg at the duke's express command because certain knights, squires, cities and fortresses had rebelled against him.[479]

The Duke of Burgundy set out from Courtrai on the twenty-fourth of the month and lodged next at Oudenaarde. From Oudenaarde he went to lay siege to a fortress called Schendelbeke,[480] held and occupied by Ghenters who were causing all manner of trouble in Hainaut and elsewhere in the duke's

---

[479] Duke Philip had been appointed regent of Luxembourg by Elisabeth of Görlitz (see note 49 above, p. 56), but her death in 1451 had made the duke's position there precarious, the duchy being claimed by Ladislaus of Bohemia.

[480] Some 25 miles south of Ghent, near Grammont.

lands. The artillery was set up to open fire with cannon and bombard, and the
Ghenters' hearts failed them and they surrendered to the duke's will – which
was that they should all be strung up and hanged. The surrender was made
on the twenty-seventh of June, after which the duke stayed where he was
encamped for three days; on the third day following, which was the last day
of June, he broke camp at Schendelbeke and returned to Oudenaarde, where
he stayed for just one night.

Next day, the first of July in the year '53, the duke went and lodged at
Courtrai, and set out on the third day following to lay siege to the fortress of
Poeke.[481] The Ghenters had installed a garrison there, and they were wreaking
havoc in the country all around, raiding everywhere as far as Bruges and
Roeselare.

On leaving Schendelbeke, the duke had ordered Sir Jacques de Lalaing
to go to the fortress of Oudenhove,[482] held by the Ghenters: they were also
holding a fortified church at a place called Velzeke.[483] Oudenhove was enclosed
by water-filled ditches, walls, drawbridges and barriers, though it wasn't the
strongest of forts; but the Ghenters were manning it and inflicting all kinds of
damage thereabouts. So it was decided that the valiant knight Sir Jacques de
Lalaing should advance upon the place with his company of a hundred lances
and archers to pen them in and ensure they didn't leave till a larger body of
the duke's troops arrived to take it by assault or otherwise.

Sir Jacques undertook the mission and set off with his men to carry it out.
He went under cover of night; and when they were still a fair distance from
the place he ordered them to dismount and leave their horses where they were
so that the men inside the fortress wouldn't hear them. Just as day was about
to break he found himself right outside. Seeing it was dawn he told one of his
men to give a watchman's cry. But no one replied. Sir Jacques and his men
were troubled by this: they thought it must be a trick, and that the Ghenters
knew of their approach and were ready to open fire with their artillery. But it
was otherwise: the Ghenters had fled leaving gates and barriers shut and the
drawbridge raised to make it look as if it were occupied. So Sir Jacques de
Lalaing had some of his men strip off and wade across the moats, lower the
drawbridge and open the gate and barriers. Then Sir Jacques and his troops
went inside, and found most of the Ghenters' belongings abandoned in their
haste to flee.

With the place in his possession as you've heard, Sir Jacques de Lalaing
sent to the duke to find out what he wanted him to do with it. The duke was

---

[481] A major stronghold, Poeke (Poucques in French) is about 15 miles west of
Ghent, and 25 miles from Courtrai.

[482] '*Auxdenove*'; Sint-Maria-Oudenhove is just south-west of Zottegem, to the south
of Ghent.

[483] '*Wellesicq*', a few miles further north.

advised to have it burnt and demolished, and duly sent instructions to Sir Jacques; he carried out the order with much reluctance and regret, for he would never willingly consent to burning. [*f. 202r*]

109

How Sir Jacques de Lalaing, having taken Oudenhove, joined the duke at the siege of Poeke, where a cannon shot tragically ended his days

After the place had been burnt and demolished, Sir Jacques de Lalaing returned to the duke his sovereign lord, who was besieging the fortress of Poeke. It was the evening of the third of July when the good knight arrived there.

Next morning he went and stayed in the duke's tent to hear three masses; and he spoke in confession to an eminent doctor of the Dominican order named Master Guy de Douzy, because the firing of the fortress at Oudenhove, carried out by order of the duke, was weighing on his conscience.

Once these masses had been said and celebrated, Sir Jacques took a horse – as he had a slight wound in one leg – and rode to see a bombard that the duke had firing, along with other powder artillery including mortars, veuglaires and small cannon, with the aim of breaching and demolishing a section of the wall of Poeke Castle between the gate and a very strong tower. The lord of Saveuse and other lords had had trenches and approach works dug in several places and the castle was under close and heavy bombardment.

While he was watching proceedings Sir Jacques spotted Golden-Fleece, with whom he was well acquainted. Smiling, in amused and jovial spirit, he told him what had happened in the taking of the fortress at Oudenhove. Then, having viewed the siege works and talked with Golden-Fleece for a fair while, Golden-Fleece said to him:

'Sir Jacques, it's time you went and rested your leg: Master Jehan Caudet, my lord the duke's surgeon, says it needs rest.'

Sir Jacques replied that he was going to dine, and after dinner would stay in his tent to rest his leg in which, as said above, he'd taken a slight wound.

But perverse, accursed Fortune would not allow it. At about four in the afternoon, Sir Jacques mounted and returned for another look at the siege works, and found Golden-Fleece in the same place he'd met him that morning. Sir Jacques was sitting on his horse in the shelter of a big tree, viewing the damage inflicted by the bombard on the wall of this fortress at Poeke. Golden-Fleece came up and addressed him, saying:

'What, sir! You were supposed to rest your leg and stay in your tent after dinner!'

The good knight smiled back at Golden-Fleece and said it had started to bore him, being stuck so long in his lodging. While Sir Jacques was talking to Golden-Fleece, Sir Adolph of Cleves, lord of Ravenstein, came and darted for cover behind the mantlet[484] of a bombard for fear of the fire coming from the fortress. He was followed by the Bastard of Burgundy clad in a paltock[485] of rich crimson cloth of gold; he had a crossbow[486] under his arm and a quiver of bolts belted at his waist. Seeing the two lords taking cover behind the bombard's mantlet, Sir Jacques de Lalaing dismounted and went to speak to them; Golden-Fleece stood close by.

Now, the fact is that on each side of a bombard and mantlet it is usual to dig trenches and earthworks to provide cover while observing the damage done by the bombard and while the gunner is taking aim. But at this bombard such earthworks had yet to be made; instead there were four pavises, two on each side of the mantlet. The lord of Ravenstein, the Bastard of Burgundy and Sir Jacques de Lalaing started peering at the impact the bombard had had on the castle wall; all three thought they were sheltered from incoming fire. But Sir Jacques was outside the mantlet, looking from behind the cover of a pavise. At that point a gunner in one of the castle's towers had a veuglaire trained on the mantlet of the bombard, and as chance would have it he had it loaded now and put the match to it. The ball from the veuglaire hit the pavise behind which stood Sir Jacques de Lalaing, and a piece of wood from the front of the pavise struck him on the right side of the head above the ear, taking off the corner of his head and part of his brain. He fell backwards and lay stretched out on the ground, stirring neither leg nor foot. A Carmelite friar went to him and devoutly turned his mind to remember God and the glorious Virgin Mary; and when Sir Jacques heard him speak of God and of the Virgin – whom he had loved so much that for her sake he had adopted the motto and device 'La Nonpareille' – he turned his attention to the friar and tried to speak; but Death was pressing so hard upon him that he was unable to form an intelligible word. But he clasped his hands and tried again to speak and could still understand, according to the friar. Just a short while later, the good knight ended his days.

It was a grievous pity, for while he was in this world his like was not to be found in any land: there was no more perfect, valiant, courageous knight, so endowed with prowess. As for his virtues, there is no human tongue so eloquent that it could ever convey them in full. He was a gentle, humble, amiable, courteous knight, and a generous and caring giver of alms: throughout his days he gave aid to the poor, the widowed, the orphaned. And God had endowed him, the flower of knights, with five great gifts: he had the beauty of Paris the Trojan; the compassion of Aeneas; the shrewd intelligence of Ulysses the Greek; when he found himself in battle against his foes he was possessed with the wrath of the Trojan Hector; but when he saw or sensed

---

[484] A substantial wooden screen or wall, usually mounted on wheels, to provide protection for gunners.

[485] 'paletot': a doublet, usually worn beneath armour.

[486] 'crennequin': see note 446 above, p. 212.

he had vanquished them there was no man more magnanimous or humble. It was a pity indeed that he did not live longer, for when Death took him he was only about thirty-two.

His death was a grave loss to his friends, especially to one of his brothers: Sir Jacques had loved him dearly, seeing in him the greatest promise and a fine beginning, his actions, words and morals all tending towards valour and virtue. Seeing such promise in his brother Philippe, Sir Jacques had resolved that, once the wars in Flanders were over, out of love for his brother he would pass to Philippe all rights and responsibilities that would fall to him on the death of his father the lord of Lalaing – in other words, the lordship of Lalaing.[487] For his own part, he was intent on devoting his body and his life to the service of Our Lord: he would go to the lands that bordered the infidels and never return, keeping only a pension sufficient to support him, such as his father and close family and friends together deemed fit.

But that was not God's will. And at the good knight's death there was an outpour of grief, a mighty commotion, throughout the army of good Duke Philip of Burgundy. When the duke was informed he wept most piteously, tears streaming down his cheeks, and his heart was so oppressed that he could utter not a single word. The army was gripped by dreadful grief; the tears and laments of all were beyond belief: everyone looked as if he had lost his dearest friend. When a great host is gathered one can well expect to hear the clamour of trumpets, men and horses, flutes and drums and everything else from at least a league away; but such a hush fell on the army, stricken and downcast at the good knight's death, that from a bowshot away no one would have known there was anyone there.

When the news of his death reached the lord and lady of Lalaing, it was very hard for them to bear. And you may be sure that his three uncles, the lord of Créquy and Sir Simon and Sir Sanche de Lalaing, who were present in the army themselves, were distressed and crestfallen when they heard – and with good cause: they could all avow they had never suffered such a loss. But despite the loss they should take comfort in this: that as long as books survive, his renown and his illustrious, noble deeds will shine on earth.

After the good knight's death his trusty, loyal servants prepared his body and, amid bitter tears and lamentation, laid it on a cart draped all in black. Drawn by fine horses it was carried and escorted to Lalaing. Its arrival there was greeted by deep mourning from the lord and the good lady, whose grief was such that all who saw her could not help but join her in her weeping; and they loved him so dearly that their mourning could not stop: day after day their plaintive laments continued for the piteous death of their beloved son.

The body of the valiant knight was taken from the litter and carried to the great hall of Lalaing, where it lay till it was borne to the church where the tomb had been prepared for his burial. Vigils and prayers were said and sung that

---

[487] Jacques having been the eldest son.

night with deep devotion. And next day, after the divine service for the dead, the body was committed to the ground amid much weeping and lamentation. Over the body was built a rich and splendid tomb, superbly carved with the thirty-two banners and insignia of both lines of his descent; and engraved in the stone was an epitaph which read as follows:

> Here entombed in darkness, hidden, lies
> One in whom Nature made a prodigy;
> His body now brings light to the shady earth
> More than gold illuminates a painting.
> The heavens open; tears rain down for him.
> How piteous, that he is covered by the earth,
> That such a piece of work is swallowed up,
> With little to replace it in the world.
> Here lies the perfect paragon of honour,
> The bright, clear mirror of a noble life,
> Inspiring good men and provoking envy
> By winning so much glory, so deserved.
> Here lies the honour of high and royal courts,
> Embodiment of all triumphant virtues,
> The burning lamp in chambers and in halls,
> The source of radiant light for every eye.
> Here lies the fount of deep humility –
> Though, when iron-clad, fierce as any in the world.
> So mean a thing has wrought his early end,
> But he was the very image of a Worthy.[488]
> Here lies one who, whiter than ivory,
> Made chastity a pillar of his glory;
> It cleared a path for him to victory,
> Knowing impurity would block his way.
> Here lies the perfect model for the good,
> Revering God, committed to His church;
> So faithful, sober, generous, such his worth
> That praise of him should fill the earth and sky.
> Here lies one who, before his thirtieth year,
> Had accomplished twenty-eight combats in the lists.[489]
> Such awesome feats, achieved by one so young,
> Amazed the world, a mighty enterprise.

[488] This hints at the Nine Worthies, the nine paragons of chivalry including Alexander, Julius Caesar, Charlemagne and King Arthur, established by Jacques de Longuyon in his hugely influential Alexander romance *The Vows of the Peacock* (*Les Voeux du Paon*), c. 1310.

[489] Some other MSS say 'eighteen', which interestingly tallies with the comment made by the Portuguese nobles above, p. 196, and is in fact the correct figure if counting the number of individual opponents faced by Lalaing as recorded here in *The Book of the Deeds*.

Here lies one whose daring nerve was such
That he would never arm his face in battle;[490]
Composed and steady, ever cool as ice,
With honour he emerged from every field.
Here lies one who in the Ghentish wars
Won honour to rival that of many a Greek
Against the Trojans in their fearsome strife;
His glory soars to heights immeasurable.
Here lies one who ever flouted Fortune,
Fearless of reverse and misadventure.
But loss of honour, earning ill repute,
He feared as much as any beneath the sun.
Here lies the very pearl of valiant men,
Whose stay upon this earth was all too short;
And no tongue in the world can give acclaim
And praise enough to match his rich deserts.
Here lies one who, single-handed, held
The passage of arms at Chalon-sur-Saône,
The lofty praise for that high deed so loud
It fills the air: the very sky resounds.
Here lies one who journeyed far and wide,
In England, France, Navarre and Italy,
Through Scotland, Portugal and through Castile,
To challenge the good and with them win renown.
Here lies one whose fame will never die,
The knight who bears the family name Lalaing,
And who in sudden fashion, without skill,
The Ghenters brought down with a cannon shot.
Here lies one whom every human voice
Should laud as gold is exalted more than barley;
His praise should ring in the heart of every palace,[491]
For nothing Georges[492] can write can match his worth.

Here ends this present volume, in which are contained the deeds of the noble, valiant knight Sir Jacques de Lalaing.

---

[490] See the repeated references to him fighting in the lists without a visor, above, pp. 135–6, 140, 160.

[491] Literally 'in the heart of the palace, not in the porchway'.

[492] *'Jorge'*. It has long been assumed that this epitaph was the work of Georges Chastellain.

INDEX

Printed and bound by CPI Group (UK) Ltd, Croydon, CR0 4YY

09/06/2025

14685702-0003